MY AUTISTIC AWAKENING

MY AUTISTIC AWAKENING

Unlocking the Potential for a Life Well Lived

Rachael Lee Harris

ROWMAN & LITTLEFIELD
Lanham • Boulder • New York • London

Published by Rowman & Littlefield
A wholly owned subsidiary of The Rowman & Littlefield Publishing Group, Inc.
4501 Forbes Boulevard, Suite 200, Lanham, Maryland 20706
www.rowman.com

Unit A, Whitacre Mews, 26-34 Stannary Street, London SE11 4AB

British Library Cataloguing in Publication Information Available

Library of Congress Cataloging-in-Publication Data

Harris, Rachael Lee, 1969–
My autistic awakening : unlocking the potential for a life well lived / Rachael Lee Harris ; foreword by Tony Attwood.
pages cm.
Includes bibliographical references and index.
ISBN 978-1-4422-4449-8 (cloth : alk. paper) — ISBN 978-1-4422-4450-4 (electronic)
1. Harris, Rachael Lee, 1969– 2. Autistic people—United States—Biography. 3. Psychotherapists—United States—Biography. 4. Children with autism spectrum disorders. I. Title.
RC553.A88H365 2015
616.85'88320092—dc23
[B]
2014043149

Printed in the United States of America

For my mother Gabrielle Harris, my first mentor and abiding inspiration. With a daughter's love and thanks.

CONTENTS

ACKNOWLEDGMENTS

My heartfelt thanks and gratitude to my husband Rudi, who urged me to share my story, for his unstinting support and encouragement during the writing of this book, and for his graciously allowing his new wife to give out to the public at large a history which had only recently been offered to him.

Thanks to my mother Gabrielle, who willingly and patiently spent more hours than she and I care to remember typing my handwritten manuscript into a neat and decipherable document. The best secretary a daughter could wish for: sixty words per minute—and counting!

Many thanks to my darling sister Sarah, for running her eagle eye over my story—of which she is so much a part—in the pursuit of proof-reading perfection.

To Professor Tony Attwood, my friend and colleague, for whom I have the greatest respect, and who kindly offered to write the foreword to this book, your belief in me, and encouragement in my professional work, continues to be a source of strength and inspiration. Thank you, Tony.

With grateful thanks to the Sisters of Quidenham Carmel, in whose company my education, both intellectually and spiritually, was—a veritable "finishing school" for my soul.

And to all my brothers and sisters in the Autism Community: it is a remarkable journey we share. May you always catch sight of the beauty in the twists and turns of your life.

FOREWORD

Rachael's autobiography can be appreciated and enjoyed on two levels. She has an amazing story to tell, and she is a talented writer. The scenes and experiences are described so richly and eloquently. As each chapter closes, the reader will be eager to find out what happens next. She is a brave and determined woman, and she describes aspects of her life, such as living in a Carmelite monastery, that are fascinating and uplifting. This book will be thoroughly enjoyed by someone who has no understanding of autism but who appreciates a well-written and absorbing true story.

The second level is Rachael's description of the world through the eyes, thoughts and feelings of someone who has Asperger's syndrome, an expression of autism. There are many autobiographies written by women who have Asperger's syndrome, so why is this one different? Rachael's autobiography is unique in that she describes a spiritual journey, and she has become a qualified psychotherapist. Some would not believe that a person who has Asperger's syndrome could be a successful psychotherapist, but I have known Rachael for several years, and frequently, and with confidence, I refer my clients to her. She has an intuitive insight into autism spectrum conditions and compassion for the experiences of her clients. As much as she has been able to unlock the potential of her own autistic characteristics, she is now able to unlock the potential of her clients. She is my hero and a valued and appreciated colleague.

Tony Attwood, September 2, 2014

INTRODUCTION

In 2007 I was diagnosed with Asperger's syndrome, a type of high functioning autism. In the years since I was diagnosed, and in particular since my becoming a psychotherapist specializing in helping others on the autism spectrum, many people have asked me how it is that I have managed so well. Reflecting on the question "Why?" led me to writing not a "case study" but a "life" in the hope that in this life's telling, an explanation might come to light.

The story of Asperger's syndrome, too, begins with a life. Hans Asperger was born on the family farm just outside Vienna in 1906. He was an intelligent but lonely boy, described variously as remote and aloof, who found it difficult to make friends. He went on to excel academically in the field of medicine, going on to study and work at the University of Vienna and specializing in pediatrics.

In his rooms in the University Children's Hospital in Vienna, he began to identify a consistent pattern of traits and behaviors in a group of about twenty boys who had, over time, been referred to his clinic. The pattern included little ability to form friendships, sensory sensitivity, fine and gross motor problems, difficulties in emotional regulation, problems with organizational skills, and a seeming lack of empathy. Indeed, Hans Asperger's uncanny ability to spot the consistent pattern present in the development and personality type of this relatively minor number of boys lay in no small part in his own recognition of the same traits within himself as a child: a realization of a personality type with which he freely identified.

It was to Hans Asperger's great satisfaction that he also noted that these same children had an inexhaustible ability to talk about their favorite subjects in great detail, subjects he termed "special interests." These were his "little professors" who, according to their abilities, went on to careers in fields as diverse as science and the arts. Some fifty years after Asperger published his landmark paper describing Autistic Psychopathy,[1] his work was finally recognized. In 1994, the condition received his name, Asperger's syndrome, in honor of his work.

My story of living the autistic experience is not, although a large aspect of my life, the whole of my life. This statement should not be revolutionary, but it is made so by examples of Asperger literature, whose unrelenting focus on extremes of behavior and attitude expressed in the content paint a picture of high functioning autism so severe that the reader cannot relate to its contents: "rollicking roller-coasters of mayhem," to which I personally have a hard time relating. This is a book that happily bucks the trend.

My Asperger life, as with all individual lives, can never be viewed in isolation; it can only be viewed through the prism of environment, upbringing, temperament, life experience, and personal values

This autobiography is very different from many in that it leads by an example of moderation almost unheard of in the catalog of Asperger firsthand narratives—that is its strength. It is a considered life, not one of simply reacting to events. I have sought to examine my own life, that my journey may give hope to the many people on the autism spectrum who are desperately seeking a way to transcend the hand they have been dealt: trying to cope with extreme emotions, abuse, anxiety, social confusion, critical thoughts, and poor choices, and to see that despite all these things, peace of mind and solid self-esteem are not only possible but attainable—a middle way not in theory, but by hard-won practice.

My autistic life is woven into a larger story of influences that far outreach those of my own limited experiences. The chapters of this book that pertain to my early childhood are a true and accurate description of my thoughts and feelings at that time. What my mature years have done is enable me to articulate them. I have sought to describe my most lucid memories—the ones that have stuck—which retain the value I saw in them at the time.

In the telling of this story I also hope to give some insight—particularly to those who have never known anyone on the autism spectrum or even heard of Asperger's syndrome—into the kaleidoscopic fragmentation of my early years and the beauty that I have experienced at each and every turn in my life's journey; a window into autism—not as it is imagined, but as it is lived.

This is a story about transformation: Where I am at the beginning of my journey is very different to where I am now! It is a slow and steady tale of maturation whose developmental Holy Grail is, perhaps disappointingly for some, the chalice of time: me being left to my own devices and the influence of those who were either in or entered into my life along the way.

Putting pen to paper, I had little idea what course my recollections would take, but soon it became evident to me that their direction was being "pushed" down a certain pathway, making me something of a ghostwriter of my own history. So I cast it out here, like a message in a bottle. It is a story no greater or lesser than that of any other person, but one, I hope, that will find its way onto another's shore so that it might do them some good.

Thank you for sharing my adventure; you, although hidden from my awareness, in a shared humanity, were and are always with me.

I

THE WANDERER

There was a time when meadow, grove and stream,
The earth, and every common sight,
To me did seem
Apparelled in celestial light,
The glory and the freshness of a dream.[1]

The word that best describes my beginnings is "precarious." My mother, because of a threatened miscarriage, was required to lie on her back for four months under the watchful eyes of a team of obstetricians. It was 1969, and one afternoon just after lunch, a nurse wheeled a television set into the ward so that Mum could watch the moon landing. For my mother, this was a welcome and exciting diversion from the doctors' thinly veiled references to my apparent lack of viability, for my existence hung by a thread. From the time of my caesarean birth, it would be two full years before I took my "one small step."

I cannot remember feeling anything in particular the morning I lay in bed at the Dickensian-sounding Xavier Home for Crippled Children. Almost two years had passed since my premature birth, when I had been transferred there directly from the infinitely more glamorous Mater Misericordiae Children's Hospital, where I had undergone numerous operations on the misshapen bones of my legs and dislocated hip, all the aftermath of not having had enough room to exercise in utero, owing to a tear in my mother's womb.

Xavier had become my "home away from home," where I received intense physiotherapy for repeated bouts of pneumonia caused by all the anesthetic that had been required. I scanned the black pipes that crisscrossed the ceiling as far as my gaze would allow. As I lay there I felt nothing except a kind of suspended bliss. I was neither happy nor unhappy. I simply "was." The pungent smell of the plaster encasing my lower limbs drew my attention back into the ward and the daily ritual of meals, toileting, and a kind word from a nursing sister as she passed my way.

I understand that it was my father's custom to drop in and see me when he finished work, although I only remember his coming once. His smiling face and company made a happy distraction in a dull day. The visit over, Dad walked to the end of the ward, then turned and waved cheerily before going home to the rest of the family. The presence of my father had made me forget my former, unfazed state. I was alone and cried bitter tears. From my earliest years, circumstance threw me back on my own resources. From the time I was cut free from my plaster, I was forced to stand on my own two feet, and how!

When all that could be done was done, I was sent home to take up "an ordinary childhood." No matter how broadly one might define "an ordinary childhood," mine continued to defy conventional description at every turn. Despite my being the youngest of five children and being born into what was essentially a warm and loving family, restlessness, isolation, and anxiety were the hallmarks of my early years. Even among my siblings, I continued to be socially isolated. My mother attributed this to my extended hospitalization, which, at that time and with no other plausible explanation, seemed to make sense.

At the age of four, what prompted me to wake, dress and wander down the corridor of our family home and out into the street at dawn, I cannot say. A mystery to myself, I obeyed rules and directives of which I was unaware. Strewing clothing as I made my way down the street, all I knew was the wet grass under my feet, the crisp air filling my lungs, and the play of dappled light through the trees. Thoughts of direction and safety never enter the mind of a child locked in an autistic fog—for them there is only the sensing.

An hour passed before my mother and sister pulled up in the Volkswagen to find me in a supermarket parking lot, naked, circled by a pack of stray dogs. Another time my compulsion to walk took me around the block and alongside the busy main road. Where I had come from and where I was going mattered nothing to me. Left foot, right foot, left foot, right foot—a mind clear of thoughts and eyes whose only object was the horizon. I walked with an emptiness of mind that would have been the envy of a Tibetan monk. When the police car pulled up alongside me with my panic-stricken mother in the back, I simply got in, bringing that day's wanderings to a close.

A few years later, my elder sister, a budding paleontologist, would help me channel this energy, taking me on her teenage expeditions to scour for fossils near a local quarry. The discovery of small fragments of fern fossils often rewarded our efforts. These treasures we took home, adding them to our previous collections. Understanding the origins of things had, from those early years, fascinated me. These feathery, flint-like images satisfied my Asperger brain's insatiable hunger for detail, becoming my first "special interest."

My physical wanderings, as I view them now, were simply an expression of my desire to reach out and make contact with the world around me, to make a connection with a world at once fragmented and very beautiful. In my world, every day presented fresh new experiences of color, scent, and form, but still, unconsciously, I traced my finger along the physical world looking for a crack, a seam, an opening that would unlock the mystery of what lay behind the beauty I could see.

"Where's Rachael?" continued to be the family mantra from my fourth year until my eighth. Where was I? Some days I would go down the street to where I had discovered a large green-ant colony. I'd sit there on the curb, watching them for hours at a time, throwing in the odd twig now and again and enjoying the new patterns their movements made with every fresh assault I made on their nest. For a child who didn't like sudden changes in her daily routine, such as an unannounced outing or the arrival of an unknown visitor, I was more than happy to see how other creatures scrambled to bring back a sense of order to theirs.

Water also held a fascination for me; a body of water was as attractive as it was dangerous. One particular incident stands out in my memory that, when I recall it now, makes me shudder for what might have been. In the early 1970s in Queensland, pool fencing had not yet been made mandatory. One afternoon as I was playing by myself at the end of our backyard, I noticed the water of our next-door neighbor's in-ground pool sparkling beyond the trees which lined the fence. Enticed by what I saw, I climbed over the low fence that divided the properties and walked over to the edge of the pool. I couldn't have been any older than five and couldn't swim. The neighbor's yard was deserted.

As I stood by the edge of the pool, I watched an inviting flotilla of pool toys bobbing and skimming over the water's surface as they caught the breeze. I stood there for some minutes. Why I did not decide to go for a "swim," I do not know. I sensed no danger, and as with all my adventures, I gave no thought to the possible consequences. Only by the grace of God did I turn away from the edge of the pool and return to my own backyard.

My nights, in contrast to my usual reckless sense of adventure, filled me with dread. Being lovingly tucked into bed by my mother and read to by my father proved no antidote to the primitive fears I held for that which lurked in every dark corner of the bedroom. Like most children on the autism spectrum, my anxieties were legion. Closing my eyes, rather than bringing comfort, brought the terrifying sensation of falling into an abyss. Fantastic shapes and figures loomed out of the darkness and made their ghostly way across my retinae. As was my custom, I would pull the covers over my head, leaving just enough room to breathe. The fact that my sister Sarah shared the same room and slept half covered, not five feet away, did nothing to alleviate my fears, but rather, left me feeling more dismayed by her apparent courage and my sad lack!

With my ears straining to hear the slightest sound in the room, I would lie there, heart beating thick and fast should the roof creak or a gust of wind rattle the windows. Down the corridor opening on to the living room, my father was busy with his own nightly rituals. Sometimes he would play his piano, and the sweet melody of "Traumerei" by Schumann would reach my bed, soothing my fears with its familiarity, sending me to sleep. Other nights my father would put on classical records, *Finlandia* being his firm favorite. My heart would constrict on hearing the opening bar, jangling my already frayed nerves. How sorry Dad would have been had he realized that Sibelius's music had become the soundtrack to my nightly terrors!

I daresay, dear reader, that you have come to the conclusion that for me now, even hearing the first strains of that childhood tune would send me into the throes of post-traumatic stress, but no; rather, I seek it out and possess my own copy! For as I have grown in years, strength, and resilience, I welcome and embrace the music that once almost proved my undoing.

For many years, my father had served as a first tenor in the Queensland State and Municipal Choir. That Victorianesque working title exposed me to the loveliest music, which, looking back, surely had the value of taking me out of myself. For a child on the autism spectrum, it is the tendency to "wind in on oneself" that defines his or her greatest challenge. I sat through interminable hours of choir rehearsals in the public seating of the city hall concert chamber as the choir prepared for their annual production of Handel's *Messiah*.

It is said that patience is a virtue, but I cannot say with any certainty that my ability to wait hour upon hour was particularly virtuous. At that time, I spent most of my waking hours in a kind of daydream. When not engaged in any particular activity or simple conversation, I would find myself being drawn back into my inner world, a half-world carried upon a stream of fragmented images and fleeting emotions. I cannot recall being the author of these reveries, but rather, I was a spectator caught up in a passing parade of mental images.

Occasionally a piece of information would break into my inner-scape and demand my attention. Well into their rehearsal one afternoon, I heard the choir sing "For we like sheep, for we like sheep have gone astray." This, as with many things I heard, left me feeling quite perplexed. I turned it over in my mind: "If they liked the sheep, why did they let them go astray?" The disconnections in my brain's wiring caused the information I received, especially social information, to come in bites, often lacking context. I was a child on the autism spectrum, and literal interpretation reigned in my perception of things.

In the home and beyond, my mother seemed to me the epitome of 1970s glamor. Even now, forty years on, I can still see her coming over the horizon, seeming to rise up out of the pavement like Botticelli's *Venus*, with long, flowing auburn hair brushing her hips as she walked up the footpath in her platform shoes toward the kindergarten gate. She sparkled in a deep-green kaftan studded with mirrored rhinestones that caught the light, transforming her into a walking disco ball. Such was the overwhelming impression my mother's style had on me that I looked to her to guide me in my growing sense of femininity. She happily obliged. Until my dying day I will never forget the orange-and-purple paisley dress my mother bought me whose white-winged collar stood out in complete disproportion to the size of the dress. The shop assistant said I looked "groovy," and by her and my mother's attentive smiles, I figured that this was a good thing and wore my paisley dress with pride.

My favorite toy at that time was a car and horse float which I ran up and down the kindergarten floor, playing "next to," but never "with" my peers. There was little else I could do; I had no conversational speech until the age of four and remained firmly locked away in my own world.

The one element in the playroom that caught my attention was a poster of counting numbers that beckoned in blue, red and yellow. As I worked my way slowly from 1 to 10, I discovered that some numbers pleased while others repulsed me. The number 8 in all its symmetry, going round and round in an unbroken line, was my favorite; 5 felt "trustworthy"; but to my mind, 3 was a dangerous number, dark and sinister. Even its mere utterance could result in calamities unknown!

I took to tapping out my "safe" numbers in an attempt to ward off harm. A tree, a table, any surface I could touch would receive an alternating pattern of eight and five beats: a mathematical prescription to allay my primitive fears. So effective was this method that one day when feeling particularly calm, I chose to do the unthinkable, beating out with trembling fingers the forbidden number 3 to see what might happen! Only a few seconds passed before I lost my nerve and found myself restoring the universal order with five quick taps on the trunk of a tree. To this compulsion I added another: having tapped the required quota, I would sniff my hands, craving any sensory input that they contained. Thus did I spend my outdoor playtime cocooned within my precious compulsive behaviors while my playmates ran, tumbled, and skipped, unencumbered by the laws that bound me.

Having worn a permanent track in the playroom carpet, I ditched my car and horse float, favoring a "Barbie Styling Head," complete with a little comb, brush and curlers with which to style the impossible sheen of her plastic locks. One Christmas, my mother presented me with a small bottle of drugstore-brand perfume called "April Violets." How its purple hue sparkled as I held it up to the light! The first whiff planted its indelible seal on my senses; to me, this was the height of sophistication. To this very day, April Violets remains my favorite fragrance, despite long access to any number of designer house perfumes. How different may have been the trajectory of my life had she given me Chanel No. 5!

My mother, however, was far more than a fashionable clotheshorse. She was, without doubt, the social heart and soul of our family unit. Thanks to my mother's influence, we grew up with a strong sense of social justice. This attitude was put into action through our family's hospital and nursing-home visits. My older brothers and sister could all sing, and they were encouraged to do so from a very early age. With this unifying talent, every Sunday morning, scrubbed, polished, and packed up with sheet music and guitars, off they went with me in tow to minister at all the major Brisbane hospitals, the Wacol psychiatric unit, and the local nursing homes, a different place each week—even on Christmas morning! Thus I spent my formative years exposed to the sick and infirm. One may have considered it "cruel and unusual punishment" for a socially impaired child; on the contrary, I enjoyed it. In this whirlwind of entertainment, I recall a particular visit to a nursing home.

We made our way through the corridors singing a few sets of carols until we reached a kind of gathering place, in reality no more than a shelter shed with a concrete floor. The residents, mainly women, sat on the benches that lined the walls. Despite their number, the room held no conversation; each person was seemingly isolated from the other. Music shuffled and stands arranged, we commenced our caroling. It wasn't long before this formerly silent space was transformed into a ballroom. Some residents danced in pairs, some happily swayed on their own. Mum encouraged my older brothers to take up partners in the dance as she herself did. How happy the women were! Perhaps they recalled their youth or sweethearts long departed. The music over, some approached me, saying, "You're just like my granddaughter." I was amazed at how I could bear a resemblance to so many! As we were leaving, one elderly resident came up alongside the fence that ran the length of the boundary and pushed a well-worn holy picture of the Sacred Heart through the wire into my hand, a picture I still possess. On the back of the card are written the words "Prayers help." As I recall that scene now, I do pray for her, long gone, but certainly not forgotten.

One afternoon while in kindergarten, I was given a large sheet of butcher's paper which the teacher attached to my easel, and a waxy, clear crayon. I was invited to draw whatever I liked. I started to write out the letters of my name and formed them as well as I could, given that they could not yet be seen. The teacher then handed me a blue-green wash of paint that I spread over the entire sheet with an oversized paintbrush. The letters rose up from the paper, luminous and alive, a revelation. My mother had just arrived to collect me. Shocked into speech, I ran to her, grasped her hand and led her to the easel. "Look Mummy, it's my name!" I could not have been more astonished by this effect had the letters written themselves! My name, Rachael, a Hebrew name meaning "ewe" or "sheep," was, I believe, a perfect fit. An Asperger child is just that: vulnerable, often silent, and ready to take another's lead for good or ill.

2

SCHOOL DAZE

The year was 1974. I remember my first day at school, standing by the entrance to the gate, hiding behind and looking now and then past my sister, my hair two bunches of copper pigtails sticking out at right angles beneath a beige rattan hat. I clung to her, terrified, as she tried to separate herself from my vise-like grip to go down to her senior school. I had to make my way through the kaleidoscope of noise and confusion that were my earliest memories of primary school. Poor Sarah, she had to suffer not only the bruises I left on her arm every morning but also the indignity of having me slink into her bed during the almost nightly thunderstorms throughout the summer. This caused me, more often than not, to be too afraid to visit the bathroom—with devastating consequences, for her at least.

The observation of my teacher during my first year was "Rachael is here physically, but that is all," graduating in the second year to "Rachael goes parallel to the class." What were they to make of a serious six-year-old who was given to wandering off, fascinatedly watching green ants for hours and entranced by the movement of water? I recall one particular morning before the commencement of school. I had taken up my usual position at the communal drinking fountains. Words cannot describe the wonder and pleasure I felt on turning the tap to witness the glittering spectacle of light and color which danced before my eyes: green, indigo, violet, and colors I had never seen before. Unfortunately, the headmistress didn't share my "special interest" in bubbling fountains. In 1975 there were yet two full decades until knowledge of the autism spectrum would come to light, opening with all the ferocity of Pandora's box.

I felt the hand of a teacher on my shoulder. Turning around, I saw that all the children had lined up on parade in ranks of two. "Sister wants to see you now." I never heard the bell ring, or if I did, it didn't register against what had already captivated my attention. I stood on the balcony next to the headmistress; before me was a sea of faces up-turned, some with their mouths open and all, no doubt, thanking God it was me and not them. "You are a willful, insolent, lazy child, you have no respect for the school rules!" I had been hauled up and corrected in front of the entire school, and now my nerves were at breaking point. Typical of Asperger children, my face displayed the opposite of the terror within: I smiled, I giggled. "You think this is funny, do you?" "No, Sister," I replied. Why was her face turning purple? I didn't like that color. "Put out your hand." Crack! Down came the strap on my arm. It was made of brown leather with white stitching. It was neither the first nor the last time I would feel it.

Children, as everyone knows, have an uncanny ability to pick out a vulnerable member from among their peers. In the animal kingdom, the weak are usually torn to shreds. Children's methods may be more subtle, but no less devastating in their outcomes. I loved words. I delighted in their sounds, shapes, and textures. Certain words held strong associational connections for me. My favorite word of all was "friendship." It was both smooth and crisp as I uttered it. Stranger still, as I pronounced it, I could *literally* taste hot French fries in my mouth and see them sizzling before my eyes! Another girl in my grade noted my love of words and suggested I write notes to the headmistress that she would dictate. This girl paid attention to me, and in my isolation, how I craved it! I faithfully transcribed everything she suggested. The theme of these notes revolved around how I was going to "end it all" and how I hated myself and her as well. The idea of "ending it all" was a vague concept for me, to say the least, and set off no warning bells as to how such notes would impact on the already antagonistic attitude the headmistress held toward me in her ignorance.

It was Holy Week when I wrote down the contents of these notes. Catholic imagery loomed large in my head and gave me strange comfort. Having written down all that my classmate commanded, in a final act of self-expression I drew a child-like image of myself crucified, a smile on my face as red crayon coursed from my side. I delivered the notes personally to Sister's office, placing them neatly on her desk as I had been directed to do so by my "friend." The next morning the headmistress came down to our classroom. I looked up from my desk to see her standing there. I was always amazed at how her face could change color. Now it was white, and a thin, sharp line quivered where her lips had been. I had no idea why she had come down to the classroom herself. The previous day's events had been wiped clear from my mind as I passed through the school gate after the final bell. "I want to see the girl Harris in my office—now!" I followed behind, with the slow steady gait of the condemned, until we reached her room. "Did you write these notes?" "Yes, Sister" (that being the literal truth). "So you want to end it all, do you?" "No, Sister." I walked away from her office, my arms and legs throbbing and numb.

I did not keep silent at school or at home owing to some misguided sense of loyalty toward the girl who had set me up; it was due, rather, to my impaired ability to distinguish between the malicious intentions of my classmate and my part in carrying them out. The general confusion I experienced in social situations, coupled with high levels of anxiety, were enough to prevent me from explaining the broader details of what had gone before. As I look back over my school days, I recall few mischievous incidents that did not involve my strings being pulled by another.

Sister's attitude toward me was not made easier by the fact that my mother, socially gifted and an extrovert by temperament, stood in sharp contrast to her socially isolated and awkward daughter. I truly believe that Sister thought me a naughty child and that she could "snap me out of it" through punishment and humiliation. Many years later, I tried to contact her to explain that there was a reason for why I behaved as I did. Unfortunately, by this time she was dying and unable to receive visitors. From my adult perspective, at first I was furious that she had subjected a child to such merciless treatment until I realized that what she had done had been done in ignorance, and with that knowledge, I forgave her from my heart. A great burden left me that day, and in its place came peace.

Not long after the incidents that resulted in my unjust punishments, my mother, on the advice of a sympathetic teacher, took me to a child guidance clinic founded by a psychiatrist and his wife. There, a kind general practitioner with an interest in pediatrics assessed my development. He asked me various questions about my family, the games I played at home, and how I got on with my three brothers. I remembered their backyard games of cricket; I was often assigned the role of "outer fielder." I suppose I stood in the outer field in every way as far as my brothers were concerned, and who could blame them? My position of little sister put me firmly at the bottom of the pecking order, and having joined the family circle a couple of years after my entry into this world, I must have seemed something of an intruder as I had not bonded with them. Because I was overly sensitive and easily provoked, I daresay mercilessly teasing me must have seemed great sport to them, with little outlay for their entertainment. Yet still, even at a distance, I admired the boyish energy with which my brothers took up their interests: now skateboards, now road bikes, now waxing surfboards to perfection, now their first cars and forming their first rock bands. I have my brother Bill to thank, too, for rescuing me from drowning.

The incident occurred during a neighborhood poolside barbeque when I was about six years old. I was floating happily on the surface of the water, my thin arms holding tight to the sides of a rubber ring while other children swam and played about me. Greased up with sunscreen, I lost my grip and slipped through the center of the ring, finding myself at the bottom of the swimming pool. Suspended in that silent watery world, I looked about without fear. What must have been only seconds later, my brother dived in, scooped me up, and raised me above the surface of the water and into the anxious arms of my mother. To my brother I owe my life.

Let me return to the little wooden chair and table where I sat drawing a picture of myself on top of a hill flying a kite. "Draw anything you like," the doctor had said, and this had been my subject of choice. While I executed my picture, questions were asked and school reports consulted. The doctor told my mother that my developmental profile was unusual. Academically, I was, in many areas, advanced for my age, yet socially I lagged far behind my peers. The possibility of medication never arose for as far as the doctor was concerned, I did not merit it; rather, he took a "let's see how she goes" approach and with his recommendation, the punishments of the headmistress, which had been so unrelenting, suddenly ceased, never to reoccur.

My difficulties were "social" rather than "mental health" issues, so neither my doctor nor mother saw my difference as "something that needed to be treated." They presumed I would mature and "find my place" with time, which, eventually, I did! There was no knowledge of high functioning autism, so there was no official "treatment" either. My mother, to which our visits to entertain the frail and elderly attested, was quite instinctive in the way she managed me. She got me involved socially and in my church community, playing to my strengths, while simply allowing me to be myself. Not for one moment was my mother frightened by my silent and withdrawn nature, and never did she try to force me out of it, thus did my interactions ebb and flow between my retreating in and my desire to reach out.

As we gathered our things to leave, the kind doctor observed, half to my mother, half to himself, "I think Rachael feels lonely in a crowd." My lone stick-figure self continued to fly her kite on the back door of the doctor's office for a long time after her flesh-and-blood self was re-immersed in the society she sought to understand.

For typical children the playground is a fun, stimulating place for spontaneous play and interaction. For children on the autism spectrum, the playground is a noisy, chaotic, nerve-jangling environment with ever-changing social rules that are totally lost on them—and so it was for me. Fortunately during my early primary school years, structured and well-organized games abounded. Skipping rope, hopscotch, and various ball games were all in vogue. In my usual enthusiasm, I threw myself into these pastimes as well as I could, despite the constraints my lack of mobility produced. I could not bend my knees properly, so bike riding and roller-skating were out, but my regular games required little conversation and put me at ease. Most of the girls in my grade made allowances for both my physical and social limitations; still I had no particular friend outside these activities.

When not otherwise occupied, I would disappear to the far end of the playground, claiming a spot under a shady tree. Once seated, I began playing with my most recently acquired companions, Chewbacca and R2-D2. Round and round the base of the tree, I would take my little plastic pals on an endless quest of discovery of alien worlds. Occasionally, my mini-figures would attract the interest of a passing child. I was pleased to be able to show them off and with the social success they promised, I began bringing toys and books to school as conversation starters. "Wookies" and "Droids" were all very well and good, but for a child desperate to express herself, their whistles and grunts meant their days as companions were numbered.

The beginning of my third year at school proved to be a turning point in my journey. On the first day of the new term, I sat at my desk fumbling with freshly backed books, pencils, and paints in a vain attempt to sort my belongings. Since the time that formal interaction was demanded of me, I found that like many children on the spectrum, I lacked the skills necessary to organize myself, no matter how great the order imposed from without.

Pushed an inch too far, my pencils tumbled from their case, sending a cascade of color over the edge of the desk, followed by a musical clatter as they struck the tiled floor. I bent down and started to pick them up and as I did so, I noticed another hand reaching to retrieve them from where they had fallen. I looked up and saw a smiling face. "Hello, I'm Helen," she said. "Hello, my name is Rachael," I responded.

That day I made a friend, and what a friend she was! In my mind's eye, I see her now as she was then. Helen had dark locks and darker eyes which always wore an expression of quiet confidence. She was mature, like an older girl, and never was she fazed by anything that came her way. With these qualities, Helen became the link between me and the world outside myself, and under her influence I thrived.

On my entering the classroom on any given morning, Helen would be there to make sure my books were in order before the commencement of lessons. It was she who, noticing my limp, would offer me her arm as we ascended the winding wooden staircase that led to the second floor of the school building. With Helen at my side, the noise and chaos of the playground gave way to the sounds of laughter and energy as she helped me navigate my way through what had previously been such an assault on my senses. Helen herself possessed an enigmatic quality, which was most evident in her capacity for silence. It was in this very quality that, paradoxically, I found my voice.

With the morning's lessons behind us and a whole hour to please ourselves over lunch, Helen and I would make our way to a shady step and there she would patiently listen while I told her about my latest find at the local quarry, the antics of my dog, or stories from the latest camping trip my father had taken us on. Looking back, I don't think Helen once showed frustration with being on the receiving end of my autistic monologues. In her generosity, she accepted my style of communication as simply my way of being in the world. However, what I lacked in the give-and-take of conversation was more than made up in the capacity I possessed to translate my vivid imagination into playtime games which, by virtue of their radical nature, drew large groups of girls who wanted a slice of the action.

With newfound confidence in my capacity for self-expression, I set to work concocting the rules for an elaborate game of "Haunted House." During free time, I would commission the most artistically gifted girls in my class to draw posters of ghosts, ghouls, and assorted specters with which to imbue "The House" with the right degree of eeriness.

Leaving my artists to their task, I set out to find a suitable setting for our game. Having searched the length and breadth of the school grounds, I was duly rewarded when I came upon a large storage area at the far end of a long stone corridor, an area hewn, it would seem, into the very earth on which the foundations of the school rested. I decided to investigate my find further. I pushed open the heavy wooden door and stepped into the dark, musty space that smelled of damp earth and appeared, as I ventured a few steps forward, to recede far into the distance before me. As I stood there, my eyes slowly adjusted to the pale yellow light that streamed through a small concrete grate high above the level of the ground. A slow smile spread over my face as I considered the possibilities. "Perfect!" came my exclamation, the only audible sound in that somber space.

Hurrying back to the hub of activity I had left, I soon related the details of all I had seen, and despite the rising excitement among my fellow playmates, I managed to swear them to the utmost secrecy. It occurred to me that our lunchtime entertainments would not be looked on favorably by the teachers, who would prefer their students to engage in less revolutionary pursuits.

The minutes ticked toward the bell that marked the commencement of the lunch hour the following day. With its shrill announcement, murmurs of conspiratorial glee ran through the ranks of girls who had associated themselves with the "Haunted House Club." With books closed and chairs eagerly pushed back, a large portion of the class filed out through the door and made for their school bags, drawing from them the artworks which were to hang from the walls of the storage room. Quantities of white and gray wool had been purloined from the sewing baskets of mothers handy with craft, all in the name of transforming the dull, dark area at the end of the corridor into a space charged with supernatural ambience, an extension, as I see it now, of my own longing for what lay behind the commonplace and mundane.

To this end, we affixed our posters and strung our wool in cobweblike clumps throughout the generous space the storage area afforded. The group's enthusiasm to enter fully into the role-play our efforts demanded left Halloween merriment in the dust. Giddy with excitement, we ran up and down the length of the room waving our arms and groaning like zombies, getting tangled up in the woolen cobwebs and laughing all the while with the sheer joy of running amok! Happily occupied, we continued our lunchtime games for several days. Fresh pictures and new balls of wool were brought in to replace those that had fallen, ripped and tangled in the joyful riotous stampede we girls gave ourselves over to in our themed revelry.

Despite our best efforts, news of "The Club" began to spread among the students, and our ranks swelled by the day. I'm not sure what it was that gave us away in the end. Perhaps the ever diminishing headcount on the playground was our undoing, or the higher-than-average enthusiasm with which large numbers of children made their way toward a far, usually uninhabited, corner of the corridor.

What I do remember with great clarity was the day my class teacher swung open the heavy wooden door, catching us like a large nest of mice, struck dumb with eyes shining in the shaft of light, our secret exposed! Without fuss, we were ordered to clean up what we had so painstakingly created and were given strict warning that our clubhouse was, from that day forward, out of bounds.

As quickly as my newfound friends had been amassed, so, too, did they disperse the moment my fantastical games were brought to an end. The bridges I had built between others and myself were made of a kind of pageantry, a theater in which many would enter to receive an afternoon's entertainment. As with all matinees, my season too came to an end, leaving me to reflect on my short-lived social performance. The days following the closure of my club brought with them a keener sense of loneliness; in stark contrast, no doubt, to the multitude of playmates with whom I had, for a time, been constantly surrounded.

I turned to the one anchor in my sea of apprehension. Helen, not having joined in the fever pitch of silliness I had invented, had become distanced from me, befriending others and thus closing a door that, by virtue of my social lack, I could not open. Helen, I know, was well within her rights to develop new friends, and even though after that time I rarely crossed her path and despite the lapse of years, I have never forgotten her consideration toward me. Helen was kindness itself.

My sister Sarah continued to follow my mother's directive to "keep an eye on her," a coded phrase roughly translated as "stop Rachael from aimlessly wandering around or outside the school grounds after the last bell." Unfortunately, this occurred far too often for my mother's liking, which necessitated my siblings doubling up as a search party.

Once found, either in some obscure part of the school grounds or down at the local corner store, I would stand there, mouth gaping and eyes wide open, genuinely amazed at suddenly seeing them before me; not once, but every time they found me. Such was my sense of disconnection. It never entered my head that my mother would be worried about my whereabouts. "Where have you been, why do you keep wandering off?" she would ask, searching my face for answers, and I, struck dumb with anxiety, could supply no response—for I did not know the reason myself. Time meant nothing to me, nor did I feel a growing sense of uneasiness as the distance increased between me and those who had the capacity to protect me. It was not that my fears were nonexistent; rather, they were archetypal in nature.

On one occasion, to prevent my wandering off, Sarah, who had yet to collect her things from the science lab, met me at my classroom and walked me back down to the senior girls' school to retrieve her books. On entering the lab, I froze with horror at the sight of a full-standing skeleton. I ran outside to the balcony and refused to reenter the room. Sarah came out and tried to alleviate my fears. "Come on, Rachael, it's only plastic!" she said. Her assurances sounded hollow to someone overwhelmed by primal fear. She tugged at my dress but my fingers clung, firm and white-tinged, to the balcony rail. "No no no—don't make me look at it!" I screamed.

What I lacked in social understanding was more than made up for in my autistic capacity for absorbing the emotional atmosphere around me. The fear of annihilation was never very far from the surface of my mind. It was not surprising, considering my perilous beginnings, for surely it must have affected my psyche. Neither then, nor since, have I taken my existence for granted, always walking a precarious tightrope between "being" and "nonbeing."

3

CURIOUSER AND CURIOUSER

Dear, dear! How queer everything is to-day! And yesterday things went on just as usual. I wonder if I've been changed in the night? Let me think: *was* I the same when I got up this morning? I almost think I can remember feeling a little different. But if I'm not the same, the next question is, "Who in the world am I?" Ah, *that's* the great puzzle![1]

For my tenth birthday, my father bought me an *Alice in Wonderland* picture book. I liked Alice; I could relate to her. She wore the same slightly startled expression on her face with each new social encounter that I wore. I found it easy to sympathize with Alice. No one seemed to follow the logic she so clearly expressed, and that which the characters deemed "normal," was anything but normal to her.

One afternoon, I took myself off down the road to visit my ants. As engaging as I found them, I realized that I wouldn't find in them the companionship I badly needed. At this point, a little girl about my age skipped up her driveway and introduced herself. "Hello, my name's Marjorie Bristlehead, what's yours?" "Bristlehead, that's a funny name," I replied. On hearing this she ran inside to her mother who, moments later, appeared in the driveway. "Bristlehead is not a funny name!" her mother kept angrily repeating. "What's your surname?" "Harris." "Harris is a funny name," she declared. She may as well have said black was white and day was night. "I do not have a funny name," I said indignantly. "It is you who have the funny name!" Like Alice's pack of cards, mother and daughter blew away.

I did not make a new friend that day, though I had longed to do so. I saw Marjorie and her mother out in their front garden from time to time, although I could never look at them without imagining straw sticking up out of their collars where their heads should have been. Perhaps, because of their difference in wiring, people on the autism spectrum never seem to lose the "Alice in Wonderland" quality in their nature and so their innate sense of wonder.

Many children on the autism spectrum have unusual sensory sensitivities, and as a young child I was no exception. Like Alice, whatever I ate, whatever I drank, became a risky undertaking with no certain outcome. The daily ritual of eating breakfast became for me a game of Russian roulette. Some mornings I ate my cereal and toast without incident. Other mornings, the roof of my mouth would start to tingle as I finished the last morsel. This tingling sensation heralded the worst nausea I have ever had to endure. At its peak, wave after wave would wash over me for up to two hours at a time. As I stood pale and overcome in the middle of the playground, I often wondered how other children managed to bear it. It never once occurred to me that they weren't experiencing life in the same way as I did. I could only marvel at their resilience, and despair at my lack.

Water, which had once held such charm for me, became a monstrous thing. To my ears, the flushing of a toilet had all the force of Niagara Falls. I would stand halfway out the door, my finger poised on the lever, ready to run. My nightly bath also required modification. On pulling out the plug, I swept as much water as I could over the plughole to prevent the formation of a swirling funnel of water roaring like a jet taking off as it disappeared down the drain. Such experiences jangled my nerves and sent my levels of anxiety through the roof.

Daily life continued to hold many mysteries for me. Having lined up on school parade, we would march to our classrooms to the accompaniment of music. Glenn Miller struck up his band, and the music poured out of speakers in the upper level of the building. I couldn't work out for the life of me where the band was. Were they assembled inside one of the classrooms? Were they set up behind the back of the school? The fact that our family had a record player at home in constant use did nothing to relieve these and other riddles that presented themselves to my fragmented mind. At this time in my development, I was unable to generalize experiences from one context to the next and I made little connection between cause and effect. Islands of information floated around in a sea of gray matter.

The routine of my days continued, and as one week led to the next, I fondly remember the Friday nights spent sleeping over at my Nan's place. Nan was an English West Country woman with a thick Gloucestershire accent. She was made up of equal parts hospitality and high anxiety, and she presided over a kitchen that always smelled of freshly baked tarts and cat food.

Nan, my father's mother, had been widowed for some years when she met her second husband—Pop, as I knew him—during a shipboard romance on a trip to the Old Country. He, a sprightly ex-military man in his eighties, having served in the British Army at Gallipoli, divided his time between tending his rose garden and trellis tomatoes and listening to the "wireless" through a small pair of earplugs. Pop would sit by the window, a monolithic silhouette, animated now and then by the drumming of his large fingers on the edge of the armrest of his chair.

In sharp contrast to her husband, Nan was a study in nervous energy. Her uniform consisted of a floral-print housedress and apron. Her days were given over to baking, knitting, and washing voluminous amounts of clothes, which she hand-fed through her wringer. At the time, it struck me as odd that a quiet, elderly couple, such as my Nan and Pop, should require such unrelenting upkeep. But who was I to argue when at night, my grandmother tucked me into the large, white, crisp sheets of the bed in the front room? There I lay, and instead of counting the phantasms that passed across my heavy eyes, I watched the amber patterns of car headlights that shone through the lace curtains sliding across the walls and disappearing at the far corner near the door until I, too, disappeared in sleep.

During her leisure hours, Nan would knit and sew and consume a steady diet of Catherine Cookson romance novels. Passing her coffee table, I picked one up and stared at the cover. A brightly colored illustration of a woman with a wistful expression on her face stared back, but her thoughts were not my thoughts. Replacing the book on top of its fellows, I ventured out into the garden and round to the laundry shed. There I was carried away by the love of "spinning objects." Grasping the wringer handle, I watched the silver cogs rotate in an eternal round of perfection. My ecstasy was shattered by an inquiring voice. "Whatever are you doing there, my love?"

How could I put into words a delight that robbed me of speech? "I'm looking at the wheels turn, Nan," I replied at length. "Lummy days! Come inside and I'll give you something to turn," she said. We went back into the kitchen, and there she proceeded to pull out various ingredients from her larder: flour, butter, jam, eggs, and a large stainless-steel sifter, which she placed before me with the following instruction. "There you are my love, you can pour a cup of my plain flour into that and turn the handle for all you're worth; mind you keep it over the bowl now." Together we spent a happy afternoon making strawberry jam tarts and I, queen of my grandmother's heart, would not have anyone steal them away.

After the evening meal, Nan and I would sit out on the small porch by the back door. At that time there was a tannery down the road which intermittently, when the wind blew the right (or wrong!) way, would send a smell wafting through the yard. I drew in my breath and said, "Mmm, that smells good, is someone having a barbecue Nan?" She couldn't have looked more surprised. "Flipping Hanover! That's no barbecue, my love, that's the tannery!" Even my Nan's cat that had been snugly ensconced on her lap leapt to the ground and slunk inside the house. Where my sense of smell was concerned, my brain continued to play tricks on my perception and reinterpret all kinds of sensory input.

The sudden stench of the local tannery or the base note of cat food in the kitchen hardly registered, whereas the first whiff of Pop's aftershave or talcum powder would unleash in me a chain reaction of queasiness, rising to panic. As with many individuals with Asperger's syndrome, with time, these sensory issues receded and found their proper place, drawing me to welcome the pleasant and spurn the repugnant.

My grandmother's kitchen table served many uses. It was a humble, laminated construction masquerading as polished pine. Upon it, Nan would serve up the nightly ritual of "meat and two veg." On its cool, floured surface, countless pastries came into being, and its generous space also held a catalog of dress patterns. But of all its purposes, none compared to the intrigue of my introduction to playing cards.

Naturally inquisitive, it had long been my habit to rummage through Nan's kitchen sideboard looking for things with which to amuse myself during the course of my stay. Thimbles, dice, and brightly colored buttons all served as fodder to my curiosity. So it was, one evening, that I reached my hand as far back into the drawer as I could, having exhausted that which was easily attainable. From there I pulled out a small cardboard box, and finding a quiet spot to sit, I examined its contents.

Fascinated by what I had found, I first became acquainted with the King of Hearts. His face wore a look of noble resignation. He clutched his ermine coat with one hand and held his sword aloft with the other. Yellow, red, and black hued, his head and torso repeated in the lower half of his black-bordered confines. I looked thoughtfully at his image and wondered if he were at war with others or within himself? His queen, similarly clad, bore an expression barely containing her outrage. Her slender fingers held a red-gold Tudor rose, but despite her beguiling gesture, to me it was quite evident that she was moved neither by love nor nature.

The Jack, a profile of perfection, looked out upon his world with disdain from under his carefully coiffured locks, grasping a standard—his standard, such as it was. But of all those inhabiting the Kingdom, it was the Joker, with upturned shoes and jangling bells which swung off the ends of his floppy, three-pointed hat, whom I found most unnerving. It was he who, with contorted grin, roamed at large, unrestrained, shaking a distracting likeness of himself on the end of a stick. His merriment belied his mischief.

If only people kept their faces as still as those on my Nan's playing cards! The human face in a social setting is a never-ending montage of gesture, movement, sound, and inference. It was not that I was incapable of reading the social cues others expressed. The trouble lay in the speed with which the information was conveyed and the time it took for me to process that information. No sooner had I grasped one point in an exchange than I would find that the train of conversation had picked up speed and moved on, leaving me far behind.

It is said that "the eyes are the windows of the soul" and in our gazing upon them, all manner of the heart's secrets are plainly seen. For my part I kept my windows shuttered firmly against the onslaught of sights and sounds—otherwise, visual information would pour through my eyes unchecked and without priority, which my brain struggled to process. What to others was a pleasant conversation, to my young mind presented as a veritable cacophony. Some read my lack of eye contact as an indication of shyness. Friends of my mother would gather round me exclaiming, "Oh look, isn't she shy, how sweet!" Thus would they offer me indulgent smiles, lowering themselves to my eye level, willing my interaction.

Irksome as their misunderstandings were, I was not then, nor have I ever been, shy. I have always been fascinated by human nature and sought to understand other people in relation to myself; no doubt, because my knowledge had been so hard won. To drop my gaze filtered out the distractions that would cut across my concentration. A dull patch of flooring would enable me to focus exclusively on the conversation at hand.

The curiosity I felt toward others was by no means a one-way street. Despite my disengagement from those around me, in some ways, I didn't escape people's attention. In fact on many occasions, complete strangers would approach me. "What's wrong?" or "Cheer up!" they would say. Once on a bus trip, a man who had sat quietly observing me from a distance, came straight up to my mother and said, "There's something troubling that little girl, are you aware?" She assured him that I was more than all right, and he made his way back to his seat. Mum and I looked at each other in disbelief and laughed. My mother, well used to my looks and ways, knew her daughter to be a very different kettle of fish from that perceived by an outsider.

I felt like wearing a badge with the message "Sorry, it's just my face." This personal observation was closer to the mark than I could have possibly known. How was I to know that the expression on my face was a social handicap? The faces of people on the autism spectrum lack the tone and animation of their "neurotypical" counterparts; that is, those who are typically wired and therefore the majority. My expression, which was simply neutral, was seen by those who did not know me as pensive or sad. I saw myself as having two layers: an "inner self," vibrant, inquisitive, full of life and humor; and an "outer self," a mask, solemn and still, which camouflaged and contradicted my inner life. It brought a whole new meaning to the expression "taking things at face value."

Returning the playing cards to their box, I slid off the end of Nan's rocking chair and found her putting away the last of the crockery from the drainer. "I see you found my cards, my love. Just let me put this apron back on the hook and I'll show you how to play." Sweeping the last of the crumbs from the kitchen table, she bade me pull up my chair close to its edge. From the sideboard, my grandmother, with a twinkle in her eye, produced a jam jar filled with one- and two-cent coins. Placing it on the table, she dutifully counted out a small sum and divided it equally. Nan's share lay in a little heap by her elbow. My love of precision dictated that mine be ordered in two neat stacks: a squat bungalow of twos and a towering high-rise of ones. With a deft hand, my grandmother shuffled the cards. The individual characters I had so carefully studied passed through her hands in a blur of color. I put my elbows on the table and watched Nan's reflection in its hard and shiny surface.

That evening Nan taught me the simple pleasure of a game of Snap. How the cards flew, one on top of the other as my eagle eye anticipated the consecutive drop of a matching pair. "Snap!" My hand came down on a pair of Jokers, stopping their mischief in its tracks. That night my fortunes rose and fell, as did the little bronze towers I had so painstakingly constructed.

As a child I loved "Tea Parties." Knowing this, one Saturday morning my grandmother pulled out from her string bag a miniature tea set of cream plastic with a cornflower-blue motif. Enraptured with the detail, I gave myself over to the quiet contemplation of the set's teapot, cups, saucers, and tiny spoons. At length, I arranged my new tea set on the living room carpet. My guests consisted, not of "Dormice" and "March Hares," but Teddy bears and Barbie dolls. Playing the perfect host, I poured their "tea" from the little pot, inquiring, "Would you like one lump or two?" "Milk?" and "Is that the right shade?"—phrases garnered from observing my mother or afternoon television. Teddy seemed unmoved by my hospitality, whereas Barbie, with her permanent plastic smile, was ecstatic no matter what the outcome. What drew me to the ritual of the "Tea Ceremony" was the sense of order it imposed. Here was a social scenario where the rules were clear and the guidelines without ambiguity. Thus contained, I felt both free and safe to practice my social side, moving from one part to the next in an orderly and satisfying sequence. To this day, I am more socially at ease entertaining and enjoying the elegance and organization of a dinner party rather than a chance meeting at the local shop.

Watching my play unfold, my grandmother would look up from her knitting and offer a kind word of encouragement. "How daintily you pour your tea, my love, I've got a good mind to make one myself!" Putting her work aside and rising from her chair, Nan reached into a small drawer in her display cabinet and pulled out a little iron key. Turning the lock, she carefully retrieved two of her best bone china cups and saucers. These I had long admired with their "Cottage Rose" design. I marveled at their refinement and delicacy, in stark contrast to their provincial neighbors the Toby Mugs. "Here we are, my love, I've made us some of my dainty sandwiches and cake. Come and sit with me by the window." My Nan was a woman of simple pleasures. Hot Bourneville Cocoa, sandwiches with the crusts cut off, and "best butter," as she called it, all ranked high on her list of luxuries. She was generous, too, swelling by her contributions the number of presents beneath our Christmas tree. With great satisfaction she would select large foiled and boxed Easter eggs filled with chocolate beanies, to the delight of her grandchildren. Yes, our grandmother loved us, but Nan was as colorful and as fragile as her teacups.

During my stays, I caught glimpses of what was to come. Nan's anxieties, which were never far from the surface, manifested themselves with ever-increasing regularity. Having lit her gas stove, she would quickly turn to the sink, dousing the spent match-head a little *too* thoroughly. The first signs of an approaching thunderstorm would necessitate her covering the cutlery in the drainer with a tea towel, lest it be struck by lightning. When I took my bath, Nan would insist I sing for its duration, so as to be sure I hadn't drowned. To cease my tune would be to invite her anxious inquiry "Are you all right in there, Rachael?"

Occasionally, I would ask Nan if she would let me examine the contents of her jewelry box. "Aye my love, that you may." My favorite piece was her engagement ring, which Pop had bought in Johannesburg on their return journey from the UK—in reality, an inferior stone in an indifferent setting. My childhood gaze imbued it with grandeur, and noticing my admiration, Nan would invariably make references to her death, which she greatly feared. "You shall have it when I'm gone," she would mournfully say.

So it was with sad eyes that I watched her slow demise until finally, she was beyond my reach. How I wish my adult self could return now to where she was then and wrapping my arms about her, speak words of comfort and reassurance into her fears! Nan, like her engagement ring, was a fleck of brilliance in a humble setting.

4

WIRED FOR WONDER

The difficulty I experienced in developing relationships with other people did, in some strange way, give me the compensatory gift of a strong connection with the natural world. The very capacity I lacked in making friends came back to me a hundredfold in forging relationships with the world of matter.

I remember my mother and father packing us all into the family car and heading up to a beautiful retreat house at Marburg, situated in the rolling landscape of the Laidley Valley, home of the Divine Word Missionary novitiate. It was an imposing house with smooth, polished, wooden floors whose vast dining hall was a focal point for guests' meals. At Christmastime, a group of my parents' friends and their children would descend on Marburg to enjoy its picturesque setting and each other's company. Large bay windows gave an uninterrupted view over the brown paddocks and ghost gums, which were typical of the dairy farms in the surrounding district. We stayed in the guest quarters, where we children were happy to claim our beds before running around the grounds and exploring the walking tracks that led in all directions.

Most of the children were drawn to each other like iron filings to a magnet. I myself felt the irresistible pull of a small stone grotto quite some distance from the manicured lawns surrounding the main house. Every step drew me deeper into a great solitude, and in the silence I was never alone. I bent down and looked into the grotto. When my eyes became accustomed to the darkness, my gaze was met by patterned wings whose markings stood out like hundreds of pairs of dark-brown eyes dilated to full capacity. I froze for some moments in an attempt to out-stare them. Their unflinching gaze suddenly dissolved as large brown moths streamed out into the light of day. All was silent again, and I noticed the darkening sky over the distant hills.

The wind rose and came up through the valley in thick gusts, making the slim gums bend and rustle with the force. A lone storm-bird started its musical acrobatics, climbing from low octave to high, almost bursting with the effort, then down to its base note to start its vocal ascent once again. Here in this solitude, I knew myself to be not a casual observer, a subject among objects, but in relationship with everything that met my eye and ear. To pick up a stick and note its twists and bends, to view the arterial filigree of the smallest leaf, was to relate to its being and give thanks for my own.

I brushed the powdery bark from my hands and saw in the distance through the trees the first lights appearing in the windows of the Grand House. So was I summoned from the grotto and its inhabitants, and making my way up the well-worn track, I caught the smell of a wood fire and watched its smoke curl beyond the main buildings.

They were happy days; the summers spent at Marburg were as close to a child's paradise as one could imagine. In the morning, accompanied by the melodic song of the magpie, I would skip along the wooden walkways running the length of the dormitories and, finding a shady grove, would listen for cicadas. First, the soloist, a single specimen, would begin its tentative *ch- ch- ch*, the sound then swelling with the chorus of the colony, rising to a deafening crescendo. If I were fortunate, I would spot one of these elusive artists, marveling at the rainbow hues reflected in its transparent wings. An afternoon storm brought out miniature green tree frogs in biblical proportions. After the rains had ceased, the frogs would hop along the verandas, carpet the stairs, and take up residence in every nook, cranny, and letterbox on the property. These were my favorites. Gently picking up one of their number, I would rest it in the palm of my hand so as to study its vibrant color and note its smooth, dewy skin. A passing girl screamed at the sight; I responded by picking up another and watched with amusement as she screamed the louder, running for the apparent safety of the dining hall. Often I would explore the grounds by myself, at other times in the company of children who were happy enough to let me tag along in their wake.

Back home during Midnight Mass, weary from a broken night's sleep, I would rest my head on the long wooden pew with my ear to its surface, listening to and feeling the vibrations caused by the singing of the choir. Great numbers of Christmas beetles, drawn to the light, would fly in through the windows. Some would hit the ceiling fans and meet their end. Others would get their spindly legs caught in the loops of the carpet. On seeing their plight, I would rise and make my way around the church on a mission of mercy to rescue as many as I could. I gently released their legs from the carpet and offered my finger to those that were struggling and spinning on their backs, flinging them out into the night.

At other times I gave safe passage to long lines of hairy caterpillars on the move, preventing their being trod underfoot by children at play. This sense of reverence for the small and the insignificant has never left me. Only a few years back, I found myself rushing to the aid of a long brown stick-insect. A group of young schoolchildren had found it on the platform of the local train station and had begun nudging it with their feet, ready to make a kind of sport of its demise. "Stop!" I cried, and ran over to the gathered circle. "Do not touch it!" I said, as I eased it onto the brim of my straw hat. I looked up to see their mothers, not three feet away, staring at me like I had gone mad. It seemed as though nothing was going to disturb the flow of their conversation. The life of a stick insect did not rank very high on their list of priorities. I climbed two flights of stairs, giving the creature sanctuary in a grassy field on the other side of a wire fence. "Brief though its life may be, it shall have its day," I said to myself as I coaxed it off the brim.

Created works of beauty, too, had a profound effect on my mind and heart. Our parish church, like many constructed in Australia during the 1960s, was built of unimaginative, beige brick. However, what inspired me afresh every time I saw it was a monumental mosaic of Saint Francis of Assisi set into the outer wall of the church. Given my childlike dimensions, I suppose the mosaic would inspire awe. What captured my attention, though, were the individual tiles that made up the mosaic. I pondered the little facets of color that, although charming, individually made no sense. It was only when I ran a good distance from them and looked back that the full integrity of the mosaic would suddenly emerge. There I saw Francis with arms outstretched, solid and towering, yet existing only for, and by, his Lord's glory. It took great courage for me to run toward his image, watching it shatter and descend into shards of multicolored chaos, and so with each and every trip to church, I would meet this spectacle with a renewed sense of wonder.

Far from me being left to my own devices, my explorations of Marburg were punctuated by many social activities. As we poured into the dining hall, its vast area and high ceilings soon filled with the sound of lively conversation. Much of what was spoken flew over my head, but what was not lost to my understanding, and indeed, what communicated itself loud and clear, was the kindness and patience shown toward me in many practical ways by the members of our little community. We would gather together every morning to celebrate Mass in a small chapel, surrounded by the rolling woodlands. My level of attention, as with all children, fluctuated wildly between observing the ritual, saying my responses, and craning my neck to look out of the window.

What I sought was a view of the large in-ground swimming pool farther down the hill which had become the happy venue for my swimming lessons. A member of our community and a lifesaver, hearing of my brushes with death, offered to teach me to swim. With great patience and attention, Paul guided me through all that I needed to learn. He encouraged me to hold my breath underwater and to use a kickboard to propel myself toward the other side. It was he who, with a reassuring hand, steadied me as I learned to float on my back. Putting each step together so that they culminated in a perfect freestyle stroke, Paul taught me in one week what most children require a year or more to achieve.

A ripple of excitement ran through the children when one morning it was announced that we were to put on a multicultural parade. This, of course, appealed greatly to my innate Asperger love of pageantry. I quickly set to work acquiring what was needed to do justice to my chosen nationality. I decided I would be Japanese. To this end I borrowed my mother's silk dressing-gown and cork platform shoes. Raiding her makeup bag, I chose a bright red lipstick and kohl pencil to imbue myself with the elegance of a geisha. Japan being a special interest of mine at the time, I had read many books on Japanese culture and had pored over countless illustrations of cherry trees framing Mount Fuji and of beautifully dressed women holding paper parasols and disappearing down the lantern-lined alleys of the Kyoto District.

One afternoon after a long session of reading, I closed the book that inspired my longings and announced to my mother, "When I grow up, I'm going to be Japanese!" The Japanese did not need to second-guess their social rules for they were laid down in the very foundations of their culture. In Japan, no one would demand that I look them in the eye. In Japan, I could enjoy the silences between words.

That night as the adults took their seats, I readied myself for my debut. Double wrapped in the silk gown, I twisted my carrot-colored hair into a bun on top of my head, securing it with a pair of lead pencils pushed in at right angles. A friend of my mother's put the finishing touches on my "Oriental" eyes. Transformed, I stepped into the cork platform shoes and shuffled, hands together, as gracefully as I could along the narrow carpet, to the cheers and clapping of our audience.

The following morning, my mother put on her own performance, although unintended. She had been given the task of defrosting the meat for the midday meal. My mother, ever a practical woman, wrapped the cuts of meat in separate plastic bags and laid them outside on the hood of her Volkswagen in an effort to speed up the process. Halfway through the morning, she returned to find the hood of her car covered with stray cats eager for a feed. She ran to the car, waving her arms wildly and shouting at them, "Get off!" What made this scene even more incongruous was Mum's choice of outfit that day, a pair of zebra-print leggings and a purple cape. Attired in this manner, Mum in her efforts to remove the cats became a parody of a nature documentary. As I looked out from the dining hall on this scenario, I wondered for a brief moment if the hungry cats might not revert to their basic instincts and "take her down" right there where she flailed and shrieked. By this time, others had gathered where I stood. We laughed and laughed before a few ventured out to rescue my mother from being the cats' second choice on the menu.

Our week at Marburg drew to a close. I would miss roaming the picturesque grounds, visiting the fascinating grotto, and basking in the company of our community. Like my geisha gown, Marburg had wrapped me not in silk but in the kindness and patience of those who were loving toward me in everything they said and did.

5

A GAZE RETURNED

I have only briefly alluded to the identity of the teacher who was to become, perhaps, the greatest influence on my social and spiritual development during these early years. As the heavy wooden door swung open on my "Haunted House Club," it was the figure of my grade-three teacher, Sr. Agnes, silhouetted in light, who stood in the doorway, gently chiding me to remove the tangled mess in which I played. The club I had formed was analogous to the inner workings of my autistic mind. Lost in a labyrinth of chaotic and fanciful whims, my mental processes crisscrossed in an endless round of random and associational thoughts that wound in on themselves, rarely making contact with the light of society.

By the time she had crossed my path, Agnes was a woman in her forties. Slim, she wore the brown habit and black veil of her order. A wisp of dark brown hair curled out from beneath her veil, framing her face, and with clear blue eyes, she looked out upon her world with a quiet sense of purpose. Despite the responsibility of having to educate a class of well over thirty pupils, Sr. Agnes, intuiting my need, found the time to pass my desk. Praising my efforts, she sought opportunities to draw me further out of my social isolation, and I, responding to her words of encouragement, began to take interest in the happenings around me. "You're really beginning to come out of your shell!" she would say, and so I was.

The education I received from Sr. Agnes, trained in the Catholic system of the 1970s, proved academically to be my salvation. In her methods, discipline and routine were the order of the day. Our class-room rang with the rhythmic recitation of "times tables" for what seemed like hours on end. Such was the regularity of these practices that, having been firmly embedded in my memory, I am to this day never lost for an answer: "Seven 7s are forty-nine, six 8s are forty-eight," and so on. Looking back on the way Sr. Agnes arranged her classroom, I see now how it helped my focus and attention. There were no pictures on the wall to indulge my love of detail, no brightly colored mobiles dangling from the ceiling to entice an already distracted mind. The long summer days in Queensland were hot, but at least there wasn't the click, click, click of ceiling fans to irritate my nerves. Her desks, too, were lined up in serried ranks, facing hers and the blackboard rather than turned in toward each other and forcing engagement with my fellow students. Teaching was very much a matter between Sr. Agnes and her individual pupil.

One morning, Sr. Agnes made the rounds of her classroom, handing back the students' papers that she had corrected. I looked at my results to see that I had received a score of ten out of ten in a math test, no small feat for a child not naturally gifted in arithmetic. It was at this point that Sr. Agnes announced my exam results to the whole class and produced from her oversized pocket—to my and everyone else's sur-prise—a chocolate Easter chicken wrapped in the most exquisite red, gold, and green foil. "Congratulations, Rachael, this is a reward for all your hard work!" She placed the brightly glittering gift on my desk and smiling all the while, started to clap, which was taken up by every girl in the class. Easter eggs (and the chickens from which they come!) sym-bolize new and risen life. Such was the life I received that day.

Strange are the fulcrums on which the levers of our lives pivot. To this gesture alone do I firmly attribute the change that took place in me that day: It was by this single moment of recognition in the sight of my peers that I was affirmed in the society outside the "half-world" I had so long inhabited, the half-world marked by my childhood compulsions, obsessions, and fears—I was ready to emerge, and the gentle and re-spectful attitude of Sr. Agnes enabled me to begin to look upon the society in which I lived with less fear and trepidation. It was, on reflec-tion, a singular moment of grace.

Rites of passage for a child raised in the Catholic tradition come in their allotted time. For weeks Sr. Agnes had, with great care and diligence, prepared us for our First Holy Communion. Lining up in pairs, we left the school grounds and walked the familiar footpath that led to the church to practice for the ceremony, which was fast approaching. Where to sit, how to approach the altar rails with due decorum, how to place our right hand under our left for reception of Communion— nothing was left to chance. The rubrics in which we were carefully schooled could not have been more in contrast to the time when I, four years before, had felt compelled to approach the altar rail in response to a long-held desire.

One Sunday after the final blessing and consequent emptying of the church pews, I lingered alone inside as I often did while members of my family chatted with other parishioners without. In the silence, I became aware of the clicking of my black patent-leather shoes on the cool, tiled floor. I made my way along the side aisle, passing beneath the roughly carved Stations of the Cross that came at regular intervals along the wall. How high they were! I stood a moment and raised my head. There I saw Jesus, a halo of wood depicting his divinity, silent and still before Pontius Pilate. Then I was moving toward the Blessed Sacrament Chapel, intimate in its proportions, where a pair of beaten copper angels kept watch over the tabernacle while the electric flicker of a sanctuary lamp announced its unseen guest.

The sun, climbing toward its zenith, cast its rays through the stained glass windows enclosing the chapel wall, scattering squares of multicolored light, claiming sovereignty over the mustard-colored carpet on which it shone. My eyes rested on patches of red and blue carpet and, retracing a shaft of light, watched particles of dust curl and fall through its beams. Raising my too-focused gaze, I stepped back startled at the sight of a pair of stained-glass arms, hands outstretched in a gesture of supplication. I reached out and traced my finger along the creases in the palm and down the thick lead support to where its being came to an abrupt end. My questioning mind wondered, At what point did this solid form knit together with its ethereal self, hidden beyond the realm of glass and lead?

I looked in the direction at which the fingertips pointed. Pale, lavender light radiated from the center of a golden monstrance. Of course I had seen it many times before and understood well its use as a vessel to hold and honor Christ present in the Host, to be raised in blessing over the people. For a long time I pondered its simplicity. Slowly at first, then with ever-increasing clarity, I realized that here at last was what I had everywhere in nature sought and never found, a portal into the mystery of what nature, fine as gossamer, covered and hid from my eyes. All that was necessary was for me to reach out with my own hand and receive.

So on the following Sunday morning at the designated time, I slipped out of the pew unchecked and unbidden and walked up to the front of the church, taking my place alongside the adults who stood ready at the altar rails to receive Communion. The priest made his way along the line, "The Body of Christ, the Body of Christ." At his approach, I stretched out a single hand and received in my palm the wafer-thin fragment of He who held the weight of the universe in His own. My mother looked up to see me receiving Communion. After Mass she took me to see the priest, who, on hearing what had happened, said, "Take her home and have a party, but I think it might be a good idea if she were to wait to make her next Communion with her class." So I did wait, and four years later, dressed in a white frock and veil, I joined those with whom I had eagerly prepared.

Everything I took in with my Asperger eyes met me with a kind of "first day of creation" freshness which renewed itself each morning on awakening. I cannot recall a single moment during those early years when I didn't believe in God. It was as though I had been wired to sense a presence in all with which I came into contact. Everything spoke to me of His beauty. It does not surprise me that I was so drawn to Him, for God was mystery and I was a mystery to myself, both of us silent and elusive; we got on perfectly well. Like Alice's White Rabbit, it was God's presence that I saw out of the corner of my eye, disappearing through the fabric of matter and drawing me to seek Him, not purely out of curiosity, but as a response to a love I had become conscious of from the age of reason.

As the weeks and months of the school year passed, my education, under the loving guidance of Sr. Agnes, continued to progress. My uneven academic profile showed me to be brilliant and lousy in equal measure. I relished music and English and struggled with math and handwriting, to say nothing of gymnastics. My continued lack of mobility barred me from achieving the high standards our gymnastics teacher, Mrs. Dubrovsky, late of Russia, demanded. I distinctly remember the dismay I felt, attempting to leap gracefully across the polished wooden floor in a leotard, waving a ribbon on a long stick and smiling all the while to the accompaniment of "Tie a Yellow Ribbon Round the Ole Oak Tree." If only I could have done that much!

In previous years, religious education was the only subject capable of pulling my autistic mind out of the window and into the classroom. I loved theology and fully engaged in any topic presented to my inquiring mind. One afternoon, Sr. Agnes, well within her rights to encourage young ladies to follow in her footsteps, put the question to the class "Would anyone like to be a nun when they grow up?" My lone hand shot up. "I would!" I said. A slow smile spread across her face. "Perhaps you will," she said, "perhaps you will."

At twelve years of age I continued to emerge from the autistic fog which had enveloped me and lingered for so many years. With this came a greater social awareness than had previously been my lot. I remembered how Sr. Agnes instilled in us the importance of considering others, and a desire to help and do good for others began to take root in me, naturally enough, beginning with my mother. I would help her dry the dishes or collect the mail from the letter box, small things in themselves, but monumental achievements for a child who had once been so unreachable. Seeing my mother's reaction and the pleasure it gave her, I redoubled my efforts. Striving to please another turned me out from myself, and in doing so, I felt connected and happy. Passing a small incinerator around the corner of the school building at day's end, I noticed that the flowers which had graced our classrooms would, after a day or two, be tossed in its mouth when the cleaner came along to light the fire. Seeing that many of the flowers, despite their rough handling, still had plenty of life and color in them yet, I set to gathering them up. These I proudly presented to my mother at her car window. "Oh Rachael, they're beautiful!" she would say. Not only had I managed to be at Mum's car on time, but I also came bearing gifts. At home, Mum would arrange to the best of her ability the blown blooms in a crystal vase. So with their petals scattered thickly around the vase, her flowers enjoyed a happy reprieve.

My own "happy reprieve" was short-lived. From the perspective that my newfound social awareness had brought, I started to look back on aspects of my childhood with a certain sense of shame, of condemnation for being the "weird" child that I was. Images of me staring at water fountains, hiding under the covers, and spaced out and strewing my clothing in the street came crowding in on me, mocking and accusing me in quiet moments of self-reflection. It was at the sight of such overwhelming evidence that I began to judge myself as being guilty of that most serious of crimes for a child on the cusp of adolescence: being different.

6

A TURN FOR THE WORST

"Stand still!" my mother said as she drew the comb in a sharp, vertical line through my hair, making a perfect part. "Ow!" I cried. "It can't be that bad," she said, willing my thick, wavy locks into submission. I can assure you that it was every bit as bad as my cries suggested and more. My sensory issues, in this case the hypersensitivity of my scalp, meant that I loathed my hair being brushed at that moment as much as I had when my sister had been charged with the thankless task of sweeping the wispy strands of my hair, when a toddler, into the likeness of a palm tree on top of my head. I stood before the mirror, anxious and excited, as my mother secured her handiwork with hair bands and bobby pins. It was the beginning of my thirteenth year, and we had moved. After packing a lunch and a short car ride later, I found myself in a new school. All eyes were upon me as I entered the classroom. I wore the correct uniform of the correct length, the correct socks, and ribbons in my perfectly plaited hair. I was "neat," but not "cool." I was doomed!

Having left the relative safety of primary school, my transition to high school brought new levels of social confusion and so increased anxiety, neither of which I was equipped to handle. Having been quickly labeled a "social misfit," I was unprepared for how nasty teenagers could be. I was lily-white when a tan was the look of the day. I stood out from the surf-bleached blondes with my carrot-colored hair. Self-tanning lotions and hair dye would have helped me blend in better, but there was no hiding the odd mannerisms of which I was unaware.

The number of students to which I must become accustomed rose from 500 to 1,500. This figure, alarming in its own right, was magnified by the sheer number of school buildings rising up out of the asphalt, double-storied and spreading out in every direction. Covered concrete walkways crisscrossed the expanse of the school grounds. At the sound of a shrill bell, these walkways, eerily silent, suddenly became rivers of shouting, jostling, running adolescence. I edged my way along the handrails, clutching a list that necessitated my marking off subjects for the year. Eventually I found my way to the Manual Arts block. I had ticked the box "Woodworking" and had purchased a triangle and drawing compass as required. I handed my list to the teacher. He shook his head, saying, "I'm sorry, only the boys are allowed to do woodwork." I said nothing, but I felt bitter disappointment. "Unjust!" I kept saying to myself, for in the home economics class to which I had been directed, I noted that in this preserve of girls, there was a sprinkling of boys with aprons and mixing bowls at the ready. To think, I could have been a master builder by now!

My capacity for organizing myself had not improved with the years, and with mounting responsibilities, it was on the decline. Like a budding street performer, I had managed to acquire the skill of keeping two balls in the air, then three, but as another ball was added the holding pattern dissolved, and they bounced off in all directions. Our home economics teacher, Mrs. Van Porten, a stout, well-built woman and a fitting advertisement for the culinary delights she directed her students to bake, would give us instructions on what to bring to the following lesson. Invariably I would forget, or misinterpret, some point of instruction. One week, I failed to bring ground beef; another week, an onion. I would bring plain flour instead of self-rising, or I would unfold a stretch fabric on my sewing bench instead of the plain cotton as requested. I cannot remember the misdemeanor that tipped Mrs. Van Porten over the edge. She drew back her hand, and *Thump!* she struck me on the back with her full force. "You slovenly, lazy girl, you never listen!" she shouted. Reeling and winded, I hardly heard the rest of her rant. This action, violent to me, seemed to have a cathartic effect on her, for she didn't repeat the blow but wrote me off as a dim-witted student and left me alone, for which I was very grateful.

My opportunity to lie low did not last very long. In our English class, the teacher had various students read a particular passage from a novel we were studying. I pushed back my chair, stood up, and started to read, the inflections in my speech, rather odd, rather formal. A ripple of laughter followed. "That's enough," the teacher said. I continued, interrupted by the odd snort of ridicule. I did not realize that I spoke differently than anyone else. Once again, I felt betrayed by idiosyncrasies of which I was unaware. Many people on the autism spectrum are wired in such a way that they have a propensity for formal, pedantic, even foreign speech patterns—foreign, not only to their country, but also to their era. I had even once asked a girl if she would like to visit my "humble abode." She declined.

Motivated as I was to find a place of belonging among my peers, I did not give up but started to talk to and hang around a group of "popular" girls. They roamed around the school grounds during recess with their socks pushed down and their skirts rolled up. They talked incessantly about their favorite pop groups or boys they were interested in. These two subjects were the mainstay of their conversations. Never did they sit quietly in each other's company or talk about books or about their individual opinions on matters. What they thought and what they did, like a hive of bees, were the thoughts and doings of the whole. I loved music and was happy enough to join in, making my contributions as I was able.

It was the early 1980s and Adam and the Ants were the group of the moment. Amazingly, one of my neighbors had managed to procure a personally signed autograph for me. I found the dynamics of the group to which I had attached myself unfathomable. If the most popular girl in the group said that she was going to marry Adam when she grew up, her friends believed her with all their hearts. When I said that I had Adam's autograph from his recent Australian tour, it was met with extreme disbelief. As with my toys and books during my primary school years, I brought the autograph to school, hoping to establish myself more deeply in their social circle. I pulled the sheet of paper from my bag, showing Adam's large sweeping As and a heart transfixed with an arrow. It read, "To Rachael, all my love, Adam Ant." They were impressed. "Oh my gosh, where did you get that?" They huddled round me and I felt the warm glow of social acceptance, feeling myself to be "well-in" with the group.

However, the ability to keep my position became harder and harder to maintain. Having spent weeks observing their actions in an attempt to emulate their behavior, it began to occur to me that remaining high in the group's pecking order would require unrelenting displays of affection, hugs, and affirmations and providing grist for their gossip. Coupled with this dilemma were changes within my own perception of things. Since hitting puberty, I had become increasingly rigid in my thinking, becoming judgmental and feeling the sting of injustice, no matter how slight the barb.

Teenage girls are rarely known for their discretion. So it was that one of my "friends" sidled up to me one day and said that another girl had said, "Rachael's got such a nice personality, pity she's so plain." These and other unwelcome remarks filtered through to me from the group's epicenter. The authenticity of these comments seemed to find confirmation in the rejection that was meted out to me every Wednesday morning with nauseating regularity in the square-dancing class. I did not like the boys in my year, but it hurt nonetheless to find myself the only girl to be left sitting on the benches after the boys had picked their partners. More humiliating still, was seeing the teacher ordering a reluctant boy to partner me against his wishes.

"One, two, three—one, two, three," round and round the covered area he would swing me, holding me at arm's length, punctuating his dance steps with horrid remarks. "Get out of my face, matchstick!" he would say, or "Gee, you're ugly!" and other delightful observations. I would zone out, and in my imagination superimpose the characters of my beloved *Pride and Prejudice* within the space I was forced to occupy. In my mind's eye, the dull, wooden benches gave way to oak wall paneling rising and enclosing the four sides of the covered area. Velvet curtains of a rich burgundy dropped from the valances and swung into place, and past them, against the last light of evening on a sliver of rolling green beyond the gravel drive, I saw the arrival of horse-drawn carriages. Within, servants lit the last of the candles in brackets lining the walls and I, resplendent in cream silk, sat ensconced in a high-backed chair, lately produced by a manservant, anxious to see to the comfort of the guests. Netherfield Park had never looked so beautiful in the soft, amber glow of the candlelit room. The scene was set and I, within earshot, heard the dialogue begin.

"Which do you mean?" and turning round, he looked for a moment at Elizabeth, till catching her eye, he withdrew his own and coldly said: "She is tolerable, but not handsome enough to tempt *me*; I am in no humour at present to give consequence to young ladies who are slighted by other men."[1]

"What are you smirking about, matchstick?" The guests swung round to see the source of commotion as the oak panels fell from the walls, ripping the curtains and allowing the harsh glare of the summer morning to fill the covered area. Before me stood a vulgar specimen of teenage boyhood, his face screwed up in confusion. The lesson over, I picked up my bag and walked away.

At night, after everyone was asleep, I would lie in bed, turning the contents of these and other upsetting encounters and conversations over and over in my head—as Asperger girls are prone to do. Each recollection, no matter how many times it had been recalled, brought fresh waves of emotional distress as I agonized over the details. "Did I say too little, too much?" or "Why on *earth* did he say that, he had *no right* to say that to me!" or again, "*Why* didn't I have the ability to say *then* what comes so eloquently to me *now* at 11:29 p.m.?" These were questions to which there were simply no answers. It seemed that I was to be constantly wounded by the unfairness of things.

Anger, too, made its appearance, an interloper, wearying and un-wanted. "*Why* am I *so* angry?" I constantly asked myself, casting around for an answer to my agitated moods. For many on the autism spectrum, intense emotions, with no middle range, are the norm, and my feelings were no exception to this rule as one emotion fed into another, taking me on a roller-coaster ride in the comfort of my own bed.

In accordance with much negative thinking, the old adage rang true: "That which I have greatly feared has come upon me." On arrival at school one morning, I went to join my "friends," but before I had reached them, one of the girls, nominated as their spokeswoman, ap-proached me and sat me down. "Um, Rachael, we think you're a really nice girl and everything, but we don't want you in our group anymore." I had not fooled them, no, not for one minute. I was not one of their kind and never would be. My expulsion, painful as it was, came as a merciful release. Socially speaking, I had bitten off more than I could chew and had been growing increasingly exhausted by my attempts to emulate their confusing and fickle ways.

Once again, I was an outsider looking in, no closer to finding a suitable set of friends and disillusioned by what passed as such. However, without a particular group of friends, I became vulnerable. The boys, who had previously been content to call me names or draw attention to my "difference," began to single me out. Sickeningly close, they would brush up against me, putting their hands up my skirt. Driven by a pack mentality, they would take turns whispering lurid comments in my ear. Victim that I was, I would freeze with terror. The girls in my class, busy about their own concerns, didn't notice or care that I was circled by a pack of boys in a corridor outside a classroom who only saw fit to disperse when a teacher clapped her hands to call them to line up.

I can hardly believe that a teacher, having to put in such an effort to bring boys to order, would fail to notice the cause of their disorder. Yes, that was the word, disorder. Those boys did it simply because they could. School had become a war zone for me, and I arrived every morning sick to my stomach and shaking with anxiety. The harassment continued, to which the teachers turned a blind eye. When I couldn't stand it any longer, I went to see the school counselor. There in her office, trembling and distressed, but determined to get help, I poured out the details of what had been going on for far too long. I will never forget what she said in response: "Maybe you could talk to the boys about it?" She may as well have locked me in a room with them and thrown away the key! I never sought her counsel again.

A reprieve lay just around the corner for me, however, quite literally. Leaving the office, I followed the walkway and turned a corner to find a small group of girls lounging, backs against the wall and legs sprawled out in front of them like speed bumps, their white socks like luminous paint marking their position. Preoccupied with recent events, I tripped. A hand reached out to stop me falling. I looked across to see a friendly, laughing face, which was a replica of the face to her left. "Sorry!" I said. Two other girls sat with them. It was lunchtime and just having met, they invited me to sit with them, which I gladly accepted. I was fifteen years old and a term into tenth grade. I found in my new friends a welcome sanctuary, as the dynamics of the playground reached new heights of complexity.

We traded the mock sophistication of our peers for girlish tricks, and in our combined difference (for we were a motley crew of twins, a teen queen, a motherless girl, and me), we found strength in numbers. Our nonconformity drew sneers and comments from teenagers desperate to conform to each other's standards, but what were their insults shared out among so many? "Here comes the Gang!" they would say, but we were more of an "anti-gang," eager to rub their conformity in their faces.

Our year had a trip to the theater. My face was "quiet," but my outfit was "loud." I arrived that evening sporting bright pink leggings that stuck out of a pumpkin-shaped dress—Cinderella past midnight. Like so many girls on the spectrum, the more eccentric my presentation, the greater was my vulnerability. During the show we laughed and giggled. "I don't care much for her shoes," I said, regarding the principal performer. Hot on the heels of this comment, one of the twins grabbed my shoe and passed it down the aisle in an attempt to remedy the offense.

United as we were by a loathing of sporting activities, the cross-country run galvanized us into action; or rather, inaction. At the pistol shot we would run along with the eager students until, out of sight of the sports teacher, we'd climb the fence and lie low, reemerging after a decent lapse of time to come in at a respectable finish in the field. Day after day, we continued to meet at the school gate, affording each other a sense of protection, our laughter and games an antidote to the stresses of our individual anxieties.

At the start of midyear, I found myself alone again. The girls, through the arrangements of their parents, had transferred to different schools. I alone was left to see out the remainder of the year as well as I could. Within this social vacuum, I found myself befriended by another girl in my grade. I do not know why she saw fit to approach me, but naïve as I was, she quickly drew me into her social scene. Unlike the people I had mixed with previously, her set was hungry for experience and they exploited their opportunities, unchecked by parent or guardian. She herself was spoilt and clearly had her parents wrapped around her little finger.

The analogy that springs to mind is that of "catching the wrong bus." In my ignorance I had purchased a ticket and had got on a bus that was to take me far from my intended journey. As I looked out of the window, the scenery became more and more unfamiliar. Turning to look at my fellow passengers, they who had once seemed so benevolent had taken on a more sinister appearance. Out of my depth and not wanting to appear foolish, I did not pull the cord to stop but allowed the bus to hurtle on, faster and faster along steep ravines and dark roads, away from that which brought me light and peace.

Hanging out at shopping malls with no particular purpose drew undesirables to me with magnetic force. With a cigarette in my mouth and my top too low, I found an older boy standing before me. Emotionally speaking, the childhood of a person on the autism spectrum extends far into adulthood, and so at that time, my emotional maturity lagged years behind that of my peers. Mine was the mentality of a child. Having lower levels of social awareness than my peers increased my vulnerability, making me an easy target for predators. My "knowing look" was an expression borrowed from a pantomime, my provocative clothing, a mere selection from a little girl's dress-up box.

In the presence of my "friend," the boy took me by the hand and walked me, like a child, out of the shopping center, across the car park, and into a nearby area of bushland. No warning bell went off in my head. To me, his intentions were a mystery. It was not until he started to unbutton my clothing that I yelled out, "What do you think you're doing?" He looked startled, thrown, and he walked out of the bush and away, leaving me stunned and trying to piece together how I had come so close to being assaulted. With hindsight, I think the contrast between my seeming compliance and violent reaction utterly unnerved him and saved my skin.

The volatility of adolescence seemed to undo the social connections with others that I had fought so hard to achieve. Anger, my unwelcome interloper, became my confidant. My attitude, once so open and receptive, became closed and unyielding. Occasionally at first, then with increasing regularity, I sought opportunities to hang out with my friend and the others who came out of the woodwork whenever she was out and about. Casting my mind back on those dark days, my memories are a montage of roaming shopping centers, railway stations, and parks and drinking wine coolers purchased by the oldest member of the set. Underage as I was, nights on the town were made possible by the lies I told my mother. "Will you be home by dinner?" she would ask. "No, I'll be staying over at Sharon's," I would say.

My first deceptions gave way to stand-up fights. I can see my mother now, standing in the doorway of my bedroom, tears running down her face and pleading for me to stay at home and stop hanging around with "that girl." Her cries fell on deaf ears. I became disconnected from those who loved and cared for me and wound in on myself in ever-tighter circles. I became completely isolated and had the rotten luxury of knowing myself to be lost—lost to myself, and to everything that gave me peace and stability. Such was the appalling state I had gotten myself into. Utterly miserable as I was, my sense of alienation was complete.

Out of my depth, rudderless, and desperate to fit in, I took on the speech and mannerisms of the gang. I tried to act tough, and I swore, matching them word for word. The more alienated from my true self I became, the more hostile I was to those who loved me the most and those who crossed the path of my narrow little world. The wide and spacious dimensions I had been created for, the sense of connection and wonder I felt for all creation and my desire to do good for others, had all but been obliterated by the mean and false world I inhabited.

But small as it was, my world collided with that of another. My friend had suggested that we spend the day at a public pool, close to the city. I sat in the changing room, sorting through my bag. Another girl came in, brushing too close to me. My reaction was swift and aggressive. "Watch where you're going, you *stupid* girl!" She said nothing and went on her way. As with all my actions, I never once was able to consider their implications. As soon as the words were out of my mouth, they were forgotten. It was as if I had never uttered them.

It was only at the day's end that I would know the full ramifications of my ill-timed and impulsive comment. I had changed, collected my belongings together, and started to walk up the passageway that led to the exit. I looked up. There, blocking the exit, was a large group of girls, including the one to whom I had made the unfortunate comment so many hours previously. I did not know why they stood there. I was surrounded; there was no time to think.

I felt the impact of a fist in my face, another, then another. I fell to the ground, instinctively shielding my face. They did not stop, but continued their revenge, repeatedly kicking my ribs. I was beyond their insults, but what I did notice was that one girl did not kick me with the ferocity of the rest but withheld the impact as much as she could, without signaling her reluctance to the others. This, I think, disturbed me more than the combined assault of the rest; this, and the way my "friend" murmured something about "not wanting to get involved" before stepping aside and leaving me to be bashed beyond recognition.

They withdrew. Covering my face with my towel, I staggered to the train station. Some passersby averted their eyes; others judged me wrongly, pointing and laughing. To them, I had "got what I deserved." No one approached to offer help. It was my mother alone who saw me through that night. Ashen faced on seeing my appearance, she took me to the hospital to be examined. As I lay in the Emergency Room, a nurse thrust back the curtain surrounding the bed, took one look at me, and brightly inquired, "Why are you crying?" I turned my face to the wall.

That night, back at home, my mother kept vigil. She wrapped her arms around me and held me close as I cried, the clock marking the hours. The following afternoon, at her prompting, I rose and dressed. I went to wash my hands. Looking up, I stared at the image before me in the mirror. I did not recognize her. Slowly, slowly, a day at a time, I started to heal, within and without.

Many weeks later I was in the city and saw the group with whom I had become so heavily invested. They walked a little ahead of me. I stepped back a few paces and appraised them coolly. Then came my epiphany. "I am not like these people," I slowly said to myself. I turned on my heels and set off in the opposite direction, leaving them to their aimless wanderings.

We can never go back and relive our past. However, each one of us can declare of our personal history, "This is the path I have trod and no other," and in doing so, we allow each past event, for good or ill, by its reality, to have its place in our story.

So I have chosen to state the facts, touching on certain relative pieces of my memory, to pass by, and to linger on nothing. This is not to preserve myself from the recollection of traumatic events, for I declare that to recall them now causes me no pain. The lasting impressions of this time in my life are ones of shock, for I shudder to think *how far* I ventured from my own truth. As it is, I can leave it all behind, not by the suppression of my memories, but by the grace to reflect, forgive, and move on. Yes, I forgave them, and in doing so I freed myself.

Unperturbed, I saw out the school year with a new strategy, escaping to the library, spending all my lunch hours studying. Come exam time, my teacher read out my results. "Guess who topped English and history for the year? Rachael Harris!" My classmates swung round open-mouthed in their seats. I will never forget the look of amazement on their faces. They had interpreted my social awkwardness and slower mental processing as unintelligence. How *wrong* they were!

So ended my schooling. As the groups of girls hugged and cried on the last day, I walked out through the gate with an overwhelming sense of relief. *It was over.* As the school gate swung closed behind me, the world and all its possibilities opened up before me.

7

"IT'S A LIVING"

Summer could not have come too soon. I took full advantage of the endless lazy days and holiday mood. Traditional pursuits such as afternoons at the beach and evenings in the backyard, filled with the aroma of barbecued sausages and onion rings—these were experiences to be cherished. That long languid summer did much to restore in me a sense of well-being, helping to decompress the accumulated stress of the entire year. The first of January, like a fresh page in a new notebook, was ready for me to make my mark.

I had heard other school leavers talking about pursuing careers. My own thoughts on having a career were hazy and ill defined, to say the least. The fact of the matter was that I simply did not have a *clue* how I was going to occupy myself. I took the dictionary off the bookshelf to see what it had to say. I read the first definition.

> **career** n **1** a field of employment in which one expects to spend a significant part of one's working life, esp a field requiring special qualifications or training and having opportunities for advancement.[1]

I read further.

> **career** v to move swiftly in an uncontrolled fashion.

Now *there* was a career definition I could relate to!

I recalled my week of work experience spent as an assistant in the ladies' clothing section of a major department store. The counter manager, keen to take maximum advantage of a week's worth of slave labor, ran me ragged. My tasks included, but were not limited to, unpacking the stock and hanging it on the clothes racks, dressing the shop windows, running to and fro between the changing rooms, ordering stock, and making the tea.

"Would you be a dear and find me an apricot dress in the same style?" A disembodied arm dangled the rejected garment through a crack in the cubicle door. "Certainly, Madam." I set off to locate the apricot dress among the unfamiliar stock. I looked out upon a sea of multicolored cloth, wondering how on earth I was going to find the lady's choice in a timely fashion. As I stood there scanning the merchandise, the colors tumbled and turned before me. How was I to pick out one shade among so many? Flick, flick, flick. I feverishly separated the hangers on the racks. As the minutes ticked away I became more anxious and desperate to find the elusive dress. The counter manager was nowhere to be seen. It was no use. I ran back to the changing room to apologize and saw the counter manager handing the lady the dress I had pursued for ten minutes. "You shouldn't have kept the customer waiting," was her curt observation. I couldn't win.

It was trouble enough employing all my skills trying to decipher a person's facial expressions and tone of voice, but the telephone was another matter. The following day I stood at the counter, quietly ruminating over some paperwork, when the phone rang, sudden and shrill. I leapt out of my skin. "Just don't stand there staring at it, pick it up!" the manager said, head in a book. I reached out with a trembling hand and held the receiver to my ear, my palm cold and clammy. The space in which I stood became a courtroom and I, the accused, took the stand and awaited questioning.

"Did you, or did you not, order the pleated skirt I asked you to order on Monday?"

"Yes, yes I did."

"I put it to you that on Monday when I asked you to order it, you in fact did not place the order."

"But I did!" I said. Order, order in the court!

"Where is that order?" the counter manager's voice broke in.

"I did place it, it will probably come in tomorrow," I said.

"It had better," the customer replied.

The order did not come in the next day and neither did I. That was the day of my Nan's funeral.

In terms of religious observance, my grandmother described herself as a "Free Thinker," a term as alien to me as Catholicism was to her. She had come from a background where analogies between black-clad Jesuits and the boogeyman were uttered in the same breath. Thankfully, those early specters vanished with exposure to our Catholic family life and the excellent care she received at the nursing home run by nuns where she happily passed her last few years.

In her last illness, she called the visiting priest to her bedside, and he, listening to her litany of anxieties, blessed her and promised that she would be buried from the home's small chapel. Visiting her later, we could hardly account for the change in her. She had cast off the fears that had bounded her like her old tweed coat, and she died at peace with her God. A few days later, family, friends, and residents filled the chapel that saw my nonconformist Nan buried with all the pomp and circumstance of a funeral Mass.

Later at the cemetery as I cast a ritual handful of sand into the grave below, I remembered the nights my grandmother tucked me into bed with an accompanying "Good Night, God Bless, see you in the morning." And so it was we tucked her into the quiet earth "in the sure and certain hope of the Resurrection" and eternal day.

That afternoon I sat at home, numb and grieving, but determined to see the week out.

Of all the questions customers put to me during the course of that week, the one that filled me with dread was "Do you think this looks good on me?" I understood from observing the other attendants that the protocol was to tell the customers that they looked "fabulous" no matter how frumpy or ill fitting, the garment. So it was that one morning an elderly lady, sporting a fluorescent orange suit with a frenetically busy, black pattern, turned from the mirror and caught my eye, her lips forming the dreaded question "Do you think this looks good on me?" Asperger folk possess a great capacity for truth and are honest . . . to a fault. In a society as politically correct and self-preserving as our own, it is astonishing to find, not just one person, but a whole population who will tell you what they *really* think, and to your face! I bit my lip, silent before her. It was no use; I could not tell a lie. "It looks *terrible* on you," I answered. Her eyes widened and her mouth became the shape of one who had sucked a lemon. I stood my ground and braced myself for the fallout. To my amazement, her mouth widened and she broke into a chuckle. "You're the first shop assistant to tell me her honest opinion. Of course I look dreadful. Come on, dear, show me what you think would suit me." I happily obliged. The old lady and I spent a pleasant half hour finding a suitable outfit that she purchased in two flattering shades.

That Friday afternoon, I sat before the counter manager, a woman not many years older than me, for a review of my week. "You could have been more forthcoming in answering the phone and of course I will have to deduct points from your performance for being absent on Wednesday," she said. "But I was attending my grandmother's funeral!" I exclaimed. She said nothing but eventually muttered something about sending the report back to the school. What a fragile, voiceless thing I was, how loath to assert myself! Confidence came slowly and painfully for me, but come it did.

The pages of the dictionary snapped to with a dull thud. I replaced it on the bookshelf and took up the local newspaper, scanning the employment section for inspiration. My brilliant career began as a bag packer at a local supermarket. I can see myself now, standing at the end of the checkout conveyor belt, carefully packing each bag as if it were a three-dimensional puzzle. I soon found a pattern in the packing: tin cans, boxes, vegetables, fragile, and frozen items. I became one with the rhythmic, steady pace needed to complete each task. "Watch my tomatoes!" "Mind my eggs!" the customers would occasionally warn. They needn't have concerned themselves. How were they to know that beneath my flesh turned cogs that spun with a precision only rivaled by a factory robot?

Inside my autistic mind, I have always stood at a certain distance from my subjective surroundings, allowing for an even keener awareness of my environment, within and without. Hence, I note patterns in my thoughts, in nature, and especially human nature. I have always viewed this slight disconnection as a great gift, affording me a precious, rational objectivity in a world gone emotionally mad.

I cannot recall feeling bored during that year, for I lived from moment to moment. Simple as my job was, I derived great satisfaction from doing it well. From that time until now, "success" has never been my motivation, but by living totally what life has given me to complete, I find that a sense of achievement has come, not as an end goal, but as a byproduct of the process.

In the calendar of events of any business, it seems that there is no escaping the workplace Christmas party. All are expected to attend, from the management down. Nervous as I was, I carefully planned for the evening. The dress code called for "smart, casual attire." Then and now, I find this criterion utterly appalling, the partygoer being exiled to the pathless wasteland between an evening gown and a tracksuit. Such was the difficulty I had in expressing myself in conversation that I found any means possible to draw attention to my presence. My wardrobe was lined with brightly colored fabrics. Sequins, beading, and layers of tulle were well represented within my collection. These ranged from the fashionable to the avant-garde. It was as though every garment served as a kind of loudspeaker, the message being "I'm here everybody, I'm here!" I wanted to shine, quite literally, and those two deadly words on the invitation—"smart" and "casual"—relegated me to an evening clothed in anonymity.

I walked out the door in a sensible, knee-length, blue skirt and white blouse; my mother, having long left behind the zebra print and rhinestones of her youth, fully approved. It is strange to reflect now and realize that as my ability to express myself increased over time, so did my style of dress recede into a darker, more tailored, and conservative cut. The bright and shiny things of my youth still lurk expectantly in the dim recesses of my wardrobe, their mirrored surfaces eagerly awaiting the light of day.

My father drove me to the venue. I watched the streetlights pass by, measuring out the distance to my destination. I caught sight of myself in the side mirror. The face that stared back was without expression, like that of a porcelain doll—pale, with lips and eyes picked out in rose and dark tints. The effect was startling, *unnerving*, even to myself. The taillights of my father's car disappeared into the night as I walked up the path toward the main door. The murmur without rose to a chatter of dozens of voices within as I entered the hall. Over the top of it all beat out the rhythm of my heart, thick and fast. How was it that no one could hear it? I took a seat by the edge of the dance floor and watched. I saw two girls approach each other, having arrived about the same time as me. On meeting, they immediately launched into animated conversation. One's mouth would move, the other responding with rapid, excited movements, jerking her head at those gathered, then quickly turning back to the other, who responded with a slap to her upper arm, both then dissolving into peals of laughter, their shoulders shuddering with the force. I could only wonder at what it all meant.

These observations filled me with a sense of astonishment at the ease with which the two girls and those around them kept up these social exchanges for the entire night while I searched for clues that would unlock the secret of how they managed it. I took up a drink and moved about the room unnoticed, picking up fragments of conversation. "She likes him, but he can't stand her." "Cost five hundred dollars, what a rip-off!" "If he doesn't watch out, he'll know about it." The air was filled with conversational confetti, thrown up to flutter for a brief moment and then be trampled underfoot. I made my way to the end of the hall, floating around its edges like a silent specter barred from the exchanges of mere mortals; they inhabiting their realm and I, mine.

I was determined to take my place in the society on whose outer limits I lingered. I decided I would get in "through the back door"—the kitchen door, to be more precise. I began a course in tourism and hospitality. As ever, I was drawn to that which offered structure and a sense of order. We students, clothed in black and white, shuffled from class to class like a colony of penguins. Reception work made for pleasant and precise exchanges; commercial cookery gave us a large variety of dishes to create and taste. However, for me, the battle lines were drawn in the college restaurant where our food and liquor service teacher, Mr. Black, had noted early that I marched to a different tune than that of my peers. He seemed determined to unmask, by any means possible, just what it was that made me tick.

Not content with keeping his ruminations regarding my character to himself, he did, on more than one occasion, vocalize his thoughts in the presence of my fellow students. "Is it *you* who changes the mood in the students, or is it the *students' mood* that changes you?" I learned to dismiss these and other bizarre comments, but perhaps due to his intense curiosity about my person, others among the teaching staff took up the general quest to account for my difference. One morning the college principal, Mrs. Herbert, called me into her office and sat me down. Without preamble, she put the question to me "Rachael, are you taking any drugs?" I stared at her, shocked and stupefied by so crass and baseless an inquiry. Such are the misunderstandings that people on the autism spectrum are confronted with as they try to navigate their way through life. I understood well enough her underlying judgment regarding my character, which ran thus: "You are a peculiar girl, a strange misfit. You do not follow the ways of your peers or show your feelings, therefore you must be without feelings. Damaged and defective by will, you are a broken specimen of womanhood." She asked again, "Rachael, are you taking any drugs?" "Of course I'm not!" I replied. She smiled, apparently satisfied with her line of inquiry. I stood a while in the corridor outside her office composing myself in the wake of such a humiliation. All I was guilty of was being myself.

Meanwhile Mr. Black, he of the dark hair, dark suit, and darker attitude, continued to conduct his own experiments during the periods restaurant training took place. My short-term memory—never my strong suit, as is typical in the Asperger population—necessitated me carrying a small notebook with which I made sure I set the right meals before the right people. I had devised a method of keeping track of orders that included drawing little caricatures of those I served, with arrows pointing to the dishes they had chosen. Mr. Black, knowing how well this worked in my favor, saw fit one day to snatch the book from my hand. "Do it in your head!" he snapped. From the corner of the room I saw him watching me as I floundered, losing my place in the order of service.

My trouble with fine motor skills meant that I could hardly keep my handwriting straight, let alone a tray full of long-stemmed champagne cocktails. I would carry the tray with two hands and then, gently setting it down on the edge of the table, deliver the cocktails intact to their recipients. Once again, Mr. Black intervened. "Serve them from the tray," he said. "If I do that I will drop them," I responded. "No you won't," he said. "Oh, but I shall," I replied. "Just do it!" he barked. So I did, taking a glass from the tray that wobbled above my fingertips. Down they came—*smash, smash, smash*—twelve in all. Did he think I modified my methods for the fun of it? Apparently so.

Graduation Night finally arrived. Students, parents, and teachers packed the function room at a local hotel. Each graduate received a few words of encouragement for their future; that is, until Mr. Black called out across the room, "Rachael, will you stand up, please?" I slowly rose and braced myself for the latest in a long line of public humiliations. "Turn around so everyone can see you." I turned my head 45 degrees. "This is Rachael, my Botticelli cherub," he declared with a triumphant smile. At that moment, the scales fell from my eyes. I realized that Mr. Black had given little consideration to where cruelty finished and kindness began. He combined the two elements in an odd brew, which evidently was much to his taste.

I applied to the Commonwealth Employment Service, which, in true bureaucratic style, called me to say that they had found me a suitable position in a local snack bar—but I had not mastered the art of silver-service to spend my days cutting sandwiches. I had set my sights on the newly opened five-star Sheraton Mirage Hotel at Port Douglas in tropical Far North Queensland. When I suggested this desire to the agency, their swift response was "Oh no, you would not be qualified enough to work there, you would require *years* of experience!" Unperturbed, I took matters into my own hands, applying directly to the hotel. The hotel's response was swifter still: "When can you come up, we have a position available in housekeeping." I was to learn that the Housekeeping Department was kept afloat by a large contingent of British backpackers from the medical professions, a veritable triage of doctors, nurses, and radiographers—the guests couldn't have been in safer hands.

At my eighteen years of age, a sense of adventure was the sap in my veins, overriding by sheer force any fear of or reticence about embarking on the unknown. Fueled with such courage to make the move, I found myself transported to an idyllic tropical paradise. However, I was happier still when my sister came to join me for the last six months of my stint at the resort. The eight-year gap between my older sister and me had closed. I had celebrated my birthday, and Sarah had become my friend and travel companion. Together we explored the lush rain forests, misty gorges, crocodile-infested waters, and coral reefs. Through sheer enthusiasm, we corralled the entire housekeeping staff into a chorus line outfitted as French maids for the hotel's Talent Night. Our chorus line was billed the "Pristine Clean and the Plebeian Perfectionists." But our combined efforts and hours of rehearsals and even more laughs, lost to a baton twirler—*Sacré bleu*!

Despite our loss, good fortune followed us. A guest who had particularly noted our good service gifted my sister and I with a bottle of Krug Champagne. Fearing confiscation by middle management, Sarah concealed it in her cleaning basket beneath the rags and polish, only to produce it later in all its "ice-bucketed glory." While enjoying choice seafood, we sipped its fruity nectar and watched holidaymakers stroll up and down the palm-lined main street. It was the first and not the last time I was to dine in such style, but under very strange circumstances indeed.

Late one afternoon, at the end of my shift, I began the walk home from the resort to my accommodation. This journey was a regular feature of my daily routine, one I had taken for many months without incident. Lost in my own thoughts, I hardly noticed when a pale yellow Volkswagen Bus pulled up alongside me as I made my way down the road. The occupant closest to me wound down his window and thrust his head through the space. "Would ya like a lift?" he called. Now in Port Douglas at that time, hitchhiking was de rigueur, a necessity for moving the vast populace of unlicensed youth from A to B. Looking past his shoulder, I was reassured to see as many young women as men in the seats behind the driver and his front-seat passenger. "Yes, thanks, my place is just down the road," I said, pointing in the general direction. "No worries, jump in," he replied.

The driver pulled out onto the road and had driven only a few yards when he suddenly announced that they were not going to take me home. My heart constricted. I looked round at the passengers' bright, smiling faces and wondered if I had not, inadvertently, stumbled upon an offshoot of the Manson Family. If ever I needed to harness the ability to read facial expressions and body language, that hour was now! "We're not taking ya home," he repeated, "we're taking ya to dinner!" The van did a sharp U-turn and headed in the direction of the restaurant-dotted precinct of Macrossan Street. The driver pulled up near steps that led to a Mexican cantina. The occupants flung back the door and piled out of the van and up the stairs with me in tow, not stopping until they had taken their places at a reserved table at the back of the restaurant.

I looked around at the Aztec deities and sombreros lining the walls and could well imagine myself to be in Mexico City, my kidnapping adding to the ambiance. I ran a swizzle stick around the rim of my margarita and listened to stories of kayaking adventures and camping sites. By this time I had judged my captors harmless. I passed a pleasant, if surreal, evening and was dropped off at my doorstep at night's end. The van sputtered as it rounded the corner, no doubt to continue dispensing random acts of kindness on its merry way.

The last few months I spent in Port Douglas were uneventful, much to my relief. I had committed myself to working there for exactly twelve months, driven by the bonus offered to employees who could endure the tropical heat for a full year. A thousand dollars was no small sum for a now nineteen-year-old, and my sister and I had already set our sights on a working holiday in Britain.

As the time ticked away, I had been given the job of polishing the vast amount of brass in the hotel's foyer, including the handrail that spanned its upper and lower levels. This I carried out diligently from early morning to late afternoon. It was interesting to note the reactions of those who observed my task. One offered a sheepish smile as he began his wobbly descent, keeping his hand from the rail so as not to spoil the gleaming brass I had lately polished. Another apologized profusely. "I'm *so sorry* to ruin your work"—this from the heart, as she steadied herself on her way to the upper level. Yet another announced, "You missed a spot!"—touching as much of my handiwork as he could on his way down.

Were the "powers that be" seeking to break my spirit before I could claim my bonus? Had I studied hard to master silver service only to find myself a slave to brass? Their efforts were futile. I had come to understand that all work had meaning, all work had dignity. In a situation where I did not seem to be doing much, much had been done in me. The daily routine to rise, dress, carry out my work, and grow by interacting with other people—despite a surfeit of social anxiety—this had shaped my capacity to grow the emotional muscle needed to meet the challenges I faced every day.

I was fortunate too, during that year, to have crossed paths with the Sisters of Mercy. They were few in number, but they managed to maintain an active presence in the community. In their simple convent, a little way out from the township, I found a place of peace and hospital-

ity; a compass in the midst of a tropical sunny playground whose shadow side was only too evident. I had watched too many of my peers
succumb to a deep boredom which they filled with alcohol and pornog-
raphy. I recall passing the common room where I found the group with
whom I was living, huddled around the television watching unspeakably
horrid images. One fellow caught my eye, declaring, "This is *real* life,
this is what *really* happens." I turned and walked out. "Not in *my*
universe it doesn't," I said to myself.

I loved listening to the Sisters' stories. We sat in their small sitting
room, the younger Sisters dutifully gravitating toward the firm wooden
chairs, while those who were many years retired sank into the armchairs
in the corner of the room. On the walls hung every item I had come to
expect in an Australian convent: a portrait of the community's founder,
a print of the Sacred Heart in an ornate frame, a large clock to witness
to the rare value which the women within those four walls placed on the
passage of time, and a small Celtic cross whose intricate, swirling knot-
work drew my eye above all else.

This tendency after the introductions have been made to quickly
scan the sitting rooms in peoples' homes has always been my lot. First
artwork, then family photos (several generations), then the contents of
display cabinets. Because I'm a highly visual thinker like most people on
the autism spectrum, these things tell me a family's story twice over,
allowing me to trace their history as far as what is displayed will permit.

I inquired where the cross came from. Sr. Anne piped up from her
armchair, "My Mam gave it to me when I got the call," she said. "What
call?" I asked, momentarily confused by her cryptic response. "The call
to join the Order," she said matter-of-factly, sipping her tea. "I left
Ireland when I was fifteen to join the Sisters of Mercy in Australia." She
spoke of her family, where she grew up in Dublin, and the day she
stepped onto the boat, renouncing every other good that lay within her
reach. I looked across the room and considered her thin, frail figure,
noting the lines in her face and arthritic hands which had seen over
seventy years' service. I wondered, "Where is the fresh-faced girl with
the golden hair who grasped the handrail, climbing the gangplank of the
ship that would take her far away from everything she knew and loved?"

In the meantime, sparked by a flood of memories, Sr. Anne had
started to sing a ditty, the rest clapping and joining in, while I, caught
up in the merriment, danced a jig in her stead. Fifteen-year-old Anne

had not disappeared, she was right there in her joy, simplicity, and unwavering faith that God loved her and would sustain her now, as then.

Months became weeks, then days, then "The Day." True to my intent, I walked into the paymaster's office that morning and claimed my bonus before handing in my official resignation. Precisely 365 days had lapsed between my first tentative steps into the world of hospitality and the strides that carried me out of the resort and on to further adventures.

8

THE OLD COUNTRY

Sarah and I had a mere week or so back home before we were in the throes of packing. Like all first-time overseas travelers, I bought a suitcase large enough to cater to the needs of several people and filled it accordingly. Jumpers, jeans, and jersey dresses threatened to burst their confines. I squashed the heaving contents into submission with one hand while coaxing the zipper, tooth by tooth, around the case. The suitcase finally fastened, I set my luggage by the front door and threw myself into bed near midnight to pass a few fitful hours of sleep.

I had barely drifted off before being summoned to wakefulness by the buzz of the clock radio. The numbers 5, 4, and 2 floated around like fireflies in the dark, rearranging themselves until they settled at 2:45 a.m. I reached out and turned on the bedside lamp, squinting against the sudden rush of light. I quickly dressed, having already laid out my traveling clothes at the foot of the bed. My mother, already up and wrapped in her velveteen dressing gown, was busy making tea in the kitchen. I polished off a few rounds of toast and Vegemite, fearing I might never taste its salty goodness again, and sipped my tea hurriedly, scalding my lip in the process.

"Have you got everything?" my father asked, emerging from the bathroom. "Bags—check, passport—check, travelers' checks—check," I confirmed. "Right, we're off then!" he said, jangling his car keys. I eased my suitcase down the back steps and, pulling the handle, trundled it toward the trunk of the car. It was still dark, and a stiff breeze came up the hill, bending the slim, tall gum trees and revealing a sprinkling of

stars. I felt my mother's velveteen sleeves encircle my waist. "Safe journey, love. Take care and ring me to let me know when you've arrived." I
swiveled around to meet her embrace. "Thanks, Mum, I will, don't
worry." Sarah and I jumped in the back of Dad's car, waving to our
mother until she was out of sight.

The long haul to England necessitated a stopover to break the journey. Sarah and I chose Tokyo. Reason had long ago informed me that
despite the best will in the world, I would not then, nor ever be, Japanese. I had to content myself with this small and fleeting window of
opportunity to sample the culture I had long admired. We had booked
an overnight stay in a hotel just off Narita Airport. Arriving late in the
evening, we were tired but still hungry and found the only option at our
disposal was the hotel bar. We took an elevator that opened onto a
plush lounge with subdued lighting, and there we found a vacant table
among the many tables filled with late-night diners.

Perusing the menu, we were horrified as it slowly dawned on us that,
in Japan, eating was financially "out of our league." We pushed the
menu aside and sustained ourselves by slowly sipping the gin and tonics
we had blithely ordered, discovering too late that they came to the exact
sum we had budgeted for our entire stay. As Sarah and I sat there,
coolly appraising the specter of hunger, a large plate of roast chicken
legs and sauce appeared like a mirage on our low table. I looked up and
saw that indeed it was real, the bar hostess smiling as she withdrew her
hand from under the plate. "I didn't order these," I said, terrified of the
consequences of an unpaid-for meal. "No, no, those gentlemen over
there ordered for you." She gestured in the direction of a large table of
Japanese businessmen, their dark suits camouflaging their presence.
"They must have seen our reaction to the menu!" I whispered. "This is
great!" Sarah responded. "No, it's not," I hissed through gritted teeth.
"What do they want for the chicken legs, *our* legs?!" Self-preservation
rose in me, overriding all other considerations. "Don't be *silly*, let's eat,"
said Sarah—so we did.

Satisfied, I dabbed the delicate napkin to my mouth. "We must
thank them," I said, any other option unthinkable. Despite my awkwardness and embarrassment, I scanned my memory for the few Japanese phrases I had garnered in Port Douglas and approached their
table. With a profound bow, I pronounced the words "Arigato gozaima-
su itadekimasu," hoping I was saying something along the lines of

"Thank you, much appreciated." The hostess suddenly reappeared, "No, no, not that table, *that* table, " as my thanks met confused but entertained faces. Deeply embarrassed, but equally determined, I repeated the whole performance to those who had the right to receive it. Their appreciative nods confirmed I had made myself understood. How kind they were, they who owed us nothing, but in giving us food, gave us everything. Bless them, wherever they may be.

We flew out the following morning, well rested—and we needed to be, with a twelve-hour leg of the journey before us. Tokyo had begun to stir, the airport already in full swing. We arrived at the check-in counter. "I'm sorry, madam, but there are no more seats available in economy class, would you mind traveling business class?" I looked at Sarah, "I wouldn't mind, would you?" I said. "Not at all," she answered. We sat between Japanese businessmen, to whom we had become so favorably disposed. We marveled at the frugality of their traditional rice and raw fish, while we gave ourselves over to a heart-stopping full English breakfast. Britain here we come!

Exhaustion had well and truly set in by the time we touched down at Heathrow. Our passports stamped, we arrived at the carousel just in time to see our cases disappearing into the cavernous mouth beyond the conveyor belt, but what were a few more minutes on top of so many hours? Eventually they were regurgitated, sliding within our reach. Somehow, despite the haze of jet lag, Sarah and I made it to Victoria Station. From there we boarded the train that would take us north to our aunt in Lancashire. I leaned my head against the window and peered out into the dark. All I could see was my own weary reflection staring back at me. I would just have to bide my soul in patience till the morning.

The rhythm of the train lulled me to sleep as we passed countless stations, indistinct names and places as yet unknown to me blending with my dreams. I felt a hand on my shoulder, "Wake up, Rachael, we're here." I must have slept for some hours. Bleary eyed, I reached for my suitcase and pulled it down onto the platform and saw a sign which read, "Preston." Roused by a thin drizzle of rain on my face and the chill of the early hour, I saw the reflection of streetlights shimmering on the wet concrete. Around me I caught the sound of my mother's northern accent, once rare, now emanating from every man, woman, and child who poured out of the train and disappeared down lanes or was carried away in taxis. A large, black hackney cab, more tank than taxi, pulled up alongside us. Our suitcases neatly stacked between the seats, we saw out the last few miles of our long journey, finally arriving outside our aunt's porch-lit home.

The luminous hands of my watch declared it a quarter past one in the morning. However, there was little evidence in my aunt's welcome to support this fact as she flung open her front door to greet us. "Hello, girls, how good it is to see you. Come on in and have a nice cup of tea. Here, give me your bags, let's get inside." Sally, my mother's older sister, was no stranger to me; I had met her when she came to visit our family when I was a child. Within half an hour of her arriving, Dad was at the piano and she and Mum were singing the songs of their youth, "We'll Gather Lilacs in the Spring Again," Sally's arm about my shoulder. She had given me a copy of Edith Nesbit's classic *The Railway Children*. Poverty had never seemed so romantic as they explored the railways in "pinafored destitution" with little more than a candlelit supper of "cooking raisins, and candied peel and marmalade"[1] to keep the roses in their cheeks and the wolf from the door. "Rachael, would you like marmalade on your toast?" Sally inquired as she brought a tea tray into the front parlor. "Yes, please." I had arrived.

I woke early the following morning, or so I thought, for all was dark and hushed. I first noted the long, mirrored dresser where my toiletries were set out, along with an old-fashioned, silver-backed hairbrush set. I unpacked and hung up a few items of crumpled clothing, waiting for gravity to work its magic. A faint hiss rose from the central heating beneath the window where deep green velour curtains hung in semicircular splendor, giving the room a theatrical air. Act 1, scene 1: First Morning in England.

I drew the curtains and looked up and down the street, the warmth within highlighting the chill without. By the pale wintry light I saw a man in a flat cap setting a brisk pace as he walked his dog. On the other side of the street, two elderly ladies in gray coats made their way up the street arm in arm, chatting as they went. I looked at my watch; it was 10:00 a.m. I slipped my arms through the sleeves of my dressing gown and went downstairs.

Sally, a widow and retired headmistress, was well disciplined and orderly in her daily habits. She was up and dressed and had set the breakfast table, ready for when we chose to emerge from our rooms. "I thought we might take a walk up to the village to get some more milk after breakfast," said Sally. My aunt, indefatigable, believed in the benefits of donning a scarf and anorak and walking whenever an errand was required. Her car sat idle in its garage, month in, month out. Sally also had a deep-seated loyalty to her country and, if challenged, would defend the English weather to the death. "Perhaps we could take the car. It's terribly cold out there?" I would say. "It's not *cold* today, it's temperate," she would reply in an incredulous tone, gesturing as she did to the petrified, frostbitten branches outside the front window. "Just tuck your scarf into your coat and button your collar up. You just need to learn to dress according to the weather."

In my aunt's mind, a well-buttoned jacket, boots, and woolen scarf were as effective in warding off the plague as keeping out the cold. As I followed at her heels, I thought I would succumb to both. I cannot remember Sally ever describing the weather as "cold." Ever upbeat, she chose euphemisms such as "bracing" or "fresh," whatever served to give a dreary, gray day a positive spin. The irony was not lost on me when I discovered that Sally had good friends in Spain and was not averse to disappearing for a week or two in the dead of winter, only to resurface near spring, sporting a tan.

Sally's love for the English weather was only surpassed by her passion for the English language. She relished words and their nuances, usage, and origins as much as I did. One day Sally received a letter from her local travel agent requesting that she "uplift" her tickets at her earliest convenience. I watched Sally standing by the hall table in silence for a half minute, eyes boring into the offending expression. Suddenly galvanized into action, she reached out for the phone, punching in the numbers. "Yes, this is Mrs. Wright calling. I am a customer of many years and would like to speak to the manager, please"—this in her most authoritative voice, which, given her career, came naturally. She waited patiently, scanning the contents again. "Yes, good morning, Mr. Aldershot, it's Mrs. Wright here. I've just received a letter from your office asking me to 'uplift' my tickets. Now I have taught English for over forty years and have never received an official letter containing such pretentious jargon, somebody thinking it terribly clever, no doubt. Why is it that a perfectly good plain-English expression such as 'pick up' or 'collect' was not used?" A brief pause followed. "Your office was not responsible for the wording?" Another pause. "Then would you please give me the number of your head office in Scotland? Thank you very much."

I stood in awe of my aunt's capacity to assert herself. Given my lack of self-confidence, I could only dream of what it took to do so. It *was* self-assertion on my aunt's part, properly and sparingly expressed, for I never once heard her argue for argument's sake. Suffice it to say, my aunt was never asked to uplift her tickets again. I came to know that if Sally was given to any type of default, it was a tendency to mine the goodness in every situation and at every moment, and that no convenience was so commonplace as to pass without due praise, whether it was produce at the local grocer's, the frequency with which the buses ran, the quality of shoes at the market, or the bargains to be had at a thrift store. "Here, Rachael," she would say, taking my arm and drawing me to her side. "This is a *great* skirt. Just feel the quality of the material. It's a designer brand, too, see? Look at the label." Then she would put it up to my waist, continuing to wax eloquent that such a bargain could be gained for a mere £3.50. Her attitude was infectious, turning a humble, secondhand store into an Aladdin's cave of treasures for the taking.

I remember the afternoon Sally and I turned off the footpath and into our favorite Oxfam shop not far from the main street. Long shafts of light picked out various items lining the walls. Sally's face was all anticipation of what "lovely bargains" we might find that day. A soft beam settled on the title of a book. My aunt picked it up, and I watched the smile disappear instantly from her face. I looked at the cover: *Disaster at Bari*. My mother's brother Vincent was the only child of the family who did not return from World War II. A seventeen-year-old radio officer in the Merchant Navy, his ship was destroyed in 1943 in the bombing of Bari Harbor in Italy. Scant information trickled through, and although his anxious parents William and Sarah were informed of his death, they were, as my aunt later told me, mercifully spared the details. Now fifty years on, the story of the horrific deaths of those who perished on the night of December 3, overcome by plumes of mustard gas and fire, was available in paperback for the cost of 20 pence.

How often I have heard it said, or seen it written, that people on the autism spectrum "lack empathy." In my own life, I am only too aware that it is merely the thinnest membrane that separates my experience from that of others. To see images of those hungry and displaced in camps is to grip the wire in solidarity with their plight. To read the pages of a history book is, for me, to turn the pages of today's newspaper. News of a person's pitiful death, whether it be yesterday or five hundred years ago, makes no difference in my perception—for me, the totality of human experience collapses into a single, present point.

I recall visiting Old Melbourne Gaol a couple of years ago expecting nothing more than an interesting historical tour, only to be assailed by the anguish of those long gone seeping out of its very stones. Clammy and shaking, I had to flee, making a quick exit through the memorabilia of a souvenir shop filled with people seemingly unaware of such unmitigated suffering. I have always experienced life in this way and have had to learn to take measures to protect myself from being overwhelmed by feelings of affliction, to temper barefaced reality—and yet, reality is all I have ever known. For those who may look at our blank expressions and assume our hearts follow suit, I assure you, they do not.

Two weeks had passed since Sarah and I arrived in England, long enough for my body clock to have adjusted from being turned upside down and inside out. Sarah had already recovered and had, a few days earlier, packed her things and taken a train up to the Lake District to seek work. Today I followed in her wake. Sally, not merely bitten but consumed by the travel bug, seemed as excited as I as we watched the train pull into the station. "Now Rachael, make sure that you see Ambleside. It's by far the loveliest village in the Lake District." I boarded the train, taking in as much of my aunt's advice as my overexcited nerves would allow. Sally waved me off, chopping the air in a large arc, and after a few moments I saw her suddenly consult her wristwatch and, looking down the road, set off into her next moment with as much passion as her last.

The journey, though not a very long one, was nevertheless divided by having to make a connection. I had left the city behind and now boarded one of two carriages pulled along a single line by a diesel engine. Its slow, steady pace enabled me to catch glimpses from the edge of a small township, of children's bikes, clotheslines, and patio furniture, which drifted by my carriage. A porcelain ballerina pirouetted in a back window, while a garden gnome in a bright yellow coat pushed his wheelbarrow by a bed of colorful spring flowers. In the distance I saw a row of beautifully painted front doors and thought, "Behind each one is a story. I hope they are happy ones." Layer upon layer of images impressed themselves on my memory, creating a montage of English domesticity.

The apprehension I felt at embarking for the new was somewhat alleviated by my sister having secured a position for me in a small hotel in a lesser-known village. The driver who collected me from Windermere Station drove at a good pace, winding along the narrow stonewalled lanes and displaying his intimate knowledge of every twist and turn. We rounded a corner, and as we were slowed by our ascent of its shrub-lined drive, the hotel, whitewashed and multileveled, came into view.

I could clearly see the dining room, for it was encased in glass from floor to roof, giving it the appearance of a large greenhouse and providing as much heat as early May could muster. Collecting my bag and walking a few steps, I noticed the dark slate tiles contrasting with the tall white chimneys that dotted the roof. A face appeared before me. "Hello, I'm Sandra, may I take your case for you?" With a crisp starched blouse and a ready smile, Sandra was all efficiency as she showed me to my room in the staff quarters across the road from the hotel. From my window I saw the bleak, high-peaked hills rising over and claiming the land on which the local inns stood. Established little more than three hundred years, they were but subtenants on nature's long-term lease.

I rose early the next morning, dressing in the striped blouse and blue waistcoat of a hotel employee, adding a knee-length skirt I had bought when with my aunt. The hotel manager's wife, Mrs. Milford, met me at the main entrance, ready to guide me through a day's duties. It was her firmly held belief that the hotel's reputation would rise or fall in direct proportion to the cleanliness of its skirting boards. To this end she schooled me in an obsessive ritual of brushing, washing, and polishing that took up most of the morning, causing me to play catch-up for the rest of the day.

Built long before any standardization came into being, the corridors I walked through bowed to meet me, stooping as I did to pass under the lintel of a door. After a few weeks, I thought myself accomplished. I had navigated each anomaly brought on by time or the rough-and-ready, seventeenth-century builder who made it thus; but "Pride cometh before a fall" and what a fall it was!

I had just started the lunchtime shift and had been given the task of delivering the pub meals from the kitchen to the bar. "Order for table

14, two ploughman's lunches," the chef called. I placed them on a tray and strode purposefully toward the bar while taking stock of the plate's contents: "cheddar cheese, ham, pickled onions, lettuce, crusty bread and butter." Deep in concentration, I failed to notice the step worn down by three centuries of hungry travelers. I wobbled and fell headlong into the bar, sending pickled onions rolling and cubes of cheese bouncing off in all directions. The guests certainly got their ploughman's lunches—I ploughed them right into the carpet where they were sitting.

Apart from my nearest and dearest, with whom I always felt socially at ease, I continued to work from a script. From my inner file, I would pull out the appropriate phrase or action as required by the context in which I found myself. So successful had I become at sympathizing with others, I could mirror not only their phrases and gestures but even their accents. I recall a particular evening spent in the company of my aunt's friends. I did not know them very well but had been invited to dinner. Throughout the course of that evening I had, by degrees, morphed myself into a carbon copy of our hostess. Every movement of her body, every nuance of her voice and character, became my own. A tilt of the head, a pat of the cheek, the rise and fall of inflections in her speech found a perfect echo in my own behavior. I was however, completely unaware of my Oscar-winning performance. It was only after our arriving home that my aunt turned to me and said, "Rachael, who *were* you tonight? I didn't recognize you!" I was shocked. Retracing my social steps, it began to dawn on me what had taken place. Like a chameleon, I had taken on the color of my surroundings, blending in to hide my social vulnerabilities.

Of course, some people that I came across could never be imitated. I remember the Welsh tourists who arrived by bus, filling the restaurant one Sunday evening. I had never heard their language before and I was enthralled by the sound of consonant after consonant falling from their lips. This would not have been such a distraction to me had I not been "silver-serving" a tray full of whole baked trout. *Splash!* A portion slipped from the serving cutlery, landing head first in a lady's wineglass. I quickly consulted my inner file, but there were no matches for "Responses to Serving a Trout in a Wineglass." Instead, I stood there, openmouthed and rooted to the spot, still grasping the fork and spoon from which the fish had fallen. "Never mind dear, I'm sure it won't drink too much!" said the lady kindly, putting me at ease. They roared with laughter and I sighed with relief.

Thankfully, the exception proved the rule. I enjoyed working in a service role and derived peace of mind in considering the needs of others, as I had long ago. Creating a routine helped to define my working boundaries and so reduced and controlled my anxiety. Despite the odd bout of chaos, I managed to create order, moving from table to table with mathematical precision. The hotel manager, Mr. Milford, noted my capacity for order. He pulled me aside into the corridor, and after looking left and right, hissed a deal in my ear. "Listen Rachael, I reckon you have the right stuff for a managerial position in this hotel. What say you?" "A managerial position?" I echoed. "Shhh, the walls have ears! Give it some thought," he said, before disappearing down the corridor. Moments later, a fellow worker sidled up to me, asking "what old Milford was going on about" in the corridor just now. Being both blessed and cursed by Asperger honesty, naturally I gave my coworker a blow-by-blow description of what had passed between us in such secrecy. News of my pending promotion spread throughout the staff quarters like wildfire. Outrage and jealousy reared their ugly heads among the more established workers, but their fears were unfounded. As flattering as the offer was, the confidence I felt in a lower position could not, at that time, translate into a level required to lead others.

On the other side of midnight, I found myself in the miserable position of having to select my dinner from the leftovers on the sweets trolley. I sat on the doorstep of the kitchen, spooning in mouthfuls of pavlova and thinking, "Time is ticking on my working holiday, too much work and not enough holiday." The hospitality industry with its notoriously long and unsociable hours had, alas, eaten up many months of my free time and had, in my reckoning, begun to wear thin. At week's end, I decided to leave the hotel. My sister and I met up to spend what little time we had left in England exploring the best the Lake District had to offer. For Sarah and me, that meant making straight for the home of Beatrix Potter.

As we drove toward Hill Top Farm, I recalled my childhood copy of *The Tailor of Gloucester*. I remembered its peach-colored cover and the picture of a bespectacled mouse sitting cross-legged on a cotton spool reading his paper. When poring over the illustrations, I was drawn by the light and warmth emanating from a tiny, watercolored candle. Seeking comfort, I imagined myself among the mice that warmed themselves under their little low roof.

Passing over the threshold of the author's door, I walked from room to room delighting in each object, practical and beautiful, chosen by her own hand, from the carved oak chest whose wooden grapevine flourished in relief above its doors to the delicate pair of French porcelain dolls, once cherished in girlhood, now sitting on the windowsill in ornamental splendor. I marveled at each piece lovingly selected, gazed upon, and treasured by Beatrix, which had nevertheless, in her long absence, been held in being by the appreciation of each and every visitor who passed under her roof.

My eye fell upon a pair of exquisitely crafted, fine-china greyhounds, each carrying a captured hare in its muzzle. What impressed me most of all about Beatrix Potter's work was her capacity to depict the whimsical charm of the natural world without shirking its harsh realities. She gazed steadily into each domain and chose the better part, leaving a legacy of beauty.

Sarah and I spent our last few days rambling in the fells surrounding Ambleside. One only needed to cover a few miles of walking track to become proficient in the opening and closing of farm gates. Gravity-defying, sure-footed sheep grazed upon the stark and hilly moorland, almost at right angles. I was amazed that the rocky outcrops on which they were pastured could sustain a single one, but they not only survived, they thrived, casting defiant looks at all who passed their way. High in those hills as we walked on, conversation gave way to contemplation and contemplation to an all-pervasive silence. Before us stretched a vast landscape whose patchwork shades of burnt orange and deepest green were illumined by long fingers of light. Rugged heights, whose immensity was only made bearable by the division of miles of drystone walls, claimed sovereignty from valley to sky. A shadow crept across the mountains, covering them in darkness, and below, in the fold of a hill, a group of small white cottages huddled together.

Sarah, keen to explore some specimen that had caught her eye, ventured farther down the track, leaving me quite alone. I did not fear the solitude, nor the silence in which I was wrapped. How could I—had it not been mine since the beginning? Solitude and silence had always been the familiar backdrop to my existence. Many had thought my silence unhealthy, unnatural even; and they had sought to school me in a way of interaction amounting to no more than froth and bubble, pandering to their sensibilities and robbing me of a quality that I valued. I had developed a healthy suspicion of noise in many of its forms, for was to fear silence not to fear one's own being?

Sarah returned, showing me a thin sliver of Cumbrian slate that she found some way off the beaten track. It was a black-green color, like that found in a child's paint palette. We made our way farther down the track, exchanging fantastic stories regarding the slate's origin. "I think it's a pendant belonging to the queen of a local tribe," I conjectured. "I'm sorry, but you're out by several hundred years, it's clearly a keepsake from a farm girl to her Roman lover," Sarah said. "Well," said I, "he didn't look after it very well, did he?" We laughed, and after our great trek, were rewarded by the sight of Stock Ghyll Falls, its crystal waters draped over the rocks like Chantilly lace.

We had left the Lake District, and the time came to board the train to Heathrow Airport. Sarah and I saw out the miles, chatting about what we had seen and sighing about what we hadn't. A talented artist, she showed me some sketches she had drawn of the Bridge House at Ambleside. I couldn't for the life of me paint a picture, but I *could* paint a face, and I directed my talents toward a new career.

9

A FORK IN THE ROAD

"**P**ale and interesting" is how I had long been described in more than one quarter. With translucent skin and a sprinkling of freckles, I possessed little protection from the harsh Australian sun. To compensate, I had developed a vampiric regimen, applying sunblock to every square inch of my exposed flesh, which, given my long, flowing dresses, did not amount to much. I would avoid the noonday sun, savoring the shady side of the street, following the buildings whose shadows gave me cool, if momentary, relief. Broad-brimmed hats were a fixture on my head, and over the crook of my arm swung a large parasol, ready to be deployed with the push of a button.

The care of my complexion, prudent in itself, rose to Aspergic heights with the seriousness with which I approached all things. As practical as my clothing was, it was not chosen without a nod in the direction of fashion. Surely my style was in vogue (for a nineteenth-century woman). I already possessed the speech and mannerisms of yesteryear—in for a penny, in for a pound! I devoured books on Victorian poetry, art, and literature and with a sure hand chose fabrics and styles pleasing to my taste. Considering myself something of an aesthete, I developed a style best described as "late Victorian," a style that I now suspect instilled fear rather than lust in men's hearts. I had a favorite black-brimmed hat with gold-and-red tapestry roses, which I teamed with dark woolen dresses that almost swept the floor. The flat expression on my face gave the appearance of one who had stepped out of a sepia photograph. So attired, I swept around a street corner to hear a young boy cry to his mother, "Look, a ghost!" I set off up the road striding purposefully through Brisbane city toward my beauty-therapy business like a mad Mary Poppins.

I had studied beauty therapy under the guidance of the principal of my chosen academy, who herself had learned her art under the tutelage of the late Madam Gatineau of Paris. I eagerly attended the principal's lectures in anatomy and physiology, relishing the details and receiving several commendations for my work as a masseuse. "You show great empathy through your hands," she observed. The hairdresser, under whose roof I had set up shop, had given me carte blanche to convert an unused section of the business into a therapy space. Commanding a small army of shop fitters, I created an oasis of peace and relaxation in the heart of the city.

From out of their office towers and off the street they came, a whole cross-section of humanity passing through my cubicle door. Under a canopy of green-blue organza and a framed print of a solitary beach-comber examining in her palm a fine pearl, I saw my clients visibly relax under the warm, sweet oils and massage, which drew away the tensions of the workaday world.

I enjoyed the one-on-one interaction with my clients and they, more often than not, slept through their treatment, which reduced the need for "small talk"—my perfect working environment. Despite such a preference, I was more than able to mirror my clients' needs. Some would chat; often we'd laugh; an unofficial book club even sprung up as we shared what we considered a "good read." Others, weary and weighed down (I sensed it as they passed through my door), poured out their troubles and left feeling better, knowing that in the silence, I listened.

Some Saturday mornings I filled my cosmetic case with color palettes, lipsticks, and pressed powder in various shades, bracing myself for an appointment with a wedding party. Snapping the case shut, I would travel to their homes, ready to transform the bride, her mother, and a bridesmaid or two as previously agreed. I had meticulously factored in the time needed to complete the makeup of each client, and I would set to work. I recall one bride who, flushed with excitement or champagne, or both, burst into the living room as I industriously plied my trade. "Rachael, my two sisters and aunt and my cousin and grandmother have just turned up. Would you mind doing their makeup as well? Thanks!" My Asperger capacity to shoulder stress and change had definitely improved with regular inoculations such as these.

On some occasions I would offer my services as a wedding singer. No sooner had I put down the lip brush, then I would pick up my sheet music and head off to the church. Ascending to the minstrel's gallery, I had a good vantage point from which to see my handiwork as the bride walked down the aisle to the strains of my rendition of Gounod's "Ave Maria."

How random they seemed to me, the processes that brought one from singlehood to that solemn state! All my adult life I had observed the flirtatious behavior women initiated, apparently conveying to men a clear and unmistakable message of attraction and interest. I had covered much ground in my capacity to socialize with others in the intervening years since my childhood, but the art of flirting remained to me incomprehensible, if not downright embarrassing. A shrug of the shoulder, a raise of the eyebrow, turning her face away, a quick glance back with a flick of her hair, and laughter—always laughter, the soundtrack accompanying these signals. Surely death itself could not be more stressful than the playing out of these moves, designed to attract and secure a mate?

I looked and looked but could not easily work out the communication going on between men and women in social settings. I myself was invisible, my presence unacknowledged. It was only many years later that it occurred to me that men, less expressive in their emotions and less skilled in reading body language—much like my good self—required from women a complex array of gestures to invite attention, gestures I was unable to express.

My days were full and I ran my business with great success, but my success came at a high price. Like many people on the autism spectrum, the mental energy I needed for social interaction, organizing myself, and coping with constant anxiety left me exhausted by the end of the working week. Arriving home, I would kick off my shoes, pour myself a drink, and lose myself in a classic black-and-white movie before shuffling off to bed. I thought wistfully of the weekend pursuits my clients had spoken of: choirs and camping, ballroom dancing and bush walking. How I would have loved to engage in any number of these activities in my own free time, but every ounce of my energy was spent, poured out in the practice of "earning a living."

The pattern of my working days continued as it had always done in the three years since I had set up shop as I performed a steady stream of facials and massage and instilled in my clients a care for their complexions *almost* as enthusiastic as my own. That was until I began to notice a change in my regular lunchtime routine. Usually I would sit and eat in the staff room or fight my way through the heaving crowds that milled around the nearby food court. Now, for some weeks, I had taken to hastily eating my lunch, and then, crossing the street, I would pass the imposing edifice of the General Post Office, its large gothic clock striking the half hour, hastening my steps. Walls of sandstone to the right and to the left of me, I would pass through the vaulted arcade and find myself in the wide-open square surrounding St. Stephen's Cathedral, which was nestled among towering, mirrored skyscrapers.

Drawn into the cathedral's cool, marbled interior, there I would find the nearest pew and sit, just sit, noting the people who came and went: a mother with a young child whose voice echoed in the high spaces; a wizened old lady wearing a black lace mantilla and hunched in prayer, barely taking up any space at all; a couple of tourists snapping pictures, taking advantage of the soft light that permeated the whole building. Gradually I would be left alone in the silence. I would close my eyes, becoming aware of my breath and the silence at the end of each breath, then a deeper silence—the silence of my childhood, of the grotto, of the church where I stood tracing my finger along the creases of a stained glass palm, and the silence of Christ, held in my own palm before receiving Him in that First Communion so many years before: "Lord I am not worthy to receive you, but only say the word and I shall be healed."

Soon I became aware of a presence, yes, definitely a presence. In the same way as when one turns off a light and is plunged into darkness until the eyes adjust, the eyes of my heart were slowly adjusting. I felt God calling me, not just "in silence" but "to silence." I hardly knew what it meant. I left quickly by the side entrance, touching my fingers to the cool, still water in the stoup by the door. I emerged from the cathedral, and the presence I had sensed within those four walls enveloped every car, traffic light, building, and office worker who went about their business in the heart of the city. It was not long before I received an answer to the question rising in my mind.

I visited one of my mother's friends (having the happy knack of turning her friends into mine) whose impressive collection of books lined every wall of the house. I drew my finger along the spines and pulled out at random a book by an English author and Carmelite Sister, Ruth Burrows, whose words resonated with that for which I had long hoped and half guessed. Never before had I read the life of someone whose story echoed so much of my own. It was not that her family or much of her personal history bore any resemblance to mine; living as we did worlds and generations apart, it did not. Rather, the familiarity lay in a quality of perception and temperament.

The author, like me, had from an early age been thrown back on her own resources: me, through my precarious beginnings; she, through the untimely death of her older sister in childhood. Deeper still ran an innate vulnerability and extreme sensitivity to the passing nature of things, of which we were both only too aware. No amount of happy distraction could avert our gaze from these realities, for they were written in every happening of nature and in the very fabric of our beings. We both possessed buoyant personalities, and as such, the knowledge we had accumulated had the effect of galvanizing each of us into a search for truth.

The author's journey was a curious one, and more curious still was the lifestyle in which it was lived. She had, in early adulthood, become a contemplative nun, entering the Order of Our Lady of Mount Carmel, one of the most ancient and honored expressions of religious life within the Catholic Church. Its roots were embedded in the lives of twelfth-century hermits living in caves on Mount Carmel in the Holy Land who later formed communities across Europe. Far from their being a fragment of medieval history, I learned that the Carmelites were alive and well and that from within the silence of their monastic enclosures they offered their entire lives to God; their hours, days, months, and years spent in prayer and simple work for the good of all humanity.

It is said that "grace builds on nature," and as I read the last page of the last chapter, I realized that I had been captured by an ideal that seemed to speak to all my longings: a life of order, of silence, of interminable routine—in short, "Aspergian paradise." There and then I made up my mind that I, too, would become a Carmelite nun; I would answer the paradoxical call of a life lived for others, from within the depths of a great solitude.

A golden opportunity came my way when a few months later, my parents announced that they were going on a vacation to visit France and to see family in England. I told my mother and father of my desire to enter a Carmelite monastery in England and that I had been in regular correspondence with the Carmelite Sister and prioress whose book had given me such inspiration. Knowing the seriousness of my intent and the happiness I could hardly conceal, they entered into my joy, leaving the sorrow that would surely come for another day. The decision made, I settled my affairs and wound up my beauty-therapy business. I gently took down from my cubicle wall the framed print of the solitary beachcomber. She had found her "Pearl of Great Price," [1] as I sought mine.

10

PARIS

We arrived in Paris in early June, the bus taking us along the poplar-lined route from Charles de Gaulle Airport to our hotel in Montmatre. My intrepid Aunt Sally had arranged our accommodation and was waiting to greet us in the modest reception area consisting of a desk, a small lounge chair, a storage cupboard, and a dark wooden staircase which spiraled to the hotel's upper floors. Sally tossed aside the copy of *Le Monde* she had been perusing and leapt to her feet. "Hello, my dears, how are you, did you have a good flight? I've already seen our rooms, rather small but, of course, that's how it is in Paris. The beds are *very* comfortable and there's plenty of hot water. Come on, let's get these cases upstairs." Sally's inquiries were punctuated by hearty hugs. There are two camps into which an Aspie falls: "Them That Hug" and "Them That Don't." I was mercifully spared the tactile sensitivity that would make one recoil from an embrace, and I was always delighted by the way that, despite the lapse of years, it was as if we and Sally had never been apart.

Staying a mere five nights, Sally was keen to show us the sights of Paris and was adamant that such an undertaking was best done on foot. The Metro was a stone's throw from our hotel. We descended into its cavernous passageways of gleaming, white-tiled walls whose every advertisement was a snapshot of French culture. An image of a young model smiled out from a glossy poster, reminding me of a snatch of poetry from the pen of Apollinaire.

Her dancing eyes like angels

> She laughed and laughed
> Her face all the colors of France
> Blue eyes white teeth and red red lips
> Her face all the colors of France.[1]

In the train that sped us to our destination, we were happy captives to the music that poured forth from the accordion of a busker who steadied himself near the door. "Padam Padam" he played, the notes soaring and diving to his touch as the train lurched in time to the music. I fumbled in my handbag, finally managing to draw out a few francs to reward his talent before the doors slid open. Emerging from the Metro, Sally set a cracking pace along the Champs Élysées, she, many yards ahead and I, bringing up the rear. "Aren't we having a good time?!" she called, a question and statement combined—and so we were.

We arrived at the grand entrance to the Musée du Petit Palais and passed through its arching, gilt doorway. I found the nearest thing on which I could sit. The large cold pipes of the central heating, redundant during the summer, served as a makeshift seat. A concerned guide approached my aunt, who said, by way of explanation, "My niece is a little delicate," a description I considered both shameful and alluring. I had seen, often enough, portraits of Victorian women, the life ebbing out of them as they lay on chaise lounges, poor things; but I was made of stronger stuff and sought a particular piece of art that I understood the museum held.

Having passed through countless chambers, I finally found Bouguereau's *The Virgin with Angels*. I had acquired a picture postcard of the artwork, which, in reality, took up the staggering proportions of a whole wall. I don't know why it drew me so; perhaps it was the Zen-like stance of the Madonna, or the authoritative gaze of the child, imparting a blessing from the embrace of her arms. Maybe it was the angels who surrounded them like a chorus line from the Ziegfeld Follies, lost in wonder, or kneeling at the Virgin's feet, raising golden thuribles whose incense seemed to waft out of the intricate latticework of the design crafted by the painter's hand.

Parisian angels were a breed apart. In the Church of La Madelaine, hewn out of marble they stood, far removed from the willowy creatures depicted in holy pictures. With rippling muscles and sleeves rolled up like dockworkers, their beefy arms strained to take the load. I saw them carrying out their duties in squares and churches and on monuments throughout the length and breadth of the city. What I would have given for an ounce of their energy!

Ever since my mother had brought me back a scarf from her travels when I was still a child—a red, blue, and aqua geometric design on a shimmering white background—I had longed to visit the city from whence it came. "It's a Parisian scarf," she had said, as I touched it to my cheek, a magical fragrance still lingering in its silk. "Pa-ri-si-an," I repeated, intuiting even then that Paris was not so much a place as a state of mind. I soon discovered that Paris had not one state of mind, but many.

Each morning during our stay, I would rise, dress, and consider which hat in my modest collection I would wear. Would it be the green felt with the upturned brim, the blue beret, which was both stylish and comfortable, or my favorite black-brimmed hat with the red-and-gold tapestry roses? That day, we were going to visit the Cathedral of Notre Dame. This would definitely be a "tapestry roses" kind of day. It was a beautiful morning as we walked along the bank of the Seine, watching the pleasure boats pass by on its glistening waters. We were happily chatting about that day's adventure when an elderly gentleman stopped in his tracks before us and appraised my hat before launching into an avalanche of Gallic compliments. It was evident that my choice had pleased him and that pleased me, but not everyone approved of "mademoiselle's chapeau."

We crossed the square and were absorbed into the wave of humanity which surged through the doors of Notre Dame. The Apostles in all their chiseled grandeur were there to greet us. My eyes had hardly adjusted to the dim light when, from out of the press behind me, rose a shrill voice. "Enlevez votre chapeau! Enlevez votre chapeau!" it kept repeating. I swung round to see a young woman coming toward me, her hand outstretched in an attempt to remove my hat. My aunt, with a ready sense of what was right and just, stepped between me and the young woman who tried to divest me of my headwear. "It is traditional for women to cover their heads in church. By what authority do you make such demands?" she asked. The young woman did not look so sure of her position and weakly repeated her request. "Are you here in an official capacity? Where is your identification?" The young woman conceded that she had no such authority and disappeared into the crowd. By way of explanation, Sally turned to me and casually said, "She had her wires crossed." Now I suppose being the subject of an altercation in a major cathedral might not "look good" on an aspiring Catholic nun's curriculum vitae, but in all fairness, Sally's quick thinking nipped in the bud what could have been an all-out row in a place of worship.

We continued on foot across the city, taking in the glories of France. On top of great buildings and in the squares, allegories of freedom and virtue took shape in monumental splendor. Here, Liberty raised her arms, imploring the nation to find sanctuary in the folds of her garment; there, a team of bronzed stallions pulled a chariot, clamoring and straining to break free from their metal footings to mount the sky. So thick and fast was the traffic that swirled around a square where we stood that it seemed to pass by in an impressionistic haze. Suddenly I felt an overwhelming sense of connection with all those who zoomed by, beeping the horns of their Citroens and other small European cars. I belonged to them and they belonged to me. This realization was *so simple* and *so startling* that it was all I could do not to wave at them in recognition!

I remember boarding a train on the Metro and taking an empty seat. Gradually I became aware of the passenger sitting next to me. He was a young man about the same age as me with a perfect aquiline profile. His skin was the color of café-au-lait; his jet-black hair swept over his forehead, crossing a high cheekbone in a gesture toward the Romantic era. His suit was a contrast of deep green jacket and pale green trousers which draped over his aesthetic frame, embodying quintessential Parisian style in his elegant couture. He was a man of extraordinary beauty, a vision so overpowering that I wanted to run in the opposite direction. I tilted my head slightly, willing myself to take in this sight, as beautiful a work of art as any I had seen in the Louvre. The next station announced, he rose from his seat and moved toward the door, turning at the last moment to afford me one last look at his stunning appearance, of which he was fully aware. I suspect that we might only experience one or two occasions in a lifetime when beauty lifts us completely out of ourselves. This was such a moment. I only rode the Metro with "Monsieur 1996" for three stations, but they are three stations I will never forget.

Climbing the cobbled streets of Montmatre, we were soon surrounded by a group of lean and hungry artists. I chose the leanest and hungriest-looking of the lot. Having agreed on a price, he set to work, executing a pleasing portrait of my twenty-five-year-old self. I had always been drawn to portraiture, and photography even more so, the older, the better. Amid the gift shops of the Place du Tetre, I found a picture postcard of a woman standing in her La Belle Époque finery, taken not far from where I was standing. What pathos there is in the expression of one who stares out from a sepia photograph! It is a moment in time, a style, and a desire to make one's mark. Even more captivating was the fleeting glimpse of a background figure: a casual observer who, for sheer curiosity, must have stopped to see what all the fuss was about. Caught forever in the photographer's frame, perhaps this was the only record that this grainy individual had ever existed, loved, hoped, and dreamed. How my heart went out to that still, solitary figure, just as it had to the inmates of the Old Melbourne Gaol and the countless stories of those whose lives inhabited the pages of history books!

How often I have thought, when closing the book of a long-gone author, that had I met them, how I would have loved them! There are no "dead authors" or "dead poets" for that matter. All words are the words of the living; the thoughts of one, through their written word, are transferred to the mind and heart of another. Words bridged the passage of time, connecting me with the whole of humanity, past, present, and yet to come. I was certain that God had given me the desire to hold them all up to him; surely my prayerful intercession would reach its mark?

On the highest part of Montmatre overlooking the city, the Basilica of Sacre Coeur suddenly rose into view, its white domes shining like a pavilion in the afternoon sun. Within, carpets of golden light shimmered at the feet of statues of the saints, golden threads woven from candles offered in prayer by pilgrims who moved about, hidden in the half-light. Illumined on a pedestal stood Saint Therese of Lisieux in plaster perfection. Clothed in the brown habit and cream mantle of the Carmelite Order, she looked out with a slight smile, the poor cousin of da Vinci's mysterious lady who lived across town behind several centimeters of bulletproof glass. Therese's elevated image drew from me a wry smile. In life, her every hessian-sandaled step trod the way of the small and mundane.

Outside on every step descending from the doors of the basilica were throngs of tourists delighting in the view over Paris whose buildings were bathed in a glorious pink-and-orange blush cast by the late-afternoon light. A ripple of applause ran through the happy crowd as a street performer added another pin to his juggling act, while a guitarist strummed a local tune. The steps of the Sacre Coeur are surely one of the most joyful places on the planet.

At the foot of the hill in the Place Pigalle, we passed by the Moulin Rouge. Crossing the boulevard I was taken aback, for there, among the sex shops lining the footpath, I saw in a window a statue of Saint Rita plying her trade in grace, as highly painted as any lady in the district. I leaned toward the window and whispered, "What are *you* doing here?" In this city there was nowhere the saints could not be seen.

That night, my last in Paris, saw us waiting for a table outside a popular workers' café that my aunt had frequented during her stays. Far from the haunts of the tourist, local diners sat at long tables covered in large sheets of white paper that served as a cloth on which the waiters could also tally up their bills.

The proprietor, a small, wiry lady in a black knit dress and a string of pearls who bore an uncanny resemblance to Edith Piaf, stood at the center of her café craning her neck and lifting her finger to alert the staff to her patrons' needs. She suddenly saw my aunt, her face lighting up in recognition. A space was cleared and a table placed, joining us to a long trestle of Parisian locals. On the candlelit tables, glasses brimming with Burgundy wine sparkled invitingly. Sally acted as translator, ordering various items from the menu with a flourish. Course upon course of exquisite French dishes arrived at our table; pâté and delicate slices of smoked salmon, bouillabaisse filled with fruits of the sea, crème brûlée, and platters of pungent cheeses with unpronounceable names were set before us on which to feast.

The proprietor brought strong coffee and spoke to us at length through Sally, laughing loudly and often over the general buzz that filled the room. She poured her best port into crystal glasses with a generous hand. "Sur la maison!" she declared, upending the bottle as the evening drew on. On that last night, surrounded by those I loved, how I wished that I could stop the clock and preserve that moment. I looked about at the happy patrons, listened to the low hum of conversation, and considered the rapid, purposeful gestures the proprietor made as she moved about the café, which was an expression of herself. How beautiful, how full of charm the world seems when one is just about to leave it! I looked at my mother and father, who looked back at me with infinite tenderness, but I could not stop the clock and within only a matter of days, my parting from them would be complete.

The following morning, having negotiated the winding staircase and placed my packed suitcases by the reception door, I had one phone call to make. I dialed and waited. "Good morning, Carmelite Monastery," intoned a crisp, English accent. "Good morning, Sister, it's Rachael here. I'm still in Paris, but I'll see you Monday evening." This I blurted out, heart in throat, a cocktail of nerves and excitement. There was a slight pause. "I'll just get Sr. Ruth for you," said the voice. "Hello, my dear, so you're almost ready to join us. I'm so looking forward to seeing you! Have a safe journey and God bless." I placed the phone back on the receiver as our bus pulled up outside the hotel.

II

THE MONASTERY

Does the road wind up-hill all way?
Yes, to the very end.
Will the day's journey take the whole long day?
From morn to night, my friend.
But is there for the night a resting-place?
A roof for when the slow dark hours begin.
May not the darkness hide it from my face?
You cannot miss that inn.
Shall I meet other wayfarers at night?
Those who have gone before.
Then must I knock, or call when just in sight?
They will not keep you standing at that door.
Shall I find comfort, travel-sore and weak?
Of labour you shall find the sum.
Will there be beds for me and all who seek?
Yes, beds for all who come.[1]

Sally pushed the key into the lock of her front door and we all tumbled in, Mum and Dad to rest and Sally and I to do what we did best—head for the village to scour the secondhand shops, this time armed with a list of "must-haves" for the discerning monastic novice. I scanned the racks of ladies' clothing with only one color in mind—brown. Brown was the color of the habit of the Order, hence all accessories were to conform to this fetching shade. I cannot say that I found this constraint terribly penitential, considering my love of color and style; rather, I found it liberating. "I have a lovely red cashmere jumper just come in," the shop assistant cooed. "Yes, that's very nice, but do you have one in . . . brown?" I inquired, taking no small pleasure in seeing the incredulous look on her face.

I drew a line through one item after another: undershirts, socks, and scarves. Sally had given me a fine, coffee-colored scarf with a light-blue stripe which I thought I might *just* get away with; in fact, I did. It turned out that the consensus of the community lay in following "the spirit of the color" rather than its letter. Consequently, my fellow nuns were decked out in a chocolate rainbow of every shade from beige to dark brown, with the occasional electric blue sock peeping out from a sandaled foot.

Swinging bags of supplies, we set off for the main street. Sally had offered to buy me lunch, which I graciously accepted, choosing a pizza restaurant. Sally had hardly settled into the booth as I snapped my menu shut. "I'm going to have the 'Meatlover's Pizza' today," I said. Sally's face jerked up from where she had been arranging the bags, a study in horror. "But Rachael, where will you get your greens?" she gasped. "Sally, the Carmelites are vegetarian, I'll be 'getting my greens' for the term of my natural life!" said I, for once justified in the face of my aunt's unerring gift of common sense. "Touché," I declared, sotto voce, raising a fork laden with beef, ham, and pepperoni to my lips.

The hours of that afternoon and evening slipped through my fingers as I whittled down my possessions into a single small suitcase, putting my hats firmly aside. Before the last light of evening, from my window I watched the villagers, people of regular habits, going about their routines. The lady next door pruned her hedge, while a young couple in luminous running shoes set a steady pace up the road. The man in the flat cap, older now, with his even older snowy-faced dog that waddled by his side, passed under my window. Because I was aware of my imminent departure, this familiar backdrop of movement, which previously would not have registered, was today something I wished to take hold of and cherish. So it was that I sat by the window, weaving a web of sentiment about people I had never met, our only connection our inhabiting the same few square miles.

My familiar claim was even more tentative, for in the corner of the room stood my large old suitcase, which contained almost every item that attested to my having been there. Despite my presence, it was as if I had already left. I lay in bed that night in the upstairs room with green velour curtains that was so familiar in a house that had, indeed, become a second home. Having come fourteen thousand miles, had I not been able to walk into the kitchen of my aunt's home and place my hand with great surety on a cup and a spoon with which to stir my tea? Agitated through excitement, I thought I should never sleep, but sleep came quickly on a tide of nameless anticipation and fatigue.

Woken by a shaft of early-morning light which shone through a chink in the curtains, I rose and listened for signs of movement outside my room. It was not long before I heard a soft knock at the door. My mother appeared around the open door's edge with a hot drink and a wide smile. "Sally's already up, come down when you've finished your tea," she said, handing me the steaming mug.

Sally, as always, busied herself with the practicalities of the day, but on this occasion, only more so. A full English breakfast was set before us prior to my heading upstairs to finish getting ready. Splashing my face with warm water and patting it dry, I looked in the small mirror above the sink. I smiled encouragement to the girl who, with an eager and anxious gaze, smiled back. I carried my suitcase down the stairs and out to the garage where Sally, with great ceremony, had parked her pristine vehicle in the driveway ready for our departure. It was only a short drive to the bus station at Preston, where Sally dropped us off before we boarded our bus. There was little time but to line up my suitcase along with the rest by the side of the bus as the passengers flowed in from all sides, separating me from my aunt. All I could do was wave to her across the sea of commuters until she was finally out of sight but certainly not out of mind. How I loved my aunt, she who had become, through familiarity, a "second mother" and mentor to me.

The journey from Preston to London, then on to Norwich took the best part of the day, the details of which are all but lost to me for as we covered the miles I retreated into my own thoughts. "Of all my adventures surely this is the greatest, to lean the whole weight of my existence on the unseen God and follow Him wherever He sees fit to lead." Entering Norwich, I was surprised to see fields of red and yellow tulips in serried rows and the turning of a windmill on a low horizon. I wondered for a brief moment if we had not taken the wrong bus, ending up in Holland? I discovered later that East Anglia had, in fact, once been joined to the Netherlands, consequently sharing its low, flat terrain.

As I looked out the window, the words of Saint John of the Cross swirled around in my head, and I found myself trusting this sixteenth-century Carmelite mystic as though my very life depended on it. In "The Ascent of Mount Carmel" he speaks of a spiritual hike to the summit where God is all in all. It was both ironic and fitting that this community of nuns would establish their house in such a place as East Anglia, for the community's vistas and promontories lay not in its geographical setting, but within the hearts and minds of its members. Our taxi wound its way along narrow country lanes with views alternating between open fields and high-walled, red-bricked farmhouses. It had been raining that afternoon, and through the mist, trees and shrubs in every shade of green glistened in the half-light, encroaching thickly on the roadsides and overhanging every wall.

We had arranged to stay the night in a bed-and-breakfast a little way from the monastery. We had not long climbed the stairs to our rooms when the clock on the mantelpiece struck 4:30 p.m. From the open window I heard the pealing of distant bells. There are no words capable of describing how I felt that evening or the next day as I prepared to join the community. A strange, enchanted atmosphere hung over my parents and I, knowing I was to leave them, never to breathe life with them in the same way ever again. That evening they were to return to Norwich, then to London and back to Australia, and I would go to my new life. Having no way of expressing the sorrow we felt, we lapsed into a silence that said it all.

The lady who ran the bed-and-breakfast, far removed from feeling the gravity that lay in my parting, bustled us into her car at the appointed time and drove along the narrow, winding roads to the entrance of the long driveway that led to the monastery. She, keen to run some errand in Norwich, dropped me off unceremoniously by the gate, but not before my mother could leap out of the car to give me one last lingering hug. I looked across and saw my father, throughout his life a man of few words, hunched over in the seat crying, stricken with grief. The sight of my father shocked me. I felt numbed, unable to comfort him. There was so little time to say our good-byes as the lady sat in the driver's seat, her engine still running. I walked a little distance, turned, smiled, and waved, for that is how I wished them to remember me, smiling—an expression that for their sake cost me everything.

I continued over a small bridge and onward up the long drive, trundling my suitcase behind me. Ruminating on what lay beyond the monastery walls, my thoughts were suddenly broken by the sound of bleating. I looked up to see that a large herd of curious sheep had left their fields and lined up along the fences to each side of the road, forming a guard of honor. "And I suppose you're the Welcoming Committee?" I called out, as a few startled pigeons hurtled into the sky.

Turning the corner of the driveway, I saw a collection of red-brick buildings. The round, stained-glass windows that ran along the side of one announced that building as the chapel. Beyond it, a tall, square tower with a simple, brick-faced clock needed no introduction, for at that precise moment, the bells of the evening Angelus reverberated through my whole body. From out of the chapel door came a woman in blue jeans and an anorak whom I later discovered was a Sister living alongside the community; a kind of go-between for the world within and the world without the confines of the monastic enclosure. "Hello Rachael, how was your trip?" she inquired in a strong American accent, her clear, blue eyes eager for my response. Still slightly dazed and numb from my ill-timed separation, I suddenly wondered how it was that she knew my name and my reason for being there. "Let me show you to the guesthouse," she said, taking the suitcase off my hands. I was ushered into a little row of guest quarters beside the monastery wall.

Within, I found several modest and neat rooms. One contained a single bed, an armchair, and a small set of shelves stocked with an eclectic variety of books where Saint Teresa of Avila rubbed shoulders with Bill Bryson and Douglas Adams. I unpacked a few things for the night, for I was to spend it there before entering the monastery the following morning. Farther up the corridor I noticed the kitchen. Throughout my life, I have found that no amount of nerves has come between me and my appetite, and that night was no exception. Rummaging through the kitchen cupboards, I found a wholesome selection of canned and fresh foods. Inside the fridge were a clutch of eggs and a small plate of sausages, the latter provision convincing me of the virtues of hospitality and self-control possessed by the Sister who placed them there. Equally hospitable was the recent guest who had left a half bottle of Bell's Scotch Whisky in the cupboard for the benefit of his fellow pilgrims. Polishing off the sausages, I poured myself a "medicinal dram" over ice and spent the evening luxuriating in a nice hot bubble bath before retiring to a good and sound sleep.

I rose before dawn and heard the morning bell summoning the nuns to the first hour of prayer. "Today's the day," I told myself—as if I needed reminding! Dressed, packed, and sipping some tea, I looked out into a courtyard blooming with purple hollyhocks and a white ground cover I could not identify and then let my eyes continue up to the bell tower visible from the guesthouse window. It was now almost 9:00 a.m.; a mere five minutes more and I was to go and wait by the large wooden door to the enclosure, the demarcation between my life up to that point and what was to follow. I drained my cup, washed it in the sink, and putting it aside, stepped out into the cool morning air. Common acts, things I had done thousands of times before were, on this occasion, charged with a strange air of finality.

As I walked across the gravel drive, I overheard a snatch of dialogue between some workmen nearby. "Pass 'em o'er 'ere Charlie," said one. "Ya won't be able t' do nowt wi' that," replied the other, and in the crackle of their car radio I heard David Essex crooning "Hold me close," the tune fading as I passed by. Odd are the things one notices and that linger in one's mind under extreme conditions. So it was that a few fragments of a casual conversation and a 1970s pop hit were that day indelibly etched in my memory.

I had only stood by the enclosure door a moment or two, enough to catch my breath, when the door suddenly opened. Beyond stood three smiling figures, the prioress and two of her councilors, clad from head to toe in the brown habit and black veil of the Order. The prioress moved forward. Open armed, she warmly greeted and kissed me as I stepped over the threshold, the door closing behind me. She took me by the hand, instilling in me a sense of assurance as we passed through the cloister. She had walked the same walk over fifty years before, and she knew exactly how I felt. This is an experience one can never really explain, or forget. Ascending a set of concrete stairs and passing through a plain door, I was astonished to find myself standing at the foot of a grand wooden staircase, which led to the nuns' cells.

Quidenham Hall, as it once was, began its life in 1606 as an Elizabethan-style house and over three centuries and more was added to and extended to suit the needs of its occupants. As I climbed the grand staircase, I wondered which ladies of title in sweeping gowns had grasped the banister, laughing and sharing intrigues as they climbed these stairs. "But vastness blurs and time beats level."[2] Of their imposing personages was left no trace. Instead, a community of silent and veiled women occupied the spaces through which they had once passed.

Above me, original Italianate ceilings graced the heights and drew from me gasps of admiration, despite the fact that the prioress of the foundation established there in 1948 had taken it into her head to whitewash its entire azure blue-and-gilt canopy in a bid to "mortify the senses." When I heard this terrible tale, my senses were duly mortified! Reaching the top of the staircase, I was amazed to see attached to the ornate plaster ceiling and hanging almost within arm's reach, a sculpture, which by some small miracle had managed to escape the iconoclastic zeal of Mother Mary of Christ. There, sailing above the stairwell, was Noah's Ark and peeping over its side were his wife, a dove, and several "beasts" of no particular description. Boldly at the helm stood Noah, wide eyed and holding out before him, for the benefit of those who cared to look up, an open book. On one page appeared the words "Peace Plentie Thou," and on the opposite page "Shalt Labor For 1619" followed, completing a message of the most extreme piety of its age. I thought it a curious statement, to "labor for peace," and it was one that would ordinarily fill me with dismay, but just how apt a statement it was I would only discover as my life in religion unfolded.

Having followed the prioress the length of a long corridor, we arrived at the door to my cell. By way of clarification, this term, "cell," is as old as monasticism itself and is not meant to conjure up images of incarceration and lack of liberty, but rather their opposite. A nun's cell is a place where she can ponder, pray, and be exactly who she is before God and herself. As the great Desert Father Abba Moses once said, "Go, sit in your cell and your cell will teach you everything."[3] And there, at the end of a day's duties, is found refreshment in the hours of sleep.

I turned the handle and stepped inside, finding its furnishings and size exactly as I expected. It was a room of modest proportions, the walls plain and unadorned, ample enough to accommodate the small bed, writing desk, and cabinet within. Unexpectedly at its end, a large, Georgian sash-window opened out onto a balcony, a window through which I could easily climb to enjoy both the view and warmth. I swung my legs over the sill to get a better look at my surroundings. Below lay a semicircle of green lawn whose centerpiece, a large wooden crucifix, stood facing the building. Farther beyond, flower beds in a profusion of color encompassed the green, in sharp contrast to the white-gravel drive that ran between the lawn and the main house. Climbing back over the windowsill, I heard the sound of a discreet knock at my cell door. The prioress welcomed me warmly again, giving me the rest of the morning to settle in before beginning the life of a postulant, the first step on the journey to becoming a fully professed nun. My immersion into the life of the community, for which I had longed, came with the stroke of a bell.

The midday Angelus rang out, after which I was collected from my cell by a kind Sister given the charge of delivering me to the refectory for lunch on time and without my getting lost down one of many labyrinthine passages which wound through the house. Through corridors and down stairwells they came, a seemingly endless stream of nuns, converging on the door to the refectory for the main meal of the day. Like all monastic practices, the ritual and routine for which I had hoped abounded and was immediately evident as each nun took her place in front of long tables, ready for the recitation of Grace before the meal.

At the center of the refectory was a large wooden table on which cold salads and hearty puddings were placed to which the Sisters could help themselves. From where I sat I could identify a large pan of bread-and-butter pudding and a bowl of baked custard—my favorites. An industrial-sized teapot sat steaming at one end of the table, and before each nun, a place was laid with cutlery, a napkin, a mug, and a jug of water to be shared with a neighboring Sister. Our meals were varied and beautifully prepared. Never once did I pine for a lamb roast, no, not for one moment. I enjoyed the pleasure of our simple and wholesome fare; even that of supper, which consisted of bread, cheese, jams and spreads, and an optional boiled egg twice a week.

The community remained seated as three Sisters in aprons carried before them large trays that contained the day's portion and pans of vegetables. These had risen from the kitchen on a dumbwaiter. The servers made their way around the refectory placing the plated meals and offering the vegetables and cutlery for each Sister to serve herself. Our main portion often consisted of fish, casseroles rich in legumes, and tofu, for which I developed quite a taste, smothering the tofu in sweet chili sauce. As the Sisters ate their meals, one, chosen for the office, would mount a small podium in the corner of the room and, adjusting her microphone, would read out loud as the community took their meal in silence.

The subject matter varied from week to week. One time I found myself immersed in the tale of a travel writer in Morocco; another time, transported into the life and fortunes of an eighteenth-century stage actress, or trying to wrap my head around the writings of a German theologian. Perhaps due to my intense concentration or natural timing, invariably I was the last to finish my meal, the others having long disappeared downstairs into the scullery to wash up. It seemed to me that I would never catch up, for your average nun had but one speed at table: very fast.

From the sounding of the first bells at dawn to the last hour of prayer at night, a rhythm was set in motion in which all activities found their proper place. On my settling in, my aptitudes and talents, like everyone's, were identified and used for the good of the community for the Sisters had to earn their keep. Over time, I held a number of appointed duties. One with which I was well acquainted was kitchen hand. Outside the kitchen door was a small storage room from where I would retrieve crates of vegetables left by the gardeners, local men who took pride in tending the growth of the harvest. Whether my work would be easy or strenuous depended largely on what hour the produce had been left in the shed. If that morning, my knife would slice effortlessly through the root vegetables which it was my job to prepare; if the evening before, the night frost produced petrified parsnips which I macheted my way through until they were diced into submission.

More often than not, my dismal capacity to complete my duties in the time allowed was further exacerbated by the summoning of the bell calling us to prayer. A fine intrusion it was into my autistic sense of order, my need to finish a task, come what may! Fortunately for me, the rhythm of monastic life worked its magic on my internal clock, bringing it, by degrees, up to speed. I would hastily hang up my apron and ascend the stairs, joining the Sisters in the antechoir. In two rows we walked in solemn procession to the place of prayer, to which we returned seven times a day. It was in choir that the real work began. With a deep bow before the tabernacle, each Sister would take her place in the choir stalls, ready to recite the Divine Office, the "Prayer of the Church." The reverberation of the bell gave way to a deep silence into which the nuns, taking up their books, would pour song, prayer, and psalm, "The Benedictus," "The Magnificat," "Asperges Me!" The chantress, who led each side of the choir in that day's prayer, intoned the note for the recitation of the office. There, united with all monastic communities throughout the world, we added our voice to the endless outpouring of intercession for the good of the Church and the world.

In the two hours of private prayer set aside in the early morning and evening, the Carmelite, either in choir or within the privacy of her cell, would enter into the inner room of her heart to pray. In those hours, solitude was easy to come by, but silence—definitely not! Rather than the "private audience with The Almighty" I had expected, my thoughts like so many gatecrashers, found their way in, disrupting my quiet prayers with their endless demands on my attention. Like many on the spectrum, my autistic brain ran hot, teeming with associational thoughts to the point of exhaustion.

I had sought to address this tendency of "winding in" on my own mental processes through a number of years practicing meditation. Each day I had chosen the discipline of making time, morning and evening, to sit in silence and stillness for twenty minutes, while letting go of all thoughts, words, and imagination by limiting myself to the poverty of one word, my mantra. Inwardly I repeated the mantra from the beginning to the end of my mediation period, which drew me steadily deeper into the center of my being. It was this daily practice that confirmed the experience of coming home to myself. In fidelity to the recitation of my mantra, I began to develop the patience and self-discipline that would continue to help me navigate a path through the most challenging aspects of my autistic nature to a place of stability and inner peace. I was coming home not only to myself, but also to all creation and the Creator. I was following a spiritual path that enabled me to gradually begin to live more and more from my center; this, a lifetime's work for a pilgrim on the inner journey.

After not too many months, the time had come for me to be clothed in the habit of the Order and to begin my life as a Carmelite novice. As per custom, I was to spend five days in retreat and in preparation for the day in a small, movable hermitage that stood at the far end of the grounds of the monastery. Every morning I collected some supplies from the kitchen and walked back down through the woods swinging a basket full of provisions, sometimes stopping to sit on a log and listen to the wind blowing through the canopy and watch the small brown birds which moved and tumbled about the floor like little animated leaves.

Near the hermitage, dating back centuries, was a walled kitchen garden. Built into the side of the wall was the later addition of a summerhouse with a pitched roof and mullioned windows in which generations of children had once played. From the edge of the roof, the head of a little gargoyle with pointed ears and a spout like a cigar protruding from its mouth looked down, grimacing with all the terror he could muster. "You'll have to do better than that," I told him as I passed through the door. Within the dark, rustic interior of the summerhouse, I saw a small fireplace set by the last hermit to have spent time under its roof. The leaves of last autumn were thick on the ground outside, forming a patchwork of dry, brown leaves at the base of the trees. Some afternoons I would go about collecting handfuls of leaves to provide kindling, adding them to the pieces of wood and newspaper from the coal scuttle which I fed to the fire. There, under the pitched roof of the summerhouse, I watched the wood blacken then glow, its sap singing its swan song as threads of fire danced amid the embers.

Beyond the wall, the gnarled branches of old apple trees hung thick with fruit beside neat, long rows of lettuce, cabbage, parsnips, and blackberries that curled around low trellises. I remembered an afternoon when we donned our gardening smocks and fetched clippers, forks, and buckets from the toolshed to give the gardeners a hand with the harvest. We had worked a little while when the wind picked up, carrying over the horizon a vanguard of dark, brooding clouds marbled with lightning. I, frightened by the exposure of the garden (for the apple trees were hardly higher than the tallest nun), suggested to one of the Sisters that we should seek shelter. She immediately obliged. "Here, Rachael, put this over your head," she said with a laugh, passing a metal bucket for my "protection." Weather aside, I assumed there was very little on the vast property that could cause any real harm.

Leaving the walled garden, I took the track down to the lake that hugged the edge of a pine forest from which any number of creatures might be poised to spring on an unsuspecting nun. A pheasant farm had long existed on the boundary, and when one was taking a quiet stroll, pheasants would launch themselves from the seclusion of fields of sugar beet, flapping wildly and piercing the air with their strident cries, a foot from where one stood. The thought had crossed my mind, once or twice, that it was entirely possible that a pheasant hunter could mistake the color of a nun's habit for a female pheasant's plumage—a similar shade of brown—and *Boom!* Turning aside from such unpleasant and anxious ruminations, I recalled a partridge I had once seen, though not in a pear tree. This small bird had favored the warmth of a courtyard. I had watched her puff up her feathers as a dozen little baby-partridge heads suddenly popped out on every side, giving her the appearance of a brightly colored pincushion.

The atmosphere of silence and solitude that permeated the land surrounding the monastery gave nature more than a fighting chance. In every field, wood, and hollow, from crawling bug to running hare to prancing deer crossing the open spaces, I had never seen such a proliferation of wildlife outside of a zoo. Strangely, one evening during private prayer in my cell, as though I didn't have enough distractions already, I looked out the window just in time to see a large, striped cat prowling along the gravel path. I stood by the window closely watching its disconcertingly large frame and rippling muscles before it disappeared through a gap in the fence through to the fields. I thought no more of it until many months later, when a Sister casually looked up from her needlework and blithely told me of Banham Zoo with its "big cats" an easy mile or so from the monastery. Perhaps the pheasant hunters with their friendly, loaded shotguns were a welcome sight after all!

I loved the lake and the mirrored sky which reflected blue and gray in the lake's still waters. Around its edge among the reeds were small jetties in various states of repair, and along its paths, worn from the boots of fishermen, lay planks of wood covering the tracks that gave way to squelching mud. Through the dusty windows of a small boathouse, I saw angling gear, nets, and more pieces of planking, witnessing to the resourcefulness of its keepers. Finding a patch of dry ground, I stood near the water's edge praying and skimming stones until I heard the snap of a stick. I turned suddenly, finding myself nose to nose with a local fisherman. Dressed in a long brown skirt and jumper, I had been, I believe, mistaken for a tree. "Sorry, Ma'am!" he said by way of apology, still staring out in shock from beneath a fishing hat whose lures and hooks glinted in the late afternoon light, his face ruddy and his mouth from which a small cry had escaped still open. I smiled reassuringly at the poor man, whose startled response had scattered a plethora of small birds from out of the reeds and surely sent his intended fish diving for the depths.

I made my way back to the hermitage via fields of wheat that rippled old gold in the fast-fading light. Walking by the west entrance to the Hall, whose silence was intensified by the sound of gravel crunching beneath my feet, I looked up at the thick, stone pillars that stood like sentinels, caught unawares by the shadows that had snuck past and hidden in the deep recesses of the porch. I hurried on past the terraced gardens and through the woods, quickening my pace as the chill of evening fell.

Finally arriving "home," I closed the little door behind me. Compared to the grand proportions of the Hall to which, over time, I had become accustomed, the paring down of things to proper scale gave the hermitage the dimensions of a doll's house. Within its cozy confines, one would think nothing of opening a kitchen drawer to find it contained a miniature rolling pin and a ball of modeling clay, or to see a cupboard lined with play provisions whose brightly labeled boxes were colorful echoes of those to be found in *real* shops, but what lay within was far better.

The opening of cupboard and drawer yielded colorful, mismatched crockery, tea sets, worn cutlery, and other oddments, cast-offs from the community kitchen. I laid a blue-checked cloth upon the small table and set a place for dinner. Above the little stove I found a tiny aluminum frying pan, ample enough to accommodate the two vegetarian rissoles that were to be my feast. The preparation of a few choice vegetables in that small space was marked by quaintness in contrast to the industrial labor and ironmongery of my workaday world within the monastery.

After dinner, happily replete but with possibly room for dessert, I took out from my basket a small shortbread tin on which a Scottish piper played a silent air atop an imposing rampart. I pried open the lid, which revealed a selection of homemade cakes and biscuits, far too many for one; and putting a pan of water on the stove, I made myself a cup of tea. I pulled back the stiff curtain and looked out on a night as black as jet. A copy of selected writings of St. John of the Cross sat upon the small bookshelf by the door. I took it up and continued "The Ascent of Mount Carmel," he, calling down from the summit, and I, barely two strides from base camp. I turned to "The Dark Night" to see if there was a shortcut to the summit.

> So dark the night
> With quickened love enflamed
> —By sheer grace!—
> I ventured forth,
> Beyond my quiet house
> By no one seen.[4]

Love and grace—these would be my guides along the way. The night drew on. I pulled a shawl about my shoulders, and, as the wind bent the silhouetted branches to its will, I struck a match, lighting the wick of a small candle, and placed it on the saucer by my empty cup. I read and pondered until the wax pooled in the saucer. Extinguishing the light, I walked the few paces back to the bedroom before settling down to sleep.

The following morning, the day of my clothing, I gathered up my things and walked back through the woodlands as the light edged over the horizon revealing the freshness of a beautiful, clear, August dawn. I watched the small brown birds emerge from the undergrowth and the creatures that lived in the hedges come out of hiding, ready to take up a day's activities. They had done this for generations, but in the course of my natural life, this was to be a day like no other, for nothing in nature could provide a blueprint for the turn my life was about to take.

Come midmorning, the bells rang out and the community gathered to welcome me into the noviciate where my training would begin in earnest. Accompanied by the subprioress, I entered the antechoir as the nuns sang in solemn greeting. There I stood, surrounded by the professed nuns and my fellow novices. Newly clothed in the brown habit, rosary, and white veil of a novice, I asked formally to be taught the Rule and Constitutions of the Order and to be formed in its spirit. I approached the prioress.

"Dear Rachael, what are you asking of us?"

"I believe that God is calling me to Carmel
and I ask to be allowed to live with the community
so that I may discern God's will for me.
I ask to be taught to follow the crucified Christ

and Mary, his mother;
how to live in poverty, obedience and chastity;
and how to remain in constant, persevering prayer:
going out into the solitude of detachment
to meet my God in loving encounter.
Please help me to be generous in that self-denial
which will free me for love,
so that I may be able to live for God alone
and enter into his loving work of redemption.
I want to be one in heart and mind with you
And strive with all my being to live as Jesus teaches."

Responding to my desire, our prioress answered,

"May the Father of our Lord Jesus Christ keep you in his love forever, and may Jesus be your unfailing light."

To which the community replied, "Amen."

Never could I have felt more welcomed than on that day, as my novice mistress came forward, presenting me to our prioress and each and every Sister who embraced me with a joy too deep for words. In the three years of my formation within the novitiate, I participated fully in the life of the community while learning the Order's history and its way of life and finding a growing sense of my identity within that unbroken line of women whom Saint Teresa of Avila, reformer of the Carmelite Order, referred to as "her daughters." Certainly women of the late twentieth and twenty-first centuries are a very different breed to the young girls who "took the veil" in sixteenth-century Spain; nonetheless, Saint Teresa described the life of her Sisters as "a very happy one," a remark that holds true now as then.

Not far from my cell was a service stairwell which had once known the constant traffic of housemaid and butler ascending and descending as they ministered to the needs of the lord of the manor and his guests. I could hardly hazard a guess as to how often I went that way in carrying out my duties or to choir for prayer, but I count them in the thousands, and it was fitting that it should have been so.

The life of a Carmelite nun is the life of a servant, and the tendency within my autistic nature to wind in on myself was addressed on a daily basis, turning me out from myself to others, where service was the key.

Having recited the Office of Terce, the second hour of prayer, and fortified by a simple breakfast of cereal and fruit, I fetched a large industrial mop and a bag of dusters from the broom cupboard and headed for the choir. In the company of my fellow novice Nicola, we would push our mops up and down the parquetry floor, covering every square inch of its surface. Then, putting our mops aside, we'd take up dusters and polish the choir stalls, a duty we performed every morning at 9:00 a.m. sharp. Outwardly, my life was a perpetual Groundhog Day; it was not very exciting, nor was it meant to be. I did not join the monastery to be entertained. The simplicity, the *sheer ordinariness* of the day's duties were imperative in preparing for a life of continuous prayer.

Ritual and routine, as it pertains to monastic life, cannot be confused with the routine favored by those on the autism spectrum. The monastic Horarium is not designed to reduce uncertainty and thus, anxiety; of themselves, the bells, the duties, and the general divestment that constitutes the fabric of a nun's life are simply an anchor to provide the outward stability needed in order to embark on the inner journey and the tremendous amount of change and upheaval such a journey implies. For me at this time, the tendency to favor routine did not come from a love of repetition for its own sake; rather, it was the perception of the freshness of life coming to meet me from moment to moment.

In the early days I took great satisfaction in my work, some tasks glowing with novelty. A Sister brought me down to the bell tower to "show me the ropes" quite literally! "The big bell is called 'Ave Maria' and the smaller one's 'Hosanna,'" she said matter-of-factly, pointing to the ropes from which the bells swung. "Now grasp the rope, that's it, not too low, and pull." I screwed up my face and pulled the rope, half expecting the lot to come crashing down through the belfry, bringing me to God sooner than the three score and ten years which I hoped for. Instead, the sound of the bell rang out deep and sonorous, filling the chapel and radiating over the grounds and across the fields. I rang it again, this time with gusto, saying to myself as I did, "Wow, I can hardly believe it, I'm a nun, in a monastery, ringing a bell! This is the life"— and so it was.

Not since the third grade had my handwriting come under close scrutiny, yet one day, the Sister whose calligraphy graced so many of our greeting cards came to speak to me directly, keen to see if she could make a "scribe" of me. In her office was a large window and beneath it, a desk filled with fountain pens and blotters peppered with ink. "Now Rachael, all you need to do is dip your nib in the pot, touch it to the blotter, and draw a line firmly down the paper, at a bit of an angle, like this," said she in her glorious Dublin brogue, proceeding to execute a flourish fit for the Book of Kells. "I'm doomed," I told myself and fulfilled the prophecy, taking up a fountain pen, filling the nib, and leaving a splotch the size of a black hole on the blotter. With a faltering hand I beat out a Morse code of dots and dashes beside the velvet ribbon which had fallen effortlessly from the tip of Sister's pen. She smiled and took up a new pen with a thicker nib, and with infinite patience, coached me in the art of calligraphy, as far as my meager talents would allow, having me repeat the Gothic letters that were little works of art in themselves.

The prioress, taking pity on my pathetic attempts at fine art, released me from this duty and introduced me to Sister Gillian, the librarian. Of all the rooms that I ever entered, none compared to that of a monastic library—the quietest inner sanctum. Upon its paneled walls, no signage cautioned the visitor to keep silence; between its narrow aisles prowled no keeper of the peace. In this inner sanctum, silence reigned supreme. Not even Sister Gillian's crepe-soled sandals dared to announce her presence as she floated round a corner, appearing like a specter at my shoulder. "Oh, Sister, I didn't see you—sorry!" I stuttered, the sound immediately absorbed by row upon row of old leather-and-cloth-bound books.

"That's quite all right," she breathed, ushering me toward a plain wooden table beneath a large bay window which cast a soft glow from a low leaden sky. Before me were pens, paper, file cards, scissors, and Scotch tape, everything I would need to carry out the task of cataloging books according to the Dewey Decimal System, whose mathematical secrets Sister Gillian set herself to reveal. As I sat there printing tiny numbers and sticking them to the spines of new acquisitions, I heard the soft thud of the wooden latch as my companion left the library.

Having finished a small pile of books, I rose and walked through the dark, narrow aisles, slipping a volume in here and there as the numbers dictated. A profound hush hung in the air and clung to a row of books whose gilt titles shone like a seam of gold in russet rock. I reached out and stroked the spine of one whose heavy Gothic artwork wove its way to its base. I drew it out and found the first page; the silence became a soapbox to the book's grievances: "'The Signora had no business to do it,' said Miss Bartlett, 'no business at all. She promised us south rooms with a view close together, instead of which here are north rooms, here are north rooms, looking into a courtyard, and a very long way apart. Oh, Lucy!'"[5] Snapping the book shut, I silenced her deafening rant and returned to my own view over the fields—north, south, east, west, I did not care. Off somewhere in the distance, I heard the bell calling us to prayer.

I have never been described as a "morning person," and few people on the autism spectrum are, but at 5:30 a.m. each morning and every morning, the sound of a handbell rung by an even earlier riser as she passed by the nuns' cells broke through my sleep, summoning the community to the Office of Lauds, the first hour of prayer for the day. I rose and attended to the demands of my newly acquired dress code. I pulled the habit over my head, slipping my arms through its ample sleeves and tightened the cincture belt from which a large, outsized rosary hung around my waist. Thanking God for small mercies, I snapped the press-studs fastening the material of the scapular to my habit. I fumbled with the pins needed to secure my veil, and having buckled on a sturdy pair of brown leather sandals, I padded through the silent, dark corridors to join the Sisters in choir.

Of all my duties, working in the infirmary was what I loved best. Following morning prayer, I would make my way toward the infirmary, pulling back the wooden shutters to let in the early light. There I dispensed medicines and prepared tea trays for the elderly Sisters, who, having risen under their own steam for over seventy years, had earned their morning brew, whose privilege it was mine to make. I have always enjoyed the company of people much older than me and have found in them kindred spirits. Many people with Asperger's can be described as "old souls," the term fitting a child as much as an adult, irrespective of age.

I remember Sister Stella; one had only to scratch the surface to find a socialite lurking beneath. She, well into her eighties, told me stories from her youth. In the early 1930s Stella, at the age of eighteen, was one of the few women in Britain to own a car, and she not only drove it, she raced it, as her father had done. As she told me her tale, my imagination rolled back the years. I could see a young, fresh-faced version of herself in racing goggles and kid gloves gripping the wheel, her blond curls flying out beneath her cap. Another elderly Sister, Joyce, told me of how, many years ago, when working in the kitchen, she reached out for a few sheets of newspaper in which to wrap some fish heads. There before her, she saw a picture of the great stage-and-screen actor Sir Laurence Olivier, her old childhood chum, receiving his knighthood that day. She raised her brows and chuckled, his debonair expression a far cry from that of the young boy who had once been her playmate.

As simple and as hidden as a Carmelite's round was, each woman who had turned aside from a thousand other choices was, within those monastic walls, giving the performance of her life for an audience of One. Jesus was always coming to meet me in the circumstances of my everyday life. I rarely recognized Him in some obvious manner; rather, I "saw" Him in a conversation with another, a passage of scripture, in my observations, or in a thought that crossed my mind. In such ways, for me, His presence, although unfelt, was everywhere to be found.

But now He came to me in a new way. Beneath the surface, the worst of my traits—my critical nature, the petty judgments I was quick to pass, the gnawing anxiety, and the odious comparisons I made between others and myself—had not disappeared; they were still there, festering away and leaving me feeling utterly exposed. Afflicted by rigidity in my thinking, I was quick to find fault, and in my mind I would leap on what I deemed a lack of charity or proper observance. Once I saw a couple of Sisters, instead of keeping the silence, making each other laugh across the refectory tables during lunch. I was scandalized, for they had "broken the rule." Another time, while I was playing a game of Scrabble with an elderly nun, she querulously exclaimed, "Oh do hurry up, Sister!" as I took time to think up my next word. Unfortunately I did not have enough consonants to spell "shut up" and was amazed by her lack of patience after so many years in religion. Obviously, I myself had a very long way to go.

For all my mental policing, if anyone else judged my behavior, I would feel crushed and mortally wounded. Irritation would turn to annoyance, then to high anxiety. Of all my emotions, I felt terrified at the possibility that someone would not think well of me, yet how easily I passed judgment on others without a moment's thought! These tendencies, of course, are not the sole preserve of people on the autism spectrum, but in us, such tendencies are *more* noticeable by their degree of intensity. Of all the things one faces within the world of enclosure, none is more confronting than having to face oneself.

I looked within myself and did not like what I saw. I did not want to think like that, to feel like that, exhausted and utterly miserable. When able, I would sit in my cell and allow myself to cry in five-minute installments before the summons of the next bell. The demands of monastic life did not even allow me the luxury to wallow in my own misery! There was no magic in how I would approach this dilemma. I had a love of truth and wanted the truth, especially regarding myself, no matter how unpalatable the revelation might be. The scaffolding had been kicked out from under me, and yet I was upheld and had a lot of "unlearning" to do.

My first teachers were the nuns with whom I shared my life. Witnessing the little victories and sacrifices they made to go beyond themselves—for we are all far from perfect—I was encouraged not to run from self-knowledge, the dark mirror into which I looked every day, but to knuckle down and simply get on with being "undone," allowing God to put me back together, piece by piece, day by day, until I was restored to myself.

I was not alone in my endeavor to allow this process to happen; I received the regular and wise council of the prioress, whose writings had given me such inspiration. "Ah my dear," she would say, having patiently listened to all I had said and leaning toward me in the seat by her desk, her pale blue eyes fixed on mine, "You judge in others what you most dislike in yourself. Open your heart to Jesus and His transforming love, and remember, it is *this world* into which He came and not another," saying this with a slow shake of her head. "Open your heart to love, hold nothing back, and you will always recognize Him coming to meet you in all the circumstances of your life." The prioress challenged my attitudes and did not sugarcoat anything she had to say. She knew I could take it, take it all, without the slightest flinch. And with eyes wide open, I sought Him in His dark disguise, the tedium and beauty of my days.

The extraordinary ideal I had sought in the Carmelite tradition was equally matched by the extraordinary women with whom I shared my life, day in day out. There was no "monastic type," no pattern among the vocations that I could distinguish. They had come across counties and across oceans, having worked in situations as diverse as taxi driving and law. Artists and academics, cradle Catholics and converts from communism, the monastery was filled with a chaotic cross-section of society whose only reference point lay in each individual's response to a mysterious inner call that would change the course of her life, and forever.

In the evenings, we would socialize during a time of recreation which broke the silence for one hour a day. I remember one evening when the Sister who received the community mail entered the recreation room waving an envelope addressed to "Mrs. C. Monastery." "Which one of you ladies would like to open this?" said she, as the whole community dissolved into fits of laughter. It was this same Sister who related to me a story about a salesperson who cold-called our phone number, launching into a sales pitch for "a new range of cosmetics in this season's fashionable colors." Sister cut him off at the pass: "I'm terribly sorry, but we are a community of enclosed nuns and have no need of your products." Silence—*click*.

I loved Wednesday evenings. On entering, one Sister had brought with her a record player and a huge selection of classics on vinyl. In the Stone Hall, whose stone-flagged floor and high ceilings guaranteed perfect acoustics, we would gather and, dropping the needle in the groove, let the music fill the space whose decorative wooden columns, arched porticos, and oak-paneled walls created a concert setting. After a day's silence, I did not always find it easy to swim up to the surface and start chatting as others did, for what I had done that day I had done the day before and the day before that and would do so on the morrow. A musical evening masked the mutism that descended on me, ironically, the moment I was at full liberty to open my mouth!

Our prioress recognized my propensity to talk some evenings, while spending others silent, though not unhappily withdrawn. I could not account for it myself and sought her advice. "It's as if you sometimes need to recharge, to give your mind the space it needs to rest," she wisely observed. "So be it and do not worry; it's the way you're made." She had pinpointed an autistic trait which had been with me all my life, articulating its essence: the need I have for the space and time necessary to allow my brain to process in peace. Her comment, almost a throwaway line, dissolved all my anxieties regarding the difference in how I related to others, reassuring me that my way of being in the world was *more than* okay.

Relating one-on-one had always been my preference, and on certain feast days, or on a Sunday afternoon, I was given the opportunity to spend some time with another member of the community. Anna was a keen artist and had the talent of being able to look at the side of a barn or a corner of the monastery wall and then transfer it in fine black ink onto her sketch pad, adding an odd detail or contour until one could almost sense the movement of a trail of ivy clinging to the page, climbing the ancient brickwork. Anna assured me that it was as easy as it looked, and although I had my doubts, I followed her instructions.

We stood a little way from the gnarled branches and thick roots of an old tree. "Just look, simply look at a small section of the trunk and transfer it to the paper bit by bit," she said. This I did, falteringly at first, then gaining confidence, until I had faithfully shaded in a shadow or a knot, low in the trunk. "That's right," she cheerily encouraged, happy to give me tips on how to raise my skills a notch or two higher than the stick figures I was prone to execute.

I remember passing through the cloister walk one dreary, wet afternoon, having rescued several lines of washing before the heavens opened. At the walk's center stood a small, wooden crucifix with a gabled roof. I stopped for a moment, considering the possibility of sketching it sometime. I watched large droplets of water cling to, then fall from its edges, gathering in pools around its base. I thought it a sweet and compassionate gesture on the craftsman's part to provide a little roof to shelter the Crucified from the elements, summer's blazing heat to winter's deepest snow.

Sketching a still life posed no problem for me; it was its animated counterpart that proved my greatest artistic challenge. If I spotted a small rabbit grazing on a few tufts of grass by the roots of a tree, I sketched as fast as I could, for by fits and starts it moved ever farther away, until it had hopped off at a pace into the woods. By early December, with light and heat fast on the decline, there was little left to sketch as the last leaves fell from the copper beech and the only creature stirring was the stoat, who with opportunistic zeal, fed on what the cold had left in its wake.

That winter I succumbed to a particularly bad bout of influenza, borne on the breath of a less than hale-and-hearty visitor, and I spent a week "holed up" in my cell, dousing the flames of my fever with doses of Lemsip every four hours. Sister Deborah, my fellow infirmarian, sustained me with a steady diet of chicken soup and checked my temperature until the thin, red line dipped below the danger zone, thus declaring me cured. I dressed and shuffled on unsteady legs, wasted by a week in bed, toward the dispensary. Returning my medicine, I caught sight of myself in a small mirror reflecting my sunken eyes and flushed cheeks. I returned to my cell, and having adjusted the window to let in the air of an unseasonably warm afternoon, I eased myself back into bed and waited for the visit from the prioress, who, despite her many duties, made it her business to see how I was getting on while out of action.

Sister Ruth, with her signature knock, appeared moments later around the edge of the door. "How are you this afternoon my dear? May I come in?" "Yes, of course," I said, happy to have her company, having missed out on a week's worth of recreation. "Apparently I'm out of the woods," I said with a rattling laugh, as the prioress pulled the chair up close to my bed. "You still look a little peaky," she said, as if considering how she might rectify the problem. "We missed you at 'games night' yesterday," she offered earnestly. "Particularly Sister Mildred, she was *lost* without her Scrabble partner!" Sister Ruth's eyes crinkled with mirth as she doubled over with laughter. Her humor was the sugar that helped the medicine of self-knowledge taste that bit sweeter.

The prioress, with as much of an eye to "the good of our bodies" as "the good of our souls," settled on a remedy for my weakened state. Returning after I had finished my lunch, she presented me with a can of Guinness as a fitting tonic to "build up my strength." I sat convalescing on the balcony for the remainder of the day, soaking up the winter sun with a warm glass of stout proving a most pleasing panacea.

The season of Advent, the time of preparation for Christmas, was upon us. I carefully trundled our Advent wreath into the center of the choir for vespers. Its foliage swayed precariously on a stand whose turning wheels rivaled those of a wonky supermarket trolley. I had never felt so grateful to be able to light its candles, a symbolic gesture all but lost on a person raised in a country for whom Christmas is the hottest and brightest time of the year.

Light seemed as crucial as air to me during those northern winters. I returned to my cell for the hour of private prayer, and through my window I watched the sun sink below the distant line of trees, taking my courage with it as I put my head in my hands and cried for its passing. I wrapped the coffee-colored scarf with the light-blue stripe that my aunt had given me around my neck and settled into my chair to pray.

The winter solstice had brought its shortest and darkest day. I marked the handful of days (if a few watery hours of light can be termed as such) until Christmas Eve arrived, and on the stroke of midnight, the nuns swung their cream choir-mantles about their shoulders and lit their candles, ready to process into choir for Midnight Mass in a chapel filled with light.

In keeping with the liturgical seasons, the community would put on its own entertainment with concerts and plays, pooling our combined talents in celebration of the feasts. At Christmas we set long tables in what had once been a ballroom, and in the corner, our tree, almost brushing the ceiling, was festooned with glittering silver tinsel and a harvest of golden baubles. The festive decorations hung down the sides of the large windows and across the mantelpiece, gracing the candlelit tables in red, green, and gold. There we merrily toasted each other with sparkling glasses of elderberry wine straight from our own cellar, a wine whose closely guarded recipe was known only to Sr. Maria-Joseph, our winemaker in residence. In the simplicity of our daily lives, our feast days were filled with a sense of occasion and were the cause of many happy memories.

When we had pushed back the tables and set up the seats, the concert began. A Sister, appointed as emcee, introduced each act. There was a piano and oboe offering to start with, followed by a Sister's amusing poetry recitation—she, hardly able to keep a straight face and with a bow, rewarded with a round of applause. An arranging of music stands announced the medieval sounds of a recorder quartet playing "Greensleeves" and other lilting tunes. I myself sang Gershwin's "Summertime"—suspending for a few brief moments the realities of an English winter—to more applause, silenced by the sound of the bell calling the community to choir for Compline, the last prayer closing the day before the Great Silence. Each nun then returned to her solitude, walking off down the dark corridors, each to her own cell, to pass the hours of night.

If the life of faith were no more than "whistling in the dark," a monastery would be a foolhardy place in which to live it; to offer no more than lip service and sentiment would be to purse one's lips in a hollow tune. For modern people accustomed to a high degree of interaction, the reduction and silence of monastic life can feel like a threat, and my perception was no different. There were no televisions, no radios, no background music—none of the usual amount of stimulation to which we are subjected on a daily basis. Even for someone like me who had a high capacity for silence, this extended silence came as a shock. The surface of my mind, like a house swept clean, began to empty out all sorts of material from my unconscious, which found its way into my dreams.

That night following Compline, I returned to my cell via the service stairs and closed the door. I fastened the wooden shutters over my window, changed, and, putting off the light, fell into a deep sleep. I dreamed I heard the sound of knocking on the shutters of my window, soft, hardly perceptible at first, then forceful, drawing my dreaming self toward the movement caused by the continual blows of that which was seeking admittance into my cell. In my dream I rose, walked toward the window, and raising my hand to the latch, I flung open the shutters. Now within my cell stood two shadowy figures, mute and shaking, whose black eyes darted around the room. They were begging to stay. I drew in a sharp breath and awoke, still in my bed, seeing only my darkened room at whose windows the shutters remained firmly closed. Another night during the hours of sleep, I dreamed I was in the hallway at the bottom of the grand staircase, desperately running my hands along the wooden paneling of the walls, feeling for a light switch. These and other dreams continued to disrupt my nocturnal hours, while the feelings of anxiety they produced leaked into my days.

During this time, a visiting priest who was also a psychologist made himself available in the parlor to any Sister who wished to seek counsel. "I must speak to him," I said to myself. "Maybe I'm not fit for this life. What if I'm losing my mind?" I could have well deduced as much, with nights brimming with crazy dreams. My Sisters, who went about their duties wearing expressions of quiet composure, only added to my growing sense of confusion and self-doubt. I stepped into the parlor, a little nervous and more than a little self-conscious, and greeted the priest, a tall, big-boned man in a "dog collar" with a warm, mellow gaze who looked at me with compassion through a pair of sturdy black-framed glasses. He stretched out his hand and gave mine a firm shake. After exchanging a few pleasantries, we both sat in silence, he waiting to follow my lead.

"Father, I think I'm going mad!" I said, pouring out the contents of my thoughts, struggles, feelings, and dreams. He listened intently to all I had to say and I, taking a deep breath, waited for him to declare me certifiable and to give me my marching orders on the spot. To my amazement he smiled and shook his head. "I think that you are quite possibly one of the sanest people I have ever met," he said, assuring me that "all sorts of muck" rises to the surface of a mind being illumined by Love.

According to this priest psychologist, he had never come across any therapy that healed and integrated the personality as thoroughly as exposure to the elements of silence, service, and prayerful reflection contained within the monastic ideal—such elements that can indeed be incorporated into anyone's mindfully disposed life-circumstances.

The life of a nun is the life of one who walks along the boundaries of the human condition. There, at the crossroads of the mind and heart, she meets not only those deep shadows within her unconscious seeking integration within her conscious mind, but in her solitude she comes face-to-face with the Living God; not the cheap god of one's own imaginings, but the One who in the depths of her heart challenges and reveals Himself as transforming Love. Thus she fulfills a vocation which means no less than this: to lay down her life like a road, a living intersection through which all the traffic of humanity with its joys, hopes, setbacks, and sufferings can pass, and be blessed on its journey.

Our prioress, out of long and prayerful experience, helped me navigate the highways, byways, and back alleys of my spiritual journey. I was delighted after the community elections to find that I had lost a prioress and gained a novice mistress. It was a role in which Sister Ruth was well seasoned, guiding a whole generation in the discernment of their vocation.

Our weekly discussions were frank and varied, and I remember the occasion in which I confided to her that on entering the monastery I had carried a certain seed of doubt regarding my ability to forgo the pleasures of family life. Over time, this seed began to take root and tear at my emotions, for I was in the unenviable position of being equally drawn to marriage and monastic life. For me, both were highly desirable, and as time went on, the joy and satisfaction I derived in learning to become a religious had its dark counterpart of pain and longing to have a husband and children.

These ruminations, which carried over from one week to the next, were no mere mental exercise. To be in two minds is a harrowing place to be, and a state that I would not wish on anyone. Some nights during the hour of evening prayer, I would drift into fantasy, conjuring up images of tucking my children into bed. "Come on John, let's put these toys away." Turning to my other child, I laughed at the sight of her jumping up and down on her bed with her Teddy almost flying out of her tiny hand. My children finally settled, I pulled up their bedclothes and kissed their warm, soft cheeks before switching off the light. All was dark and quiet. The voice of my daughter broke from the silence, "Mummy, I'm scared," "Don't worry, darling. See, I've left a night-light on for you here in the corner of the room." As my eyes adjusted to the dark, I saw the low, red burning of the sanctuary lamp throwing just enough light by which to discern the silhouetted figures kneeling at prayer.

Our house had, by the will of its nineteenth-century occupants, acquired two large baths whose generous proportions are rarely seen in a modern bathroom. At the end of the day a hot shower was very welcome, but the nuns had designed a roster so that at least once a week, each sister would get the opportunity to have a nice, long soak. "One dark night," wrapped in my toweling dressing-gown, I made my way through the empty corridors until I reached the bathroom at the top of the stairs. I drew a bath and, removing the stopper from a small glass bottle, poured a decent measure of aromatic oil, whose sweet scent filled the room.

Draping my towel and gown over an old wooden chair, I inched by degrees into the bath's deep, steaming waters and settled down to watch a lightshow of rainbow hues swirl and spin in a galaxy of soapy spheres. As the evening drew on and the bubbles began to disperse, I was given another object to contemplate—that of my own body. I ran my hand down my breast and across my abdomen, painfully, agonizingly aware of the potential that teemed beneath my skin. I was twenty-seven years old and looking steadily into a future that involved the renunciation of the capacity to bear my own children, and as my slender fingers reached the length of my thigh, I wondered if I would ever feel the touch of a hand, stronger and firmer than that of my own?

I recalled a book which had caught my eye on a shelf in our library, written by a rabbi on the character of my namesake, Rachel, the wife of

Jacob. Hers was an iconic image of womanhood, and as I lay in the bath contemplating my future, the words of the Prophet Jeremiah came back to me in all their stark and shocking simplicity.

> A voice is heard in Ramah,
> lamenting and weeping bitterly:
> It is Rachel weeping for her children,
> refusing to be comforted for her children,
> because they are no more. [6]

According to the rabbi, Rachel is the archetype of every woman who, through no fault of her own, is passed by and ignored by her male peers who are either too frightened, too selfish, or too lazy to play their part in fulfilling her dreams.

This thought stayed with me, and now as I consider it, on approaching the well of their meeting, it was Jacob who was strong enough and curious enough to remove the stone so that Rachel could draw water for him to drink. For many women with Asperger's syndrome, it is the stone of social confusion and the difficulty of expressing themselves in the manner that men expect that covers their beauty and too often seals their fate. The Rachel in every woman with Asperger's waits for Jacob and longs for him to see her, value her, and remove the stone so that she can share her life with him. It is he who has the courage and curiosity to look into the well of her soul and see just how deep those waters run. Long after the fountains of mere flirtation run dry, the man who comes to know and love a woman on the autism spectrum will find in her a faithful partner whose curiosity, conversation, and character will refresh and delight his soul for years to come. That night as the bath turned cold, it was Rachel's legacy that soaked into the very marrow of my bones and her tears that ran down my face, splashing into the waters below.

I continued to test my vocation for a further two years before deciding that mine lay elsewhere. I was well aware in making the very difficult decision to leave the place and people I had come to love and respect so wholeheartedly that the trajectory of my life would change dramatically and forever. Now, "change" was the least of my concerns. I was leaving a lifestyle whose utter stability had, ironically, prepared me to adapt to any change that life might present.

I clearly remember standing in my cell one afternoon and the thought occurring to me that I had led the life of an enclosed nun for long enough to know that I could carry its essence into whatever the future held for me. You can take the woman out of Carmel, but you cannot take Carmel out of the woman. During Mass, the morning that I left the monastery, I watched the priest raise the Host and the Chalice in what seemed that day, to me, like a toast: "Here's to you Rachael, to all your joys, hopes, setbacks, and sufferings; in embracing yours, you have embraced those of all, and all are embraced in me."

At the end of Mass and with little over half an hour before my departure, I made my way up the service stairs to my cell. There, without ceremony or fanfare, I removed the habit and veil which had become an extension of myself, hanging them on the hook on the back of the door. Now I stood in my street clothes, packed and ready to leave. Occupied or empty, my cell remained the same—the four bare walls, the single bed, the writing desk and wooden chair in which I had sat and prayed for many an hour. I would miss it, although it would always remain within me.

On the way down I slipped into the library, finding comfort in its dark, narrow aisles. There, for some minutes, I savored and breathed in that singular quality of silence that only a monastic library can produce. A distant clock chimed the half hour. It was time. Passing through the lower hall, I looked up and saw the Ark charting its 380-year-old course through the air. Noah was right, I had "labored plentie for peace"; and, once established, peace took root in the depths of my being, never to depart.

I met Sister Ruth at the top of the stairs that led down to the cloister. Without a word she took my hand and walked with me those last few yards that led to the enclosure door; for as much courage as it took for me to enter, it took far more courage to leave. Standing by the door she turned to me, holding both my hands firmly in hers. Sister Ruth had walked this walk before, although the mixture of pain and love in her pale blue eyes told me that it was a duty to which she would never become accustomed. "God go with you, my dear," she said, holding me close. She reached out and grasped the handle to open the door, and I passed over the threshold of the enclosure into the world without, dissolving in one step all formal ties with the Order.

12

MIRAGES AND MINARETS

I chose to leave the monastery, catching a train that hurled me into an unknown future. I can still see myself now, stepping into the train carriage in the blue-cotton dress with faded white floral print that I had worn on my arrival. It was a particularly warm April morning, and I had plunked on my head a straw hat in which I had spent many a silent afternoon gardening. This was preferable to having it crushed among the items I had elected to take with me in the small suitcase which had sat so long in the corner of a storeroom gathering dust.

I edged along until I found a space between the commuters and grasped at the nearest handrail, steadying myself as the train pulled away from the station. A kindly lady smiled at me from her seat. What must I have looked like? Stunned, I suppose. I had been hit by a wall of chatter and movement the likes of which I had not been exposed to for years. It all seemed incredibly, wonderfully indulgent and assailed my senses like the crescendo after a long, quiet interlude.

In the midst of so much upheaval, it was perfectly natural that I should return to the home of my aunt. I arrived on her doorstep in the late afternoon, and having been greeted with her customary enthusiasm, I headed upstairs to freshen up. I fashioned my hair into some sort of bun and pushed a large pair of plain gold sleepers back through resistant earlobes. I looked at my reflection, satisfied that I could pass for someone who had just returned from a casual day out.

On entering the dining room, I was confronted by the sight and smell of a huge joint of roast beef. I hadn't foreseen this and wondered how I would tell my aunt that I held at least vague notions of remaining vegetarian. Sally backed through the kitchen door carrying a large gravy boat which she placed on the table; and taking up her carving knife, began to tell me just how special this occasion was and how she had spared no expense in finding the best roast money could buy. I quietly converted; after all, wasn't mustard a type of vegetable? My aunt had arranged my itinerary—for I was to fly out the following week—and told me the details as I mopped up the last of the gravy with a slice of bread.

I laid low for the next few days, spending the warmer evenings on the garden patio in the company of my aunt, rising occasionally to turn over a record. Sally, ever the hostess, mixed the gin and tonics and sliced the cheese, and through the French doors, Jussi Björling and Robert Merrill sang "The Pearl Fishers Duet." "Listen!" she urged, and in one of the rare moments when I saw my aunt show her vulnerability, I witnessed a bright tear roll down her cheek.

The following morning, packed and ready to leave, I saw the shape of a yellow taxi wobble into view through the mottled glass of the front door. Arriving at Manchester Airport, there was little time but to check in and make my way to the departure gate. Sally saw me off, brushing my cheek with a swift kiss and giving me a firm hug before the call to board my flight. I understood her ways well. By temperament, Sally was not given to long good-byes, that burden being mine alone to bear. "See you, Sally, see you!" "See you, love; now have you got your boarding pass ready? You just need to make your way to the gates down that escalator there." Our precious time together ended in a flurry of practicalities.

Sally turned on her heel, anxious to return to the waiting taxi that was to take her home. I watched intently the last few steps and casual wave she gave before disappearing beyond the barrier. It was the last time I would ever see her.

I settled into my seat for the eighteen-hour flight to Brunei, where I was to spend the night before boarding for Brisbane. I had never been to Brunei and held no expectations, for in the haze of rapid change that hung about me, what was one more? Into this kindly chaos came the announcement "Ladies and gentlemen, before taking off, we would like this flight to be blessed." A hush came over the cabin, and as the stewardesses, resplendent in white veils, made their way down the aisles, a recorded voice deeply intoned an Islamic prayer: "In the name of Allah, Most Gracious, Most Merciful," and with these words the cabin was transformed into a sacred space.[1]

The prayer's English translation gently scrolled down the screen: "Glory be to Him who has brought this under our control, for we could never have accomplished this by ourselves. And to our Lord, surely must we return"—a truly sobering thought as I stared out at a wing. "O Allah, You are our companion on this journey and the protector for the family we leave behind." As the plane began to taxi down the runway, the faces of my aunt and of my sisters in Carmel swam before my eyes, and putting my face in my hands I prayed that one day we would merrily meet again, God willing.

As with all long-haul flights, the minutes melted into hours, and in the no-man's-land between departure and destination, I was surprised to see that I was never at a loss as to the direction of Mecca, thanks to a small indicating arrow that swung round in the corner of my in-flight entertainment screen. Fascinated by this perpetual piece of information, I fancied for a brief moment the papal plane showing the direction of the Vatican.

When the request came that we straighten our seats and fold up our trays, I had almost forgotten that we were to have a short refueling stop in Dubai, and there pick up passengers for the onward journey. As we descended into Dubai, I saw through my window, as straight and as far as the horizon, a highway through the desert whose blazing streetlights turned nighttime to noon. This lavish use of light was made all the more remarkable insofar as the lanes on which it shone were completely empty.

Emerging from a tunnel, I came squinting out into the light of a mirage of sparkling pale marble. Moving silver stairways carried commuters between multileveled malls. The wares sold in these markets left the buyer in no doubt that *this* was an oasis of opulence. I approached a counter, and there beneath the gleaming glass I beheld diamonds in settings the size of trinkets from Blackpool Beach. Elsewhere, chains of yellow gold, sold by the meter, to my Western eyes, gave the double illusion of being both precious and cheap.

It was not only the wealth of Dubai that impressed itself on my memory, but also its people. I sought "shade" from the beating artificial light under the fronds of an Alexander palm fashioned from metal and watched the passing parade of humanity. After a time, I noticed a young couple, he, like a sheik in white and she, a few paces behind, in black. They were tall and slim and distinguished themselves from the crowd by their elegant bearing. Bringing up the rear, their Filipino nanny escorted the couple's three young sons.

I watched the lady as she walked by; as a woman intimately acquainted with the feel of monastic serge upon my skin, I could spot the quality of the cloth of her burka at fifty paces. As she moved along the concourse, I noted the cut and fall of the fabric; it was beautiful, expensive. Imagine my delight when this same woman took her seat on the plane directly opposite mine. Of course I was itching to talk to her, for what would I not have given for a window into her way of life! Unfortunately I was too late. A well-meaning women who sat the other side of her with a screaming infant on her lap kept up a constant patter on the price of diapers and the cost of formula for the best part of an hour, to which the veiled lady graciously responded. Further into the flight, I figured from her quiet and withdrawn manner that her conversation quota had been used up—I was not surprised.

It may seem implausible that I could divine the demeanor of a woman concealed by cloth, but having spent three years in the company of women whose only exposure were their fingertips and faces, I had become by necessity a master of micro-signals. Each of us in the monastery being uniformly clad, I recognized an individual Sister by her posture and gait, the slope of her shoulder, an oft-repeated unconscious gesture, the fall of her feet upon the flagstones in the hall. Her moods, too, were not her private property. At table and beyond, my Sisters would, to my increasing awareness, trail clouds of contentment or consternation in their wake, and thus, I was ever open to my neighbor's blessing and burden, which is surely the purpose and essence of intuition?

In the early hours of the morning, I alone saw the lady in the burka remove a long black glove to attend to her youngest child. What I had not expected and indeed came as a complete surprise was that this simple action revealed a slender, well-manicured hand of rich, red-lacquered nails and fine jewelry which sparkled on skin the color of mahogany in the dawn light that slid through the cabin windows.

The arrow moved again, pointing the faithful in the direction of Mecca. Out of the corner of my eye, I watched the lady begin her morning prayer. She bowed several times in her seat and sent up a silent litany to Allah. I was struck by the depth of her devotion and joined my own hands in prayer.

Arriving in Brunei, I went to collect my bags. I retrieved one and waited for the other, but the other, to my horror, never came. I stood by the carousel pouring out my anxious inquiries to an airport official, then waited some more. "Perhaps you could take one of mine!" I turned to see the young sheik gesturing grandly in the direction of his gathered luggage, smiling a wide, white smile. I smiled weakly, but I was beyond humor. I took the courtesy bus to my hotel with reassurances that my suitcase would eventually reappear.

To the weary traveler, percale bed-linen, a kettle, and a selection of coffee and tea are little more than compensation on one's journey. Having come from a lifestyle where one's choices are paired down to the point of poverty, these modest conveniences on tap were, to me, luxury indeed! From the thrill of six-hundred-thread-count sheets to eeny, meeny, miney, moe-ing my way through several varieties of Twinings teas—I was a happy woman!

I pulled out the hotel directory, keen to see how I might amuse myself in the time I had left to discover the Kingdom of Brunei Darussalam. Turning its pages, I saw a grand, gold-domed mosque not far from the hotel. Its beautiful description bade the visitor welcome, and having never entered a mosque, I knew this was a sight I wanted to see.

I studied the dress requirements carefully. Women were to wear long, covering clothing and to cover their heads on entering the mosque—this was familiar territory. Unzipping my suitcase, I was pleased to see that it contained all my long, layered clothing. Dragging out my dresses, skirts, and tops, I tried on combinations until I settled on an ensemble worthy of worship. I stood in a floor-length, sage-green skirt and a matching high-necked top that flowed down to my finger-tips, with a large gray-and-white scarf wrapped about my neck, ready for the veiling—absorbed in this foreign culture, I felt completely at home.

Venturing out of my hotel, I strolled down a wide thoroughfare filled with sleek, modern cars and long limousines. I was curious to see a little ahead of me, a small group of walkers turning off the footpath, so naturally I followed. To my astonishment I found myself in a thick jungle whose high canopy rang with the chatter and screeching of monkeys. The sudden contrast almost hurt my head as I stood there wondering if I had crossed the border into Borneo.

Climbing the hillside path, I caught the smiles of the local women as they walked by. "Who could not feel happy walking here?" I thought, for this place was the stuff of children's storybooks. It was only a few steps that brought me back to the center of civilization, and from a minaret the call to prayer cut through the humidity that hung thick in the air. The cry of the muezzin slid through a scale of notes that measured every sound the human song could muster and stopped so suddenly that the cry by its very silence lingered.

The golden dome of the Grand Mosque came into view and shone like the sun in the midmorning light. I crossed the wide pavement that surrounded the mosque and, finding a bench, I sat and stared up at its magnificent white edifice, its arabesque colonnades beyond number and minarets that drew the eye higher and higher to the heavens. In the distance, I noted a gathering of women in white hijab—whether they were coming or going I could not tell. I patiently waited for the hour when I, as a visitor, could enter.

A scattering of locals stood about quietly keeping their own counsel, when from seemingly nowhere, a young, jeans-clad and white-jacketed man not many meters away twisted and twirled on the spot, shattering my serenity. He shuffled his feet and snapped his fingers, looking very pleased with himself indeed! It was an odd little dance designed, I think, to drum up the kind of Dutch courage needed when attempting to engage a single woman in a conversation that could only lead to no good. I did not like it. You may suppose that I was blind to his purposes, that his intentions were beyond my reckoning. His behavior, however, was painfully, embarrassingly obvious, his every step driven by an unhealthy excitability, and from that moment I was on my guard.

He strode toward my seat and sat himself down. "Hello, my name is Michael. What is your name?" I doubted that was his name but grudgingly gave mine up. "So Rachael, where have you come from and how long will you be staying in Brunei?" This fawning familiarity was simply too much. The phrase "Go away and leave me alone!" sat at the door of my lips, but I was a stranger in a strange land and did not know the parameters within which I could deal with this pesky person. "My husband and I are here on a short stopover. He's back at our hotel." The young man did not buy a word of it. I tried a more straightforward approach, "I'm just here to visit the mosque, good-bye." I got up and walked away but heard him behind me. "I can come with you!" he called. "Oh no, you can't" I thought, but he did.

Arriving at the entrance, I slipped off my shoes and draped the scarf around my head and shoulders with all the dexterity of one accustomed to religious dress. Inside, I prepared to take in the beauty of the mosque's Arabic design, and on seeing the interior, I was struck not by what the mosque contained but by what it didn't. Accustomed as I was to navigating my way in and out of long, narrow pews in European churches filled with votive candles and depictions of the angels and saints in stained glass and stone, the emptiness within the mosque came as quite a shock. Instead of all those things, carpets in muted tones covered a vast floor whose space was repeated in high, whitewashed walls where long, pale-glass windows illumined only light itself.

Within this airy vault was the one focus of attention. Above me, suspended from the ceiling, hung a large, white disc on whose still surface ran the quicksilver energy of Arabic script, swooping and turning in grand curves, suddenly shooting up to burst its boundary before coming to rest in a single dark dot. I considered the skill of the calligrapher and remembered my own futile efforts to command my pen and the black ink which ran unbidden through the nib. The artisan had achieved what he set out to do: directing all his energy and talent to creating a visual prayer.

Meanwhile, the young man edged closer and closer, distracting me from my quiet contemplation. "You would look very lovely in the veil," he said smoothly. "How ironic," I thought. To my right, an old man in a white gown and turban sat cross-legged in the corner, watching the scene unfold. "Perhaps you could study the Koran," said the young man, but his low tone and penetration of my personal space, gave me the sneaking suspicion that he was not as devout as his words would have me believe. I turned to the old man, pleading my discomfort with my eyes.

The young man, suddenly tiring of his small talk, turned, and, looking me full in the face, said, "Perhaps I could book a hotel room and you will sleep with me?" I was not for sale; this man's sense of entitlement knew no bounds. The phrase that had sat at the door of my lips flew out: "Go away and leave me alone!" I stood my ground as the sound of my reproaches echoed around the marbled walls of the mosque. I quickly signed the visitors' book, slipped on my shoes and drew the veil around my face, allowing just enough space through which to see. Making a beeline across the wide pavement toward my hotel, I heard him calling over the distance, "Miss Harris! Miss Harris!" His voice fell silent, and looking back I saw the old man, outside now, waving his arms wildly at the younger and shouting all the while.

On reaching the sanctuary of the lobby of my hotel, I threw back the veil uncovering my face, much to the incredulous stares of my fellow travelers. I did not bother to explain myself, but headed straight upstairs to my room to recover from the shock with a strong, sweet brew.

As I sipped my tea, I replayed the scene from the beginning and saw myself poring over the details of the dress code, failing to notice the growing gap between what was offered and the unspoken social considerations of such an outing. Would a typically wired foreign woman make her way to the mosque by herself? I doubt it. Prudence would curb her curiosity, or she would gather a group of fellow travelers to ensure her personal safety. I, on the other hand, in true Asperger style, set out for the mosque unaware that my solitary venture would open me to victimization, for I had not noticed that even the local women gathered in groups.

As I sat there, examining the events of those last few hours, cradling a cold and empty teacup in my hands, I felt the sudden sting of humiliation: "How was it?" I asked the air, "that I could be so foolish as to go alone?" and swift on its sting the consolation came: I may have been blind enough to dig myself a ditch, but I also had the presence of mind to dig myself out of it. I replaced the cup on the saucer by my side and thought what a pity it was that I had been unable to spend more time taking in the beauty of the Grand Mosque, thanks to the whispering campaign that "Michael" kept up in my unwilling ear.

The following morning my second suitcase arrived just in time for the onward leg from Brunei to Brisbane. Boarded and buckled up, I settled back for the now familiar in-flight prayer: "In the name of Allah, Most Gracious, Most Merciful." I pondered my short sojourn in the Islamic world, and in my mind's eye I saw the desert sands lit up by streetlights, the elegant and devout young couple from Dubai. I heard the call to prayer coming from the minaret and the women in white. I saw, too, the old, turbaned man, faithful and focused, and the young man, sick and rudderless, and once again came a verse of familiar prayer: "O Allah, lighten our burden on this journey and bridge the distances between us." To which I said, "Amen."

13

HOMECOMING

After I touched down at Brisbane International Airport in the early hours of the morning, an opaque glass wall slid back to reveal the sight of my long-suffering parents, who spontaneously gathered up their thin and fragile daughter. Back at home, having slept almost as many hours as I had traveled, I rose and took myself off to the bathroom, setting a hot shower in an attempt to wash away the jet lag that had set in some time before. Without, I heard the sound of my sister's voice. Sarah had let herself in, and as I came down the corridor rubbing my wet hair furiously with a fluffy towel, I saw that she had set a small stack of videos on the coffee table, eager to initiate me in three years' worth of pop culture that had, apparently, passed me by.

I threw my arms around Sarah, surprising her as she winced and shrank against the onslaught. Dear Sarah, now as in the past, she was the sole object of my avid affections, she whose constant cry was "Give me some space!" I stepped back a few paces and smiled. "Hello, my darling, it's so *nice* to see you!" "Nice to see!" she replied, standing at a safe distance and patting my back with her hand.

Sarah sat me down in the manner of a games-show host and began to quiz me on cultural matters spanning the years 1996–1999. "What do you know about the Spice Girls? The movie *Titanic*? 'Macarena'?" My face didn't show a flicker of recognition, and I confessed my ignorance in these matters and more. "Do you mean to tell me that you have never even *heard* of Posh Spice?" "No," I answered. "Is it something like garam masala?" Sarah frowned slightly and putting her hand upon my brow with a dramatic flourish pronounced that I was suffering from "The Dark Night of the Spice Girls." Quick to remedy the affliction, she rifled through the little pile on the coffee table and pulled out a music video to fill the gap in my education before quickly replacing it with her copy of *Titanic*. As I sat there combing the snarls out of my long red hair, I watched Rose climb the gangplank, beautiful and blissfully ignorant of her fate.

One morning after a few days had passed, my mother, who was busy preparing a snack for me in the kitchen, remarked how well I was adjusting to being back home. However, I could see by the way she threw me a glance now and then as she went about her day that she suspected that I was adjusting a little *too well* considering the circumstances—and she was right. The familiarity of home, the company of my parents, and the small conveniences and little luxuries designed to impart comfort and reassurance were, alas, too little, too late.

My mother came and touched my shoulder with one hand. With a kind word she placed a hot brew before me with the other hand. As I looked out the full-length windows at the panorama of bushland before me, not even nature could console me as it once had, such was my strained frame of mind. A vague sense of foreboding had, for a day or two, begun to nibble away like a rat at the edges of my equilibrium. I grasped my cup with cold hands, hoping to restore some heat. Having left the rarefied but familiar routine of monastic life and come home to my own country, I began to suffer double culture-shock the way one might suffer double pneumonia.

As I sat there, with all the afternoon before me to do with as I pleased, I couldn't help but think that I should "be somewhere doing something." I suddenly heard the sound of a distant bell. I sprang to my feet ready for deployment to the card office or kitchen. Across the air I caught the metallic melody of "Greensleeves" coming from an ice-cream van; it was ludicrous, laughable, and laugh I did for a long time, out loud.

What I could throw off during the day could not so easily be discarded at night. Not long after the sun went down, the gnawing, nameless fears which I had managed to fend off found full expression as I settled down to sleep. On that night and for three more to follow, on turning out the light I was seized by a trembling and a terror that rose like a tide, reaching the level of my eyes. "If it rises any higher I shall drown and all shall be lost!" I thought to myself, but with the morning the dark tide receded, leaving behind the debris of a broken night's sleep.

Over breakfast, my mother noticed that I seemed withdrawn and pale. Her voice seemed far away, and I could hardly find my own. "I'm taking you down to the doctor," she said, putting the plates in the sink and searching for her set of car keys. I went willingly enough, throwing on what clothes came to hand and slipping on a pair of my well-worn sandals.

"The doctor will see you now," said a young receptionist whom I didn't recognize. I had sat there in the waiting room scanning an article in a women's magazine—it could have been written in hieroglyphics for all I cared, for I hadn't taken in a single word. My doctor had known me since my teens and had always possessed an unusual air of intuition. His turn of mind made the four walls of his office more confessional than consulting room, and so it was that he sat there by his desk in silence, considering me for some moments before he spoke.

I fixed my gaze on a scrap of silver paper on the floor; it shone lustrous under the florescent light. I resisted the urge to pick it up to examine it more closely; that sort of thing was "not done." "It's been a long journey for you, hasn't it, Rachael?" It was a simple statement from one who had watched my comings and goings for over a decade. "Yes," I said, "yes, it has."

He asked me how I felt, and I told him of my threadbare nerves, the sleepless nights, and of the precipice that stood at the very edges of my own skin—one wrong move, *any* move, and I would slip to my death. I looked up and met his dark, unwavering eyes whose very stillness imparted a sense of stability. "You're suffering from anxiety," he said. "People who have anxiety tend to get lost in it." "Anxiety!" I repeated, quite shocked. Anxiety—that most common of common complaints—had become a monstrous, unchecked jungle whose canopy blocked out every trace of light!

For me, a little knowledge has always gone a long way. I did not doubt him, for he knew me and my propensity to worry too well. No sooner had I heard his diagnosis than the thicket of my fears began to draw back to its proper proportions, and the light of self-knowledge shone on my understanding. Aided by a short course of sleeping tablets, a nightly cup of Horlicks, and the establishment of a set bedtime routine, I began to find my way out of the forest.

What the doctor told me that day was not the last word he had to say. My mother saw him sometime soon after, spending her therapeutic fifteen minutes telling him how I was faring after coming home. He summed up my situation thus: "Rachael left a girl and came back a woman." Despite my feelings of falling apart, firmer foundations had been steadily laid, foundations as solid and as sure as the concrete cloisters I had once walked. My soul stood on solid ground, and from there I began to build a new future, embedded in the workaday world.

I turned the pages of the weekend paper, hoping to find a suitable position, something familiar that would cause me no stress, so that I could ease my way back into society. I ran my finger down the employment column and found just the job I was hoping for. A cosmetic consultant was required for a city department store. "That will do nicely," I told myself, reaching out for the phone to arrange an interview.

I arrived a few mornings after at Human Resources, wondering what on earth I was going to say—my interview skills were a little rusty, to say the least! I smoothed my skirt and checked my makeup in a nearby mirror. A face with kohled eyes and copper lips stared back. "Good Luck!" I whispered, as I pushed a straying bobby pin back into place.

No sooner had I stepped through the door than a hand was thrust out to shake mine while its owner followed after. "Hiii, I'm Carolll, come on innn!" Her voice was high pitched and each word ended as though she were asking a question. Her face was frozen in the position of one who had said *cheese* for a photo and whose punishment was to maintain it for her unspeakable crimes. Despite the flurry of words that followed, her eyebrows never moved but remained arched in an expression of permanent surprise. I'd met people like Carol before. She was a mature lady, a veteran of the retail industry and the company for which she worked. A sleek, black bob framed her face, and around her neck hung a string of large white pearls whose size, I noticed, were in direct proportion to her seniority, thus denoting her as a "Grand Master" of the establishment.

She gestured where I was to sit and taking her own seat, she popped on a pair of slim, framed reading glasses and began to peruse my application. "It's Rachael, isn't it?" "Yes," I said. "I have a niece called Rachael," she remarked. "This is good," I thought. "Surely she will not cast off the namesake of her own kin, unless, that is, they never got on." In any case, it was odd how often I seemed to remind people of their aunt or sister or niece or cousin or some random public figure. "Aren't you that lady on the television?" an elderly gentleman once inquired as I waited at the bus stop in the pouring rain—strange for one whose life was so shrouded in obscurity.

I chose my strong suit and talked of the beauty therapy business I once ran a few blocks away, of the importance of customer service, and of how I tailored my treatments to suit the individual client. Carol smiled at my answers, but of course this was no guarantee. "That's great!" she said, smiling even more widely, if that were possible. She looked down at my application again, looking a little puzzled before inquiring about my most recent employment. "Ah, yes," I said. "I spent the last three years living in an enclosed monastic community in England, but I assure you my cosmetic skills will have not suffered for it." "That's great!" she repeated. Carol didn't seemed fazed one bit, she was evidently satisfied with my interview and immediately offered me a position working at the Elizabeth Arden counter in the Cosmetics Hall. I was to start the following week. So it was that I found myself gaining employment in a parallel universe—the glamorous, airbrushed world of high fashion.

A friend of a friend of my mother's had recently retired and set off on a grand tour of Europe and the Far East, and she was not expected to return for many months. It was arranged that I would house-sit her very smart apartment that backed onto the Brisbane River at Newfarm. The apartment had the park on one side and an uninterrupted view of the water on the other, and I was filled with gratitude for landing so softly on my feet!

In the mornings I would make tea, and drawing back the curtains, I would sit at the breakfast table and watch the school rowing teams slide past my front window. Smaller boats followed, while a ferry that crisscrossed the river picked up trusting souls on one side and dispensed them safely on the other. I could not have wished for a more welcome start to my day.

On my first morning of work I pulled on a pair of tights that immediately laddered. I maneuvered the telltale track until it was hidden beneath the hem of my pencil-line skirt. Then, tucking in the ballooning polyester fabric of my blouse, I flattened it into submission under an oversized jacket—the only one that had been left on the uniform rack. Though irritated by such claustrophobic clothing, in the end all I noticed was the *click click click* of my pumps—so confronting after years of crepe-soled squeaks—as I ran down the street to make the bus.

Arriving early at my counter, I set to dusting the shelves and replacing the stock from the previous day's sales. The pace with which I took up my tasks was slow and steady, without the slightest hint of haste. I would be the first to admit that I had spent so long in the quiet, deep backwaters that I was totally unprepared for the raging rapids of commerce.

A little way into my shift, a woman in a power suit stepped into my space, letting off questions like a string of firecrackers. "Have you spoken to the floor manager yet? How much stock do you have left in the storeroom? What position on the leader board are we this week? How many units are you averaging per sale?" I blinked a little, trying to work out who this woman was. Yes, it was coming back to me now. I'd met her the week before over coffee; she was my area manager.

Like many people on the autism spectrum, I have always been subject to a degree of "face blindness." I may remember you in a certain setting, but if you're out and about, or if you change your hairstyle, I cannot guarantee that I will know who you are. Should you approach me, at least I will offer you the kind of politeness reserved for complete strangers.

I answered the manager's questions as well as I could for someone who had just started her first day on the floor. "Two units per sale?" she said, raising her eyes in astonishment. I steeled myself for the reprimand that would surely follow. "Fantastic!" she said, but the damage was done. I exhaled heavily on the spot as she turned on her heel, all her questions spent.

Sometimes, when things were quiet, I would stand at the corner of my counter spritzing swatches of card with my company's signature fragrances to entice passersby. I marveled that those who stopped to sample my cards needed to raise the newly sprayed swatch right up to their nostrils, inhaling as deeply as they could to catch the scent. My own senses were so overwhelmed that I quickly came to the conclusion that it wasn't that I was oversensitive but that the majority were under. However, just turning up to work offered me the kind of exposure therapy I needed, for after a week or two, I found that I had built up a considerable tolerance for the kaleidoscope of scent, light, and sound that swirled around my place of employment.

From my first day on the floor to the very last, I understood that only the thinnest veneer of practicality came between the customer and the sentiments of their soul. In the eyes of my customers, I was no mere hawker of lipsticks and lotions; to them I was a purveyor of dreams, a handmaid of Venus, having the ear of my mistress and dispensing beauty to the faithful in small, shining palettes and pots.

Of the thousands of people I served or spoke with during the two and a half years that I worked for the House of Arden, only four stand out in my memory, and it is to them that I dedicate the following passages.

One morning as I stood by my counter, a frail, elderly lady in a lavender twinset and pearls sidled up to me, rather conspiratorially, and said, "And what does Miss Arden have to sell today?" Her inquiry took me aback. The easy familiarity with which she spoke the name put flesh back on what had become a subsidiary of a large corporation. I drew out from my drawer the latest shade of lipstick and noticed that her own makeup had been impeccably applied. A rose-crème blush glowed in the hollow of her cheeks, and a mauve-colored shadow shimmered on eyes deep-set with age.

I turned the barrel of the tester and smoothed the crimson color on the back of an arthritic hand. "You know, it wasn't always like this," she said, admiring the color, then gesturing toward the well-lit displays. "During the war when I was living in Europe, cosmetics were very hard to come by." I listened as she told me tales of Elizabeth Arden products arriving in brown paper bags via the black market.

In my imagination I saw her sunken features flourish with the bloom of youth, and behind her, the bright lights faded to a back alley near a pub. Deep in the shadows she stood there, shifting from one leg to the other, waiting for the exchange. Presently her contact came, slipping her a plain parcel and pocketing her hard-earned pound for face powder and a pot of rouge. Her cosmetics kept her going then, and I daresay they kept her going now, as she placed the small package in her handbag and steadied herself with her walking stick as she went on her way.

Another time as I filled out my client cards, recording their purchases for future reference, I looked up to see a tall, middle-aged woman inspecting a product she had just taken down from the shelf. Of course, there was nothing unusual in this; that is, until I saw the size of her wrist. It stood out, thick and strong, clearly visible just beyond the cuff of her delicate sleeve. Woman's intuition drew my eye above the lace collar of her dress, confirming my suspicions by the sight of a large Adam's apple protruding above a fine gold necklace whose dainty charm rested in the hollow of her throat.

All her attire—dress, shoes, handbag—had been chosen with great care, and beneath the curls of a brunette wig, she had matched her foundation perfectly to her own complexion. She had formed a delicate bubble of femininity about herself, and who was I to apply the pin? Whether by fancy or conviction, her ways were not for me to judge. The very sight of her filled me with a strange reverence for her predicament.

I approached her and began to explain the finer points of the product in which she had taken an interest. She didn't look at me at first, nor did she speak—her silence was her last line of defense. I took a cotton tip and applied the cream to the smooth underside of her arm. She raised her heavy-lidded eyes and smiled secretly, accepting a sample before mingling with the morning shoppers.

Some time after, I saw another make his way around the Cosmetic Hall. He was young and frail, and hardly covering his thin, wasted frame were a pair of tight blue jeans and a crop top bearing the confronting image of the Immaculate Heart of Mary. In true Italian style, Mary's alabaster skin was clothed in blue and red robes, and her amber eyes gazed out with sweet sorrow as she gestured toward a heart wreathed in lilies and surmounted with flames of love.

The floor manager saw me watching him and came across to fill me in. "His parents are terribly well off," she said, and she told me of how they had sent their only son to an exclusive boys' school and of the bright and promising future that lay before him before the days of drugs and prostitution. "Just ignore him," she counseled, but I could not. As he approached my counter, I saw that despite his gaunt, thin features he was yet beautiful, and in his slurred speech I heard the last traces of a first-class mind sinking fast into the hell of heroin addiction. "I need some makeup to cover these spots," he whined, pointing toward skin beaded with sweat. "I'm working tonight down at the Valley and I can't go out looking like this!" he cried in a tone of rising panic. Fortitude Valley, with its Chinatown just outside the city, beckoned shoppers by day and dance-club patrons by night, and somewhere between the dark and the day, the young, fading figure of a man stood in the doorways of its dimly lit streets.

I rummaged through a box and found an almost full tester of foundation. "Here, that should last you a few months," I said, putting the bottle into his hand. He stared at the bottle a moment, then lifting his head, looked at me in disbelief. "Take it, it's yours!" I urged. He smiled the faint echo of a smile that had once graced a school photo, and turning, moved unsteadily toward the street entrance. Stripped as he was of every vestige of dignity, I knew that nothing he could do would add a single ounce to the weight of degradation that was his alone to bear, and so he went his way with the Virgin's image to stand at the foot of his cross.

Of all the people I noticed who passed my counter, one is etched more deeply in my memory than any other. I see her still—a young woman who walked slowly by, searching my face with each step. I recognized her immediately, though I had never seen her before, because my own features were mirrored in those of a complete stranger. Rebecca was my niece—at least that was the name my sister had given her at her birth. Sarah had become pregnant during her second year at college, and having spent months agonizing over what would be best for her daughter, she gave her up for adoption.

I had expected to meet her. On turning eighteen, Rebecca had made contact with my sister through the adoption agency, which had given Rebecca a small parcel of photos, a letter, and a golden bracelet that had once encircled Sarah's infant wrist. My niece lived near where I worked, and it was only a handful of days between Rebecca meeting her mother and meeting her aunt. We held each other's gaze as we met, our smiles and laughter barely contained by the constraints of my workplace. "Look at you!" I exclaimed. "Well, look at you!" she repeated, both of us openmouthed as we took each other in from head to toe. It was a happy meeting and the first of many family gatherings since.

The Cosmetics Hall was indeed a place of dreams, and for none more so than the staff that worked there. The girl from the counter behind me had her heart set on becoming a flight attendant. Ever resourceful, she told me of how she had worn the elegant navy jacket with cream piping of her uniform to her airline interview, clinching the job with borrowed style. Another secured employment as a masseuse on

a Mediterranean cruise ship, while another girl who walked like a ballerina and had the habit of singing "Stormy Weather" theatrically on her
way to lunch was silenced by her sudden departure to marry an
American and was never seen again. One daring lass responded to an
advertised position in China for a dancer, but what style of dancing this
entailed remained something of a mystery to the girls on the floor.

My own dreams were slightly more pedestrian, but deeply desired
nonetheless. Thoughts of having a family had continued to simmer beneath the surface. As a teenager, I couldn't understand what all the fuss
was about. Whenever a young mother appeared on the scene, groups of
girls would gather, pouring out an avalanche of sentiment toward mother and baby alike. Cast ahead to the age of thirty, and I was suddenly
consumed by the need to have a child of my own!

Into this potent mix of potential came an invitation from one of the
shopgirls. "Me and my brother and his friend are meeting up for drinks
on Friday night. I've told my brother all about you! Would you like to
come?" she said with a smile. Yes, I would.

14

A CAUTIONARY TALE

In the book of most people's lives, unless mercifully spared, there are at least one or two chapters that they would rather forget, but whose retelling can serve as a cautionary tale to some, or a consolation to others, in knowing that after the fact, they are not alone in the execution of a poor choice. This is that chapter.

I stood before the mirror smoothing the sky-blue crepe dress I had bought especially for the occasion, tugging at the hem and untwisting the spaghetti straps that edged their way along my sloping shoulders. "This fellow could be 'The One,'" I thought, my brain in a fever of anticipation; and therein lay my undoing.

I arrived at the café and found my workmate, her brother Greg, and his friend, seated around a table in the courtyard. A nearby tree festooned with fairy lights cast a pleasing glow about the company. I pulled up a chair and took my place at the table. My workmate and her brother's friend kept up a lively patter about their shared history and how each of them was to spend Christmas. Meanwhile her brother sat back with hunched shoulders and head down. Whether he was bored or sulking I could not tell, but he seemed to show no sign of the curiosity or interest in me that his sister had given me to believe.

Still, his appearance pleased me, so rather than interpreting his lack of interest in me as a lost cause, I took this as a cue to see how I might gain his attention and set to serving up various topics until I found a subject that made him sit up. He had taken the lead role in the school play in his senior year, and seeing this small flicker of interest, I redoubled my efforts to win his favor.

So began a whirlwind courtship, driven by my desperation to settle down. The few hours I spent with him and the many he gave to his workplace and friend rang no warning bells in my mind. I had no experience and therefore no blueprint of how a healthy relationship should progress. In the realm of dating, like many women with Asperger's syndrome, I was chronically unsure of myself. Even though there was nothing in my upbringing to predispose me to putting up with so little, I found myself making constant excuses for his poor efforts at showing his care.

Our engagement followed some months after, his proposal coming like an afterthought over a few drinks. The lobby of a hotel was the stage, and as he awkwardly dropped to his knee, he was once again the lead role in the school play. "Rachael, will you marry me?" "Yes, I will." The curtain closed to the rapturous applause of our captive audience.

My fiancé's friend arranged our engagement party at his rather swank apartment. The view over the city was enchanting as I watched light sparkle in the windows of distant skyscrapers as night descended. Numbers of our families and some friends chatted happily while enjoying the trays of hors d'oeuvres and champagne that flowed freely throughout the night. Greg came late and spent the evening looking flustered and preoccupied. He seemed to regain his composure and chatted happily enough, drink in hand, pleased with the turnout.

A couple of hours had passed when his friend broke the flow of conversation, tapping his wineglass with a small spoon. "Come on, Greg, time for a speech!" All eyes turned on him expectantly, and as I looked at Greg, I saw the color drain away from his face. His hand shook as he grasped at the stem of his glass, sending a cluster of bubbles fizzing to the surface of his champagne. I wondered if he would manage to say anything at all. I weaved my way through the guests and took his arm. "Thanks for coming everybody, hope you've had a good time." That was it, and not a word about his "bride to be." It was painful, humiliating, and was, in all honesty, the first time that I really saw through the fog of my desperation and questioned his sincerity.

As the months turned into weeks before the wedding, I had seen sufficient "red flags" to make enough bunting for a street party, but his displays of tears and the trauma of his protestations overrode common sense. My window of opportunity closed and the wedding went ahead.

The wedding cake had hardly been cut when small snippets of information began to emerge regarding Greg's state of mind immediately prior to the day. His best man, aided by a mix of drinks, told of how Greg had gone missing for a few hours on the morning of the wedding. "I thought he'd done a runner!" he bellowed over the music, red faced and apparently amused by his revelation; but this was but a tremor compared to the quake that hit one morning a few days after.

My parents had arrived at the office of Greg's friend to give him a copy of the wedding video. They stood in the reception and waited, for they had heard the low murmurings of some kind of meeting within between Greg's friend and a colleague. My husband's friend suddenly turned round to see them standing there and did not know how much they had heard. "I was just saying to Bob, I never thought he'd go through with it." My parents were shocked. "What on earth do you mean?" my mother asked, but his friend simply repeated what he had already said. My mother and father left his office, horrified by what they had heard. The marriage that had been bound only a few days before began to fray from that day forward.

The following month I found myself pregnant and in a union that was already showing signs of strain. Greg was hardly there, but my new state was solid, real, and ever present. I went down to my local lending library and borrowed every pregnancy book I could get my hands on, relishing the details in true Asperger style, following my baby's progress from one week to the next. I felt quite sure I was having a boy and at my sixteen-week scan, I asked the technician to confirm my suspicions. She hesitated a little, but I reassured her that I was no fan of surprises. "The birth will be surprise enough!" I told her, hopping down from the bed in the darkened room. My much-loved son was on his way, and I named him "Laurence" from that day.

Laurence was my constant companion. I cooked with him, cleaned with him; I read, sang and talked to him. On my way to work, or to the grocery store, I felt myself so tuned into his presence that I forgot that in stranger's eyes, I was the madwoman who muttered to herself in the street. A few weeks of pregnancy turned into forty weeks plus, and with no sign of the baby's arrival, I was admitted to the hospital to have labor induced. My antenatal classes had touted the benefits of packing barley sugars, board games, and books to keep ourselves amused while our labors progressed, but who were they kidding? As the contractions hit hard and fast, I would have hurled a checkerboard at the wall and propelled chess pieces like missiles!

They say the pains of labor are forgotten with the birth of a child, but I can assure you dear reader, due to my Asperger capacity for detail, that every sensation, every minute of those ten hours, is as fresh in my memory today as it was then, accompanied by a kind of "whale song" that I kept up for the duration.

The only real respite throughout that long night came to me by way of an unprecedented incident that I will now relate. As much physical energy as had ever been asked of me in a lifetime was compressed into those slow hours, and in the final stage I thought my strength would fail me, for I had nothing left to give. It was at that precise moment and without warning that I suddenly became aware of the presence of a multitude of my dearly departed pressing in from all sides, a benevolent curious crowd, eager for my good. I could not see them, but sensed them waiting just beyond the wall of myself. As intrusive and alarming as that might seem to any women in such a state of undress, I took great comfort in their obvious concern for me and my little one, as they departed as suddenly as they came with the final "push."

Through the haze of exhaustion that followed, I remember the midwife leaning over me and asking, "Would you like to walk to the ward?" So physically weakened I was, that it seemed to me that she had suggested I fly there. I suppose she read the reaction in my face, for a moment later she fetched a wheelchair and pushed me and my precious cargo up to the ward. I thought I was doing quite well, until another woman on her way back from the labor rooms overtook me in a pair of jeans and court shoes, her baby tucked under her arm like a football. Greg hovered somewhere on the outskirts of my maternal drama, bringing up the rear in the odd procession that led back to the ward.

I fell asleep the moment I was settled, and in the early hours of the morning as the sun filtered through the slim venetian blinds by my window, I turned my head to see the tiny bundle of humanity that lay in the crib at my side. I watched a while, and then suddenly the little creature stirred and opened its eyes and looked at me. Two emotions came rushing in; one, overwhelming love, the other, sheer terror! For in the little mewling sounds he made, I could almost hear the hydraulics of the "Mythic Ten-Ton Truck of Responsibility" that parks above the head of every first-time mother.

I swung my legs to the side of the bed and, wrapping my baby in a bunny rug, stepped out into the corridor to fetch a towel from the trolley. Laurence started to cough, turning an alarming shade of puce, quickly followed by silence and bug-eyed terror. I thrust him into the arms of a passing nurse. "Do something!" I cried, beginning to panic. The nurse looked taken aback, then annoyed. "What are you worrying about? All you have to do is give baby a gentle pat on his back, like this." Laurence gave a little burp and settled back into his former serene state. The nurse passed him back, shaking her head as she disappeared down the corridor to do her rounds. Undiagnosed as I was, neither she nor I could make sense of how overwhelmed I felt as a first-time mother. Everything was new, everything was different, and to cap it all off, I alone was responsible for his every need, whether I could read the signals or not.

As I gave Laurence his first bath, washing away the dust of his long journey to the outside world, I was struck by the perfect symmetry of his features, but there were other matters brewing to which I had to give my full attention. Greg's visits were few and far between and came within the dying minutes of visiting hours. A casual word, a quick glace at the crib, and he would set off down the corridor, sounding the silent death knell not of what I had, but of what I had hoped for.

A few mornings later, I sat by the reception desk at the end of the maternity wing, waiting for Greg to collect us. I put on a good show, smiling and responding to the questions the nurse asked me while she filled out the discharge forms. Inside, I felt the last of my frayed nerves snap, cutting me adrift on an ocean of uncertainty, yet, deep down the waters were still and upheld me before an infinite horizon. "So you have someone to pick you up?" the nurse broke in. "Yes," I said, "My husband will be here shortly." "Very good," she said, smiling and handing me a copy of her paperwork.

Greg came and took us down to where he'd parked the car. I strapped the baby in the carrycot and we set off, stopping only once along the way to pick up some supplies from a pharmacy. Greg sat in the car while I walked toward the shop entrance. Little dark dots began to swim before my eyes. I put my hand out, steadying myself against a brick wall. As I looked up, I saw a street full of people going about their business, and as I watched, I was suddenly struck by the realization that all these people had been born! That everything they said, everything they did, flowed from their first cry and the instinctive grasp of a tiny hand. The vision faded and I entered the shop, fumbling for the change purse at the bottom of my bag.

We returned to the home of my parents. The house I shared with Greg had long gone. Two weeks before I was due to give birth, I found out that he had sold it from under me, without my knowledge, to one of his friends as an investment property. All our possessions sat in self-storage, waiting for another roof under which they could fit. Meanwhile, I set up the nursery, tucking the quilt that my sister had made by hand over my sleeping son and placing Greg's soft blue toy elephant (a memento from his childhood) as guard over the crib.

Every morning, shortly after dawn, Laurence would pull down the thin cloth that I had draped across the bars of his cot against the sun, ready to greet the day. At four weeks, I remember the thrill of watching him work up to his first tentative smile—muscles twitching at the sides of his mouth until pulled into the shape of a small crescent moon. This he practiced again and again, waxing and waning, spurred on by my smiles and the kind of singsong praise one usually reserves for small excitable dogs.

What wiped the smile from my face and indeed left me speechless was the deep and meaningful relationship that Laurence developed with the blank brick wall by his cot. It was not that he didn't want to offer me his smiles; he simply preferred the company of baked clay. He would give me a cursory glance, then roll toward the wall. Moving round to the foot of the cot, I watched him, his gaze transfixed in the direction of the brickwork. Moments later his face lit up, smiling and gurgling, then looking intently before breaking into a wide smile once again. As quickly as he had been captivated, he would suddenly lose all interest, turning away from the wall. This behavior lasted several minutes, every morning, for weeks.

Keen to know what was causing his curious antics, I studied the brickwork. Perhaps patterns of morning light played upon its surface, but no, each and every time I was confounded by the dull and the plain. Laurence had reached nine weeks when what had claimed his complete attention suddenly ceased, a sweet mystery hidden forever in the pathways of an infant mind.

Meanwhile, as though I were working with a set of building blocks, I spent the weeks trying to create something solid, pushing the pieces of our family life into some kind of order in an attempt to stabilize my wobbling tower of dreams. Time and time again, Greg came along and pulled them apart with his frequent unexplained absences, and once again I would gather them up, starting from scratch. By the time Laurence was born, Greg had all but dropped any pretense of engagement in family life. Having gone to the trouble of putting on my makeup, styling my hair, and greeting him at the front door with a glass of wine and a willing ear to hear of his day, I suffered the humiliation of seeing him take the glass and slump in front of the television. To sit with his private thoughts, a world away from his wife and baby son, was beyond the pale. His late nights and absences without explanation were too much to bear.

I remember the morning I suggested that we take the baby for his first swim. Down at the public pool, I eased myself down into the water and reached out, taking the baby in my arms for a little paddle. Laurence loved the water and began to splash his hands over its surface. Overjoyed to see his reaction, I turned saying, "Look, Greg, he loves it!" but Greg had drifted off to the other end of the pool, removing himself through sheer lack of interest. A few weeks later, in much the same way, Greg drifted out of our lives.

I recall the night we separated. There had been a blackout, and with nothing else to distract him, Greg and I sat down after putting the baby to bed. "Did you regret getting married and if you had your time again, would you not have done so?" I asked, to which he simply replied "Yes." By fits and starts, he began to tell me that "he could not do two things at once," that is, he could not be married *and* apply himself to his work at the same time. This was the only explanation he gave, and now full knowing him to be an inadequate personality, the shining qualities that I believed he possessed became tinsel and dust: instead of being resourceful he was manipulative; instead of being gentle he was weak; instead of being present, he gave the impression of not being quite "there." I had no reason or desire to delve any further or prolong the inevitable.

He started to cry and I managed to grope around in the dark until I found a box of tissues near the cot. As he wiped his tears his mood changed again; a lightness came over him with the realization of his impending freedom.

For the sake of dramatic narrative, it may have been more satisfying had I rent Greg's business shirts in two, or taken the scissors to his silk neckties, cutting them in twain; but I had no such fuel for fits of passion. Rather, I felt a crushing sorrow for Greg that rent my own heart and cut me to the quick—that he was so incapable of appreciating his little family and the opportunity that we brought to his future.

There are no words to describe the moment you realize that nothing you can do, nothing you can say, nothing you can produce—not even a man's firstborn son—is enough to hold his interest or draw out a single ounce of his affection; but it would be remiss of me not to say a word in his defense. Those who knew him better than I did nothing to caution him against entering into a commitment that they *knew* lay entirely beyond his capabilities at that time; and those who had the moral obligation to tell me were either too distracted or too embarrassed to do so.

Now that I knew the depths of his inadequacies, the only mature response was to let him go with good grace with the hope he would make some kind of life for himself. I wished him no harm and would find no personal satisfaction in grinding him into the ground because he had bitten off more than he could chew. In the end, what he knew best won through. I retired to a fitful disturbed sleep and in the morning, Greg took himself, his clothes, and his toy elephant with him. I recall the particular Canon of Church Law that annulled my thirteen-month marriage: Grave Lack of Discretion of Judgment in the Respondent. Never had a truer statement been made.

A few days after Greg's unceremonious departure, I took Laurence down to the local shopping center with the intention of establishing some normality into my recently upended circumstances. As I sat on the bench cradling a small bag of groceries, a man carrying his own bundles sat himself down beside me, passing the time while his wife continued to compare the merchandise in the shop beyond.

After a few moments, he noticed Laurence in the pram at my side. "What a lovely baby," he said, smiling at Laurence in his little hand-knitted hat. "They're beautiful at this age, aren't they," he went on, inquiring kindly of his sleeping patterns, playtime routines, and other such considerations of a baby's daily life. All the while, he gazed appreciatively in response to Laurence's gurgles and squeaks.

Presently his wife came along pushing her own pram, and before saying our goodbyes, we exchanged pleasantries about our respective infants. I watched as he and his wife walked off happy and content in each other's company. This stranger at the shops paid more attention to my tiny baby in those handful of minutes than his own father had done since the time he had been born. This kindly man had inadvertently held up a mirror to my life, that mirror becoming a shard of glass that carved out in me a hole the size of a cave into which the black dog of depression crept, claiming its new territory.

As the man and his wife disappeared down the concourse, I slowly put my head in my hands and began to cry and cry and cry for the pitiful circumstances that my son and I had inherited. I did not sign up to be a single mother, I did not sign up to have the wheels set in motion for the dirty business of divorce courts and bailiffs and the fresh realization with every form of divorce proceedings filled out that my marriage certificate was not worth the paper it was written on.

But I would not be beaten. I would struggle through it and not let the darkness take away what I had left: the wonder and pleasure of raising my little boy. Laurence became my focus. I was not about to "live-down" to what others might expect but would pour the energy I had into my relationship with my son.

So I bring this sorry chapter to a close. The scene: my thirty-two-year-old self sitting in the sweltering heat on an upturned crate outside a locked self-storage unit, breastfeeding my four-month-old baby, while my father goes to foot the bill that Greg had neglected to pay. Above my head, the hands of angels held back the Mythic Ten-Ton Truck whose handbrake had finally failed.

15

LIKE MOTHER, LIKE SON

Thou art, my child, a soul received in trust
To keep and guard, from every taint of sin.
Be my resolve to plant no vices in
Thy virgin mind—Nor teach but what is just.
As ope's the blossom on the Hawthorne Bough
When May's sweet zephyrs waft the meadows o'er,
May thy young mind expand and may it store
The choicest gifts a tarnished race can know.
Then when the sunny days of youth have passed
And Winter skies shall frown on man's estate,
Thy special page within the Book of Fate
A record clean shall show—from First to Last![1]

Today as I lift the lid on the box of keepsakes from my own child's infancy and turn them in my hands, the unbridled optimism echoed in my grandfather's nineteenth-century sentiments and the wonder of those first few weeks of motherhood come rushing in to meet me. It is strange that I should feel so, for then there was nothing in my outward circumstances capable of producing the kind of buoyancy that was to pull me through—heart, home, and bank balance having been withdrawn from under me.

With the help of my parents, I managed to scrape together sufficient funds to secure the rent of a small apartment, dark-bricked and airless, into which I moved my few possessions the week before Christmas. From the hearty exclamations of the estate agent with clipboard in hand who showed me through, I was given to understand that in no way was the securing of the property a misfortune for it was the last on his list at a time of short supply.

Having pushed the last piece of furniture into place and placing the last can on the shelf in the pantry, I returned to the nursery where my infant son slept under a small, revolving canopy of musical stars. As I watched, the music and mobile wound down to its inevitable end, stopping just short of its resolution. To me it seemed to mirror the winding down of my own circumstances, the sense of reduction that is inevitable to new motherhood, and single motherhood at that: twenty-four hours worth of time, talent, and energy funneled into the formation of a brand-new being.

A life of maternal service suited me well. It was simply a variation on a long-lived theme. Monastic life had, oddly enough, prepared me for motherhood in the best possible way—helping me to go out from myself in the moment and therefore miss nothing of the little life that was unfolding before me.

Laurence lay motionless beneath his bunny rug on which a large herd of sheep, unconstrained by the laws of physics, leapt across a pale blue sky. Once again I was struck by the perfect symmetry of his features, and by association I found myself back in high school in a "mothercraft" lesson, sponging water over the vinyl brow of my plastic progeny. "Mind you don't get bathwater in baby's eyes!" cautioned Mrs. Bloomfield as great droplets slid into the winking bright-blue orbs that stared up at me. My hand shook as I rubbed away, hard enough to remove my charge's retinas before the critical gaze of the instructor. I was sixteen years old and rather resented being called to give an account of my parenting skills—my hour had not yet come. I was to live another sixteen years before rising to the challenge. I remember receiving a mothercraft certificate giving me a score of 72 percent and a rating of Average, thus was I damned with faint praise in the pursuit of parenting.

I looked down at my sleeping infant. My baby was still and quiet, too quiet. I suddenly feared the worst and woke him on an anxious whim. His pale marble features flamed crimson as startled limbs sprang to life. Laurence filled his lungs and let out a cry as I picked him up, wishing that I had let sleeping babies lie.

Laurence loved music, and with Christmas fast approaching, my mother and I decided to take him to what was to be his first and last carols concert. It was a lovely rural setting, and with the lowing of cattle across the fields and a dozen or so "little angels" running barefoot with wings askew, it was impossible to foresee the distress that was about to erupt. No sooner had the emcee introduced the choir and band than the yuletide revelers broke into spontaneous applause, sending my baby into paroxysms of sensory pain. Laurence began to cry at the top of his lungs and louder still as the brass band began to play.

I looked around and noticed that none of the other babies present gave any indication that they were uncomfortable with the volume; in fact, at that very moment, a lady I knew whose baby had been born the same week as mine came up to chat while her infant daughter never stopped smiling and turning with obvious delight at the din. "Laurence must be tired!" she yelled consolingly. "No, not at all," I hollered back. "He slept like a top, couldn't raise him!" "Oh," she mouthed, disappearing into the crowd. I on the other hand grabbed my mother and headed away quite some distance from the bandstand. Crossing the road we found a quiet seat where poor Laurence began to regain his composure. Once he settled, we headed home to a "silent night." Laurence looked both relieved and exhausted as I lay him down in the cot in his quiet room, pulling the door to behind me.

From the very beginning, Laurence defied much of what I had read of child development. His trajectory proved far more puzzling than the routine entries in the annals of baby behavior. I had noticed it first while still in the maternity ward: Laurence sleeping when all the other babies were awake, or Laurence giving a startled cry every time I ripped the Velcro fastening of his diaper bag.

I admit that my Asperger eye for detail allowed me on many occasions to suspend feelings of wonder or pleasure in favor of the pure observation of my subject. Thus I came to view my son's milestones with a certain scientific relish, noting where his development converged with or departed from what I had read.

I would sing Laurence little ditties, which I made up on the spot, and he, with intense concentration, would turn from his changing mat toward the wall (so as not to be distracted or embarrassed) and start to *eh* his way through, repeating what I had sung, note for note—no small feat for a four-month-old baby. He was giving several repeat performances one afternoon when my mother walked in to hear him. "He'll be singing arias by the time he's one!" she said in complete astonishment; but the precocious speed at which my child's brain was developing left me uneasy, and at the age of thirteen months, he began to lose not only his songs but also his words.

Laurence loved a trip to the seaside, and with Grandpa a willing chauffeur, I packed the diaper bag and dressed Laurence in a rather twee sailor suit and matching hat that someone had given me and which I kept for such outings. Completing this nauseatingly nautical ensemble, I buckled a little pair of blue shoes on his feet, saying, "Guess where we're going Laurence—to the beach. Say 'beach'?" "Beach!" he repeated, and again, "beach!" This was his first word and one that set a sense of expectation stirring behind his bright blue eyes. "Ma-ma" came soon after. Combined with "milk," as I took to naming the contents of the fridge, it was his favorite and oft-repeated request.

These simple words were to me talismans against the fears that brewed at the back of my mind, and fears not without foundation. I recalled the occasion when Laurence at nine weeks failed to react to the slam of the bedroom door, blown violently shut by a sudden squall of wind. I took up my concerns with the clinic nurse who, seeing his lack of expected response, wondered if he were deaf, and the doctors who, noticing Laurence's lack of eye contact, consulted among themselves using the term "blind." But here was my son at thirteen months, vocal and active, giving the lie to their predictions.

A few weeks later, Grandpa in his kindness offered to drive us to Sandgate, and Laurence's favorite playground. I picked up Laurence, who wobbled toward me on unsteady legs. "Hey Laurence, we're going to the . . . beach!" But Laurence did not say "beach," or "Ma-ma" or "milk." That day Laurence lapsed into silence, becoming withdrawn, and that day I was scared.

My parents had moved to within a few suburbs of where I was currently renting, and having purchased a house which came with a self-contained "granny flat," they offered to provide us with a place where I could feel more supported in looking after Laurence and yet retain my independence. I gratefully accepted and moved in the moment my lease expired. Mum "visited" us most mornings around breakfast time. Laurence would be sitting in his high chair as I fed him his cereal. All would be well until Mum entered the room. "Hello, my darling boy!" she would say in greeting. Laurence would suddenly start to cry, arching his back, sometimes to the point at which he was unreachable. My mother and I quickly came to the conclusion that Laurence was terrified by changes to his routine; anything untoward was capable of tipping him over the edge. Mum still came, but she approached him by degrees: first, sitting silently just by the door; then slowly moving over to the sofa; and finally edging toward him and taking the small spoon, helping him finish his breakfast. In this way, Laurence and my mother played their own version of Grandma's Steps, culminating in blessed calm.

Laurence's life was filled with paradox. At home, things were to be "just so." Out and about, variety seemed the spice of life. Looking through the local paper one day, I came across an advertisement for a baby show. Maternal instinct, parental pride, and a healthy dollop of ego all contended in my decision to enter him in the competition. It was winter, and I dressed him in baby-blue corduroys, a matching fleece, and white skivvy. I brushed his blond curls and the blunt fringe that framed his perfect features. Laurence looked the animated version of the vinyl doll I had cared for in mothercraft all those years ago.

Arriving at the hall, I could hardly believe how many mothers had turned up. I took my place in the long line and waited to register my baby in the "under twos." The hall was filled with crying and tears and stamping of feet—and these were the mothers! One could almost smell the seriousness of their intent. I was sorry to see one woman storm out of the hall with her child in tow; fairy-outfitted, the little girl strewed falling stars and gold glitter in her wake.

Turning around, I found myself in a lineup, the official ready to judge "The Cutest Smile." "Come on, Laurence," I encouraged, "give the nice lady a smile." The corner of his mouth began to twitch, and after some effort it set in a style most enigmatic. Against all odds and to my complete surprise, the judge suddenly slapped a blue ribbon on his coat and handed me a small, shining trophy. Tears welled up in my eyes. I alone knew the cost of Laurence's effort to make contact and was so moved by an award so generously given. However, Laurence's smile had become the bittersweet exception to the rule, and I could not ignore the fact that other people's children did not need to be coached or coerced into self-expression. A pattern was forming. I made an appointment and took Laurence down to the local community center where I sat in the waiting area with a shopping list of developmental deviations born of long observation.

Concerns about Laurence

1. Lack of and lost speech
2. Little eye contact
3. Sensitivity to certain sounds
4. Extreme emotions
5. Distress on change in routine
6. High anxiety
7. Limited facial expression
8. Socially withdrawn
9. Does not initiate hugs or cuddles

Taken in isolation, such behaviors might be put down to an "off day," but together they started to build up a picture that could not be explained away. On being called, I took the list and saw a psychologist who was completing her internship through the center. By anecdote and explanation I worked through the list, ticking off each item as I went. I did not want to miss anything for I wanted to be sure that I presented the young healthcare worker with enough information for her to put a name to his perplexing behavior.

I suddenly asked her if my son had autism, for I had, at least, a vague knowledge of the sort of children whom I had seen in documentaries, rocking and "shut in" in corners, unable to make contact with the world without. "Oh no!" she assured me, "Laurence hasn't lined up *anything*; he doesn't go around on tippy-toes, or flap his hands," but I was not convinced. There seemed at least a tenuous connection between aspects of autism and my son's behaviors at their most marked.

In the meantime, Laurence wandered the room until he spotted a toybox in the cupboard. Rummaging around, he pulled out a shiny red train that he ran up and down the psychologist's desk awhile before losing interest. Turning, Laurence suddenly stumbled on the carpet, flinging his arms toward my leg before regaining his balance. "See, he's come to give you a cuddle," she said by way of explanation for the last item on my list. I left the community health center that morning with my observations unacknowledged.

Laurence had barely blown the candles out on his second birthday cake when it occurred to me that I had a wish or two of my own. The time was right for us to find a house, to put down roots. I searched online real-estate sites within an ever-expanding radius and with an ever-contracting budget until I came across a property that I thought would suit us nicely. The property viewed and signed for and the deal sealed, I hired a mover and a pair of burly employees, making the two-and-a-half-hour journey by car, following behind as the moving truck lurched and swayed on its way up the range.

We pulled up outside a wooden worker's cottage in the regional city of Toowoomba, a hub of urban country living that gave way to the West with its cattle stations and great expanse punctuated every six hours' drive or so by a township of the "blink and you'll miss it" variety. Within our cottage, polished wooden floors reflected ceilings whose height more than made up for the rooms' modest size. With furniture in place and boxes stacked by the door, I laid down some cushions and a bunny rug before putting Laurence, exhausted by the excitement, down for a nap.

The warm afternoon sun slanted dull, yellow beams through a bedroom window, and apart from the odd passing car, all was silent. I slipped off my shoes and felt the cool polished floor under my feet. I cannot say for certain whether I crept about the house for fear of waking my child, or timidity toward the timber dwelling with whom I had just become acquainted. In my mind, places seemed to hold as much personality as people.

I moved from one room to the next, my eye, as ever, drawn to detail. One ceiling was painted "hospital green," and from it hung a long cord which dangled a pretty art deco light fixture like an upturned pudding bowl poised over the dining-room table. Through the bathroom door, the colorful swirl of a lead-glass window caught my attention, its sweeping purple and yellow palette reminiscent of something old and familiar. I looked around another door and spotted a curiosity in the corner that had somehow escaped me on first inspection. Partway up the wall, a dark-brown curtain had been strung across the gap, and behind it, a single hook stood out from the wall, ready to receive some long-departed farmer's "Sunday Best." I was amazed that this improvised wardrobe had lasted so long, like a museum display that had never been dismantled.

I reached out and rubbed the coarse curtain between my fingers, and pulling it toward me, I watched the fabric fall, habit-like, to my feet. Within an instant, the association transported me back to the quiet recess of my cell. I was once again a novice, newly clothed, ready for a day's duties, awaiting the peel of the Angelus bell. "Ma-ma!" The scene vanished as a cry like that of a drawstring doll drew me back to the here and now. Laurence was stirring in the other room. Straightening the curtain, I left the room, pulling the door behind me.

Laurence, at two and a half, had begun to find his voice again. Slowly at first, then more frequently, he started to string small, sweet syllables together. "Ma-ma, I chilly," he called, shuffling from his bedroom one cold winter's morning. I wrapped around him his little blue dressing gown on which fire trucks, helicopters, and other emergency vehicles sped toward an undisclosed location.

In the kitchen, Laurence would follow me around as I cleared the breakfast things away, stuttering requests about riding his bike or going to the shop, all the while his gaze firmly fixed on the floor. I pulled the coffee table away from the couch and placed his little red bike, ready to race. Having put on his tracksuit and strapped on his sandals, I watched him run for the starting line and spend the next half hour pedaling round and round the coffee table, training wheels taking the bends.

Life with Laurence unfolded over the months, and I continued to take note of the little habits and preferences that he displayed in certain settings. After dinner, I would bring out a large bucket of wooden and plastic trains and pieces of track for us to play with. Initially I helped Laurence set up large, looping tracks and establish within them a thriving village of schools, farms, and a police station whose solitary blue constable became an avatar to my son's exacting desires. We took turns, changing the signal from "red" to "green," and all the while Laurence watched to make sure my train waited its turn before continuing on its journey. To move off a moment before the signal had changed would have Laurence reaching for his little blue lawmaker, who would admonish my train with threats of incarceration.

Night after night, Laurence applied precise "rules of play" and became anxious if I deviated, such as by suggesting that we let the village schoolchildren go home early, or have a sheep jump the fence and stray onto the track. My toddler continued to rule a bonsai society, where everything had to be "just so." It was not long before Laurence solved the problem of his less-than-precise mother by building his own small, circular track and insisting that I do the same. So it was that we spent our evenings playing beside, but never with, each other, he with his trains, and me with mine, and never the two should meet. In these matters and more, I found myself adjusting to him, appreciating his uniqueness, and above all, allowing my son to be himself. For my part, my Asperger traits, of which I was not consciously aware, became the very key with which I helped unlock his potential.

Well aware of Laurence's preference for and benefit from routine, I sought to run my house with a nod in the direction of monastic order. Mealtimes, play, books, and bedtime, all found their proper place in our domestic day. In and out of our home, Laurence was a great companion—he suited me. Sometimes we would sit in the lounge room, he on the floor with his blocks and I, feet up on the sofa with a book in companionable silence.

Walking to and from the shops, I would point out little things that I thought would interest him: a cat curled up in the sun, an industrious garden gnome, a fragrant red rose that we would stop and smell along the way. Laurence eagerly responded to these and other sights. Unfortunately, his powers of observation had the unhappy knack of focusing a little too keenly on details that would be better ignored.

I remember a particular incident in the supermarket. I stood by a display of products, overwhelmed by a wall of Bolognese sauces. My hand hovered in the air, ready to choose one of the infinite varieties, when I felt a tug at my sleeve. I suddenly heard Laurence exclaim in a booming voice, "Look, Ma-ma, that lady is fat!" I looked up and indeed, a lady almost as wide as the aisle stood not two feet from us. Of course she heard, and what did I do? I turned my cart round and raced like the coward I was to the far end of the aisle, not stopping until we were around the corner and out of sight. I struck while the iron and my cheeks were hot. Lowering myself down to him, I slowly said, "Laurence, you must never, *ever* comment on how big people are." "But she was fat!" Laurence chimed in. "I know she was." I sighed at his cast-iron logic. "You can *think* it," I said, gently tapping his forehead, "but *never* say it with your mouth"—slowly shaking my head and putting two fingers to his lips—"because that would hurt her feelings." Laurence gave a little nod of recognition, the lesson learned.

Laurence loved the shops in any season, although come Christmas, he would crane his neck to see where Santa was and having once located him, would huddle on the other side of me, apparently embarrassed by the drama of it all. No amount of cajoling on my part or pointing out the happy line of children waiting to tell Santa what they wanted for Christmas could dissuade him from rushing by. The sight of a big white snowman walking toward us, guided by Santa's pretty helper giving out candy canes from her basket, was also to no avail, as Laurence pulled me to the other side of the concourse. Amusement rides, too, held their terrors. Despite seeing gleeful children enjoying their two-minute ride in a little shiny car and beeping imaginary traffic out of their way, Laurence would have no part in it. My son may have been unusual, but at least he was cheap!

Laurence was always keen to help, and on the way home he would whine until I let him pull the shopping bag on wheels that I took on such outings. I pivoted the bag and he pulled it happily behind him, like a dray horse pulling a cart. An elderly couple passed us on the footpath, but not before scowling at me and mumbling something about "putting my poor child to work." I couldn't please everybody, but I no longer felt I had to. I remembered the stories about my grandfather working as a child "half-timer" "down the pit" in the Lancashire coal mines, and I thought how I might have some fun with Laurence when we got home.

Ruminating on thoughts of the Industrial North, I postulated a "Monty Python theory" that ran something like this:

First Man: "Our family were so poor, that father had to make a play fort out of old tea chests from down mill house."

Second Man: "Play fort! You were doing well to have play fort. We only had seesaw, and we twelve had to sit six on each end."

Third Man: "Seesaw?—Luxury! We were so poor, that we had to make do wi' brick and plank a wood, *and* were grateful!"

Satisfied by the result, I put the groceries away and turned theory into practice. Under the side of the house, I found a long plank of wood and a sturdy brick on which to pivot the plank in Laurence's favor. Thus Laurence and I spent a happy afternoon, he standing on one end and I the other, rising, falling, and laughing beneath the canopy of the carport.

Sponging the soil of an afternoon's garden play into the bathtub, I wrapped a soft towel about my son's shoulders. Pulling the plug, I instinctively began to sweep water over the hole, to spare him and myself the sound. At day's end, Laurence bathed and ready for bed, I tucked the warm flannelette sheets around him and pulled out from the little low bookshelf Laurence's *Mother Goose Nursery Rhymes*, on the cover of which a circlet of fantastic characters held hands and danced merrily.

One would consider the telling of nursery rhymes a pleasant enough pastime, but in Laurence's case, it was an undertaking fraught with danger. I remember the fateful evening I began to sing "Humpty Dumpty" with gusto. No sooner had the unfortunate egg met its sticky end than Laurence's face, firstly shocked, crumpled into unpacifiable distress. I lifted him onto my lap and rubbed his back. "Don't cry Laurence, it's only a rhyme!" but Laurence would have none of it, dissolving once more into tears. The following morning, I sat my sleepy, spent toddler at his little table and brought in the breakfast. "Here Laurence, we're having scrambled e—." I bit my lip. "We're having omelet for breakfast!" said I cheerily, placing the steaming plate before him. "Well saved," I muttered beneath my breath, tying the bow of his bib.

Laurence's heightened emotions were nothing new to me. When he was a baby, it worried me that on being read a story, he would thrill with excitement, his arms and legs extended and quivering like those of a marionette until the last page was finished. Now, with Laurence at two, I noted the curious ways in which his emotions were expanding. That evening, not to be put off by the previous night's performance, I chose a selection of rhymes, censoring those I deemed too violent, carefully picking my way through a minefield of children's verse. "Rock-a-Bye Baby," *flick*, "Old Mother Hubbard," *flick*, "There was an Old Woman," *flick*. Ah, here's one!

> Georgie Porgie pudding and pie,
> Kissed the girls and made them cry,
> When the boys came out to play,
> Georgie Porgie ran away.

Laurence sat up, knitting his brow with righteous anger. "He's a *bad boy*, that was *naughty!*" he said with as much wrath as he could muster. Laurence held the most extreme moral convictions of any two-year-old I had ever come across. I quickly turned the page in an attempt to distract him out of his tempestuous mood.

Hey! Diddle, Diddle,
The cat and the fiddle,
The cow jumped over the moon;
The little dog laughed to see such fun,
And the dish ran away with the spoon.

The last line particularly pleased him, and he made me repeat the verse over and over with no sign of its impact waning, his pleasure renewed each time with the punch line. My son's emotions swung like a weather vane, and in his current jolly state, I conducted a little experiment, singing,

Five little ducks went out one day,
Over the hills and far away,
Mother duck said, "Quack, quack, quack, quack,"
But only four little ducks came back.

My son's expression became increasingly anxious with the disappearance of one duckling after the next. As the last chick headed over the horizon, the situation was suddenly saved.

Mother duck said, "Quack, quack, quack, quack"
And all her five little ducks came back.

Laurence's relief was palpable. What was simply a children's counting aid, in my child's mind took on the sinister proportions of a murder mystery. It became clear to me that I could slip in a less-than-sunny song, now and then, as long as it resolved in the character's favor. So did I tend to my young son's fragile feelings, grafting them to the sturdier stock of a mother who knew that to bend was not to break.

After putting out the light, I went into the kitchen and made a pot of tea, pondering my social circles which, granted, had always been small, but were now nonexistent. I was well aware that both Laurence and I needed more stimulation than a brick, a plank, and the pleasure of each other's company could provide, and I set to remedying the situation, starting with my son. Searching around the house, I found the local directory in the bottom of the broom cupboard. In its pages I stumbled across "The Childcare Center that Time Forgot." Of course this was not its real name, but having arranged a tour of the center, I came away with the impression of a level of care not seen since circa 1973.

I bundled Laurence up in his winter woollies and a beanie and started up the road, passing a girls' boarding school where he ran the gauntlet of young ladies patting his cheeks with exclamations of his cuteness both now and in the years to come! We arrived at the door of the childcare center, and on our entering, the warmth of the central heating was only surpassed by the warmth of the greeting we received from the administrator. Dorothy came around from her desk and, bending down to Laurence, spoke soothing words to ease his obvious anxiety. Looking up, she smiled at me and, seeing something of the son's nerves mirrored in the mother, addressed me, too, in a most kindly manner. "Are you new to this area?" she inquired. "Yes," I said, "I've not long moved here from Brisbane with my son. I've bought a little house just down the road." "Well now, you can drop in to see your little man any time you like," she said, taking my hand. "And if you're ever feeling lonely, come and have a cup of tea."

Beyond the balm of the administrator's heartfelt hospitality, I caught the unmistakable aroma of home-cooked meals being prepared in a kitchen on the premises. Today would be beef and vegetables. I didn't think such a setup still existed. At that moment another lady of middling years introduced herself as Miss Jane, the head of Cockatoo Corner, the group to which Laurence had been allocated. Miss Jane, like the rest of the childcare workers at the center, struck the delicate kind of balance between sweetness and authority usually reserved for a *Romper Room* hostess. So it was that Laurence spent a half-day here and there, being gently ushered from one activity to the next in the company of children his age.

On my collecting him in the afternoon, we'd walk the few minutes to our house, but despite my enthusiastic inquiries, Laurence did not want to talk about his day, preferring that bits and pieces of his activities come out at odd times of his choosing. Fortunately, Miss Jane arranged regular reports, popping them into his little backpack for my perusal.

Date: Tuesday 20th July
Name: Laurence
Setting: Playground
Laurence watched Tim and Liam playing for about five minutes, he then went over and roared like the boys were doing. The three of them then continued to follow each other around playing a "tiger game" for about twenty minutes.
Goal: For Laurence to initiate play.

Follow up: Encourage Laurence to start role-play and get others to join in.

Date: Tuesday 24th August
Name: Laurence
Setting: Olympics
Laurence ran around and around the track till he fell over dizzy. He then got up and started chasing Bryan around the track laughing.
Goal: For Laurence to build gross motor skills.
Follow up: Small fort inside

Date: 28th September
Name: Laurence
Setting: Water trough
Laurence loved playing with water. He splashed around and laughed at peers who were next to him.
Goal: For Laurence to talk to peers.
Follow up: Water play, with ducks, etc.

That evening after dinner I facilitated the quantum leap between "water play" and "washing the dishes," adding sufficient dishwashing liquid to make it fun. Laurence stood on a little stool, earnestly rubbing the plates before dipping them in the rinse water while I placed the plates in the rack to dry.

Mum's goal: Laurence to do all the washing up after every meal!

Despite his social immaturity, in some ways Laurence overshot childhood altogether with spikes of sophistication in speech and behavior. Arriving home in the afternoons, he would drop his bag, saying, "What's for dinner?" like a workman home from the fields. At other times, seeing his milk and biscuits arranged neatly on his little table, he would throw up his hands and exclaim, "Oh Ma-ma, how lovely!" It was lovely indeed watching him grow, looking at the world through his eyes. Laurence's tendency toward literal interpretation was something to witness. While in the kitchen one night, with half an ear to the news, I heard him blurt out, "I want to go to the party, I want to go to the party!" "What party Laurence?" I asked. "The political party!"

Life with Laurence, for the most part, was very sweet, and seeing the benefits of connecting him with others, I sought out a mother's "play group" in the hope that it might encourage a friendship or two, for my own sake as much as his, for as consoling as Laurence's companionship was, it could not compensate for the need I felt for adult company. I walked the mile to the hall as Laurence rode his little red bike by my side. Stepping inside, Laurence spotted a selection of toys scattered about the hall and ran to a bright orange dump truck which he pushed up and down the floor before him, but far from a group of toddlers who sat in varying degrees of proximity.

I was happy to see Laurence settled, and looking about the room I saw groups of mothers standing in well-defined circles and chatting animatedly, stopping now and then to sip their coffee, the flow of conversation never ebbing, for they were never lost for words. I went to the table to make my own drink and felt, as I did on this and similar occasions, a growing sense of unease, ever out of my depth where much "small talk" was required. I stood a little distance from one circle of mothers observing the ebb and flow of their conversation and yet found myself barred from a social dynamic that I could not easily decipher.

At that point another mother, just arrived, entered that circle, becoming immediately plugged into whatever it was they were talking about. "Surely it can't be that difficult!" I thought and, sipping my coffee, stepped into a space in the nearest group. "Darren skidded into the flower bed like a complete fool! Then he made it up to me by inviting Patty and Sam around for a barbecue before the Reds thrashed the Blues at the Finals." "Terry and I saw that round at Marg's." "Marg Lewis?" piped up the new lady. "I know Marg from junior athletics, her eldest, Bobby, trains on Saturday afternoons with my boy up at Rangeville." As I stood there it became immediately clear to me that these women were, even on acquaintance, bound by camaraderie based on subjects and interests in which I could have no part.

In a rare gap of silence I submitted my own contribution to the mix. "My son's just started at the childcare center up the road. They make the most fantastic meals on the premises." The women smiled benignly at my social offering, making a few inquiries about who I was, where I lived, and how I'd come to move there before turning back to their previous line of interest, reinforcing bonds based on what they felt and who they knew.

I don't believe for a minute that there was an ounce of malice in these mothers toward me. The distance between them and me was far more fundamental—I did not speak their language. Mine was the mother tongue of one whose delight was detail, who warmed herself by a glowing fire of facts.

What had started out as fierce independence soon began to wear thin. Isolated and alone, I eventually chose to move back to Brisbane where I had family and the support I was sadly lacking.

16

MY BRILLIANT CAREER

Having sold my cottage, I thumbed the pages of a local real-estate booklet until I spotted a small town house described as "neat and tidy." I smiled at the description, wondering if such qualities might not rub off on me on purchase. My own life could hardly have been painted in such well-defined terms; but surely what it lacked in precision was more than made up for in experience.

As Laurence lay in the back room having his afternoon nap, I sat on the couch watching the instant-coffee granules spin in my freshly stirred cup. Into my quiet thoughts the wise words with which my prioress had once counseled me came into focus: "Open your heart to Jesus and His transforming love, and remember, it is *this world* into which He came and not another." "This world," I repeated. Suddenly the thought struck me that all the roads I had walked, all the choices I had made, all the lessons I had learned—even those that came by bitter experience—could be used in the service of others. Any lingering vestiges of depression dispersed like a morning mist.

"I'm going to be a counselor!" I told my mother as I pushed through the front door and made my way down the corridor to her office with Laurence in tow riding his red push-bike. I had a newfound sense of purpose in the opportunity to help others for whom life had not been kind. Consulting my mother's computer, I found that I could study by correspondence. This suited Laurence well, and as he had just turned three, I would yet be able to keep a keen eye on his development and note his needs.

I set myself to study in earnest and loved to hear the sound of the courier's van as it swung around the corner of my road every few months, delivering thick parcels of books brimming with psychological theory and practice. For most people on the autism spectrum, study comes not only naturally but as a way of life—we sift for particles of choice information the way early prospectors would pan for gold. Freud, Rogers, Maslow, Erikson, therapeutic process, therapeutic goals—I vacuumed them all up during the hours that I allocated to the course.

As I worked my way through my psychological studies, occasionally I came across concepts that seemed to contradict my way of being in the world: "Habituation—learning not to respond to unnecessary repetitive stimuli, the simplest form of learning. Gradually ceasing to respond to it, and eventually ignoring it, rather than having your attention diverted, by such as common household noise." I shut the book. I never habituated to household noises. I never habituated to anything!—ticking clocks, the hum of the fluorescent light in my kitchen, the bird outside my window that woke me up every morning without fail. I opened the book again, and its next line rose like a reproach: "Obviously, responding to a stimulus of no importance wastes time and energy; even animals that have very primitive nervous systems are capable of habituation." "Great," I said to the four walls of my sitting room, "apparently I don't even have the adaptation skills of a mollusk!" I started to wonder if these small but general ways in which my brain failed to shut out unnecessary bits of information (like the rest of humanity) could explain why I felt so tired so often.

I turned to classical conditioning and took comfort in the knowledge that ever since a balloon burst in my face as a young child, I have never ceased to grimace and flinch in the anticipation of further explosions when confronted by colorful, overinflated rubber. I felt a certain sympathy for Pavlov's poor dogs. We had both been conditioned to respond to bells: at that precise moment I pricked up my ears and pulled out my purse as I heard the tinkling tune of the ice cream van as it rounded the corner, ready to dispense its sweet treats.

Over the six years in which I conducted my studies, I took regular trips across town to fulfill practical components of my work and took heart that many of my fellow budding counselors, certainly in the early days, didn't seem any less nervous and excited than me. As I got to know their stories, I realized that there was a wealth of lived experience in each one—nurses, mothers, foster-care workers, financiers, psychologists, and farmers, to name a few! Each one came to walk with others on their journeys, to counsel them in their troubles, and to encourage them in their successes.

As a counselor, I discovered that I myself would become the best tool in my trade, drawing not only on tried-and-true therapeutic techniques but also on empathy, self-awareness, and, given the serious nature of the counseling process, the lighter side that puts the humor in the human condition. These were the hallmarks of my own personality that pulled me through my own challenges and helped me intuit the needs of others. I loved it all, absorbed it all, and as I sat down to conduct yet another role-play, polishing up my skills, I became aware that I had set my feet on a sure and steady path into my future.

My mother, father, and I continued to watch over Laurence, who had recently celebrated his fourth birthday. He consistently exhibited the kind of behavior that made us wonder about his social development. What had galvanized me into further consultation was that even though he continued to attend a few days of childcare for the sake of his socialization, a childcare worker explained how one day he threw a box of puzzle pieces, and even though the other children "snitched on him," he offered no assistance and wandered around the group watching the other children pick up the pieces he had thrown.

On another occasion, I heard that Laurence followed another child and put a toy on top of his head. Laurence's little playmate repeatedly said, "Don't," without any impact on Laurence's behavior until the child pushed him away, saying, "I'm not your friend." Laurence was not in the least bit distressed by this, nor did he attempt to change the child's feelings—he simply walked away. On the other hand, Laurence seemed to enjoy the group storytime, insisting on sitting so close to the teacher's feet that he had to crane his neck to see the pictures. In an attempt to see the book, he would wriggle back until he practically squashed the child sitting behind him.

As far as his attempts to communicate with the children were concerned, his shoves were many and his words were few. "Use your words, not your hands!" I would say. Each and every time I walked him down the path to the local daycare center, he would repeat his anxious litany "Are you going to pick me up, will you pick me up?" until we reached the center's gate. At home our games continued as they ever had, as Laurence dictated when I was to play beside him, or the rare occasions when he welcomed me into his personal space. The way I handled him seemed to calm him, and his happiness at home gave him the courage to face the confusion of the world without. He had no friends to speak of, but after his having shown interest in the goldfish at the local pet shop, we brought one back. Laurence loved to watch Mr. Bubbles do circuits of his bowl, but being as goldfish and little boys are, he lost interest by the time Mr. Bubbles III swam to the great fishbowl in the sky.

I continued to raise Laurence by myself, taking on the roles of mother, father, playmate, and disciplinarian, which proved quite a challenge over the years. Yet a house of two is still a home, and I made mine a safe place where my son could be himself—valued, accepted, and reassured, because under all circumstances, the positive attitude of a parent is worth a thousand nightlights.

It was 2005, and at this time, recognition of the traits of Asperger's syndrome in very young children was still filtering through to healthcare workers. I had brought Laurence to the attention of doctors and other specialists first at the age of nine weeks, then at ten months, thirteen months, and three years. As someone who was always with him, it was easy enough for me to note his differences: little eye contact, sensitivity to certain sounds, extreme emotions, distress on change in routine, high anxiety, limited facial expression, social withdrawal, not initiating hugs or cuddles. But within a clinical setting, perhaps the differences were not obvious enough to cause his presentation to be without question. This was understandable, but I kept watch over his traits until at last there could be no doubt as to what it all meant.

Armed with a list of Laurence's social faux pas and my own observations, my son and I set off, perhaps fittingly, for the Mater Misericordiae Hospital where I was born. The pediatrician kindly ushered us into his rooms and read thoughtfully through the copious notes and observations I had compiled over four years. "Yes, Laurence has Asperger's syndrome," he said, as easily as one might observe that a child has blue eyes or curly hair. This "matter-of-factness" momentarily soothed my nerves. I had never heard of Asperger's syndrome. I sat there slightly numb, and as our doctor passed me the diagnostic report, I saw that Asperger's had already been allocated a place by "the powers that be" in the lexicon of mental disorders, verifying Laurence as having a formal diagnosis of Asperger's disorder. I stared at the word "disorder" and the small cross in the box that marked my son for life. I put on a bold front at first and felt genuine relief that Laurence's pediatrician had recognized his profile. I was pleased to be able to "put a name" to Laurence's way of being in the world. After all, I had dutifully attended various parenting programs that were offered to address Laurence's "difference," but they did not address it anywhere near as satisfactorily as I could in our day-to-day life. However, in the light of Laurence's diagnosis, the Mater Hospital greatly helped in assessments in speech and occupational therapy.

We made our way back to the train station and, finding a seat as the doors slid to, settled in for the long ride home; Laurence spent the time we sped past the stations gazing serenely out the window while I stared into the middle distance, everything in my brain awash with the enormity of the diagnosis that had just been delivered.

That evening, scraping up every ounce of energy, I prepared Laurence's dinner: two meatballs for eyes, a carrot nose, spaghetti hair, and some long green beans whose smile was set in the style of the incurable optimist. As I set the plate before him, my own expression crumpled with the blow I had received to my maternal hopes. I turned away and blotted my tears on a tea towel. I simply did not have the luxury to go to pieces in front of my son. Somehow I pulled myself together before sitting down beside him and chatting cheerily about the things we had spotted out the window as we journeyed home.

Later, as I pulled the covers up and kissed my sleeping son's angelic cheek, I recalled the fantasies of "my children" I conjured up in the monastery in the hours of evening prayer. Only a day ago I was "living the dream"; tonight it had morphed into a nightmare!

"Disorder"—oh the power of that one little devastating word! Closing the door and making my way to my bedroom, I felt my legs turn to lead and buckle beneath me as I curled up on my bed.

If only I knew then what I know now! How much unnecessary suffering I would have avoided and how much I would have been spared! In describing what Asperger's syndrome is, it is imperative to begin by declaring what it isn't. Contrary to much of what is written on the subject, Asperger's syndrome, a type of high functioning autism, is not a neurological disorder. It is a difference in the brain's wiring, observed in the way an individual processes information. It is "peculiar" only insofar as the individual's way of perceiving the world differs from that of the majority.

Unlike the terrible affliction of mental illness, where the mind's perception of reality breaks down—taking the sufferer to where, if given a choice, they would rather not go—the lifelong and stable condition of the Asperger mind with its preference for detail takes the bearer to a place to which they happily return again and again. It perfectly fulfills the function for which it was made—a function which is shared by countless numbers of successful people.

How ironic. That night I lay in bed sobbing my heart out for what I would soon discover *myself* to be!—a person on the autism spectrum, uniquely gifted, and needed in the society in which I lived.

A few months later as I sat with an impressive stack of textbooks and papers on Asperger's syndrome on my coffee table, I heard a familiar knock at my door. My mother had arrived to spend time with Laurence and to see how I was getting on in the wake of his diagnosis. "I'm beginning to see him in a new light," I said, placing the tea and biscuits at a safe distance from my precious new books. "In many ways, I'm looking after Laurence just as I've always done: following his routine, involving him in daily chores, having our little conversations, and respecting his need for silence and space."

Almost as an afterthought, I said, "It's very much in the way you dealt with me." Mum and I stared at each other in complete silence, and as I sat there, all the pieces of my memory began to fall into place: me—wandering aimlessly with an empty mind in childhood; me—desperate to fit in with my teenage peers; me—instinctively enclosing myself in monastic solitude to connect with all; me—warming myself by a glowing fire of facts; me—weeping for not seeing the red flags; me—finding my joy in motherhood comes at great cost.

Our stares turned into smiles, and our smiles into uncontainable laughter. "Of course!" I cried. "How obvious can it be?" I declared, pacing around the room, a fever of energy with this new revelation. "That's *you!*" my mother said, picking up the book and backhanding the front cover. "Here, give that to me!" I said, reaching for the book that my mother held to herself with an air of mock ownership. We sat together, huddled over its contents, reliving almost four decades of my personal history while Laurence sat at our feet on the rug, running his favorite red engine around the floor.

The pennies started to drop, and I came to recognize that autism was nothing new to my family—the thread went way back: my father, for example, so hardworking and so humble, who moved his family from England to make a life in Australia. His comfort was, and still is, to make his lunch at 12:00 p.m. precisely. And there was his father, the quietest of quiet men, whose solitary sporting career saw him win gold medal after gold medal in boxing and become the uncontested king of the Gloucester County 100-yard sprint in the 1920s. Goodness knows how many of my forebears sat on the spectrum, but what I did know was that there was much to be proud of in my heritage and much pride to take in my own son.

During the last year of my study, I met many adults and children on the spectrum, immersed myself in their stories, felt their sorrows, and rejoiced in their triumphs. I attended conferences populated with angelic-faced children, and adults, often in black, behind whose impassive expressions, I knew, teemed quicksilver creativity and academic pursuits of the highest order. "These are my kind of people," I murmured to myself as I took in this incredible sight—I belonged to them and they belonged to me. To me it was obvious that there was only one thing left to do: to stand with them in solidarity.

I remember the morning I took a seat in the consulting room of a young French Canadian psychologist with "old school" enthusiasm for her subject. I wondered for one wild moment, "What if she says I haven't got Asperger's syndrome?" This thought to me, ironically, constituted my greatest fear: "If not that—what?" My mother and I had already furnished her with a comprehensive report on my development and social interaction as a young child and teenager, a time in which autistic symptoms are at their most marked. It was all there: my social and general anxiety; my sensory issues with food and certain sounds; my propensity for literal interpretation; my difficulty reading facial expressions and challenges with organizational skills; the vulnerability that led to my victimization; my inability to "play the game" when it came to romantic relationships; and, in my favor, my love of nature and writing; my excellent long-term memory; my incredible attention to detail; my love and sympathy for human nature and my ability to think outside the box—no—for me there was no box, with the possible exception of Pandora's. What would happen when the lid was lifted?

After long discussion and the consideration of my personal history, the psychologist said, "It is quite clear to me that you are indeed on the autism spectrum. Congratulations, Rachael, you have Asperger's syndrome!" she beamed. This was not said in a spirit of sarcasm; she knew that I had taken my rightful place in a long line of the great and the good.

It was in this way, the history of my social abilities and deficits assessed, that I could put a name to my way of being in the world, a label, as it were, on the suitcase of my circumstances. I found it difficult at first to enter into the "celebratory nature" of my new diagnosis. It suddenly raised many questions in my mind: What does this mean for me? Was I somehow a different person than the person who walked into this office only an hour before, and if I am different, who am I now?

It doesn't surprise me that such "existential musings" came to mind. Asperger's syndrome was not an add-on, something additional to who I was; rather, it ran through every aspect of my being like letters through rock candy. Reflecting on the course of my life, I clearly saw that there was, indeed, much to celebrate in the gift of what made me, me. The confirmation was cathartic, and I was surprised to find myself dissolving into tears and crying with relief as I received the key that unlocked the mystery of my son and of my early life.

The day of my graduation dawned on a cloudless sky and a whirl of activity. By midmorning, minding my makeup, I slipped on a black cocktail dress with golden leaves scattered through the fabric. "This should suit my academic robes," I laughed over my shoulder as my sister did up the last few buttons and stood back to see the finished effect. "Rachael, you look fantastic!" she said, handing me my purse before we joined Mother, Father, and Laurence who waited in the kitchen, ready to depart.

The auditorium was a buzz of anticipation. "Here're our seats," I said. "I'll just go and get dressed." As I received my gown and sash and gently placed the mortarboard on the crown of my head, a great stillness came over me. "No, it was not all in vain," I told my myself. Everything I had suffered, everything I had learned, every humiliation shouldered, every personal battle won had brought me to this point, this place, where it could all be used in the service of my brothers and sisters on the spectrum and those who loved and cared for them.

The ceremony began, and as I listened to the various speeches, my heart quickened with the realization that the vocation to which I felt called was not a "one-off" chance; it had come to me by many paths, over many years—one layer building on the next and the next into that state we call "experience" and its un-identical twin, "aptitude," without which, even with the best will in the world, we can achieve nothing.

My name was suddenly called, and as I walked down the long aisle, I saw my childhood self wandering by the main road, in the valley at Marburg, in the train stations of my youth, and in the solitude of those high rugged hills of The Lakes. I saw myself drawn into the cool, marble interior of St. Stephen's Cathedral and stepping over the threshold of the monastery's enclosure door into the silent world within. Now as I walked onto the stage, I reached out and received my diploma, full of confidence for my future and my brilliant career.

So it is that I began my work as a registered psychotherapist, specializing in Asperger's syndrome and high functioning autism. Drawing on my life and clinical experience, I continue to improve the quality of life of children and adults on the autism spectrum and also the lives of their carers and partners through my private practice, speaking engagements, and women's retreats.

There have been many presentations and seminars in which I have been professionally involved over the years. A few of the highlights of these years have been a world inaugural seminar in Brisbane celebrating and exploring the unique profile of females on the autism spectrum; a presentation, at the invitation of Professor Tony Attwood, made at a seminar for Asperger women at Griffith University's Autism Centre of Excellence; the great privilege and joy of returning to Mater Misericordiae Hospital where I was born to present at the "Grand Rounds" on behalf of the Autism and Related Disorders Clinic; and my own signature Asperger Sisterhood retreats—taking a contemplative approach to personal growth on the autism spectrum.

By the time I received my diagnosis at the age of thirty-seven, I had worked through many or even most of the challenges that I had faced as an individual on the autism spectrum. I sought a diagnosis not because I *had to*, but because I *wanted to*. In doing so, I found that I could build a powerful sense of rapport with my clients, born of a shared perspective.

For their carers and partners who were not on the spectrum, I set myself to address their needs by being an intermediary, bridging the gap with "an insider's point of view."

As a mental health professional, I found it no small thing to declare myself a person on the autism spectrum, to risk the inevitable prejudice flowing from a poor understanding of the wide range of capabilities of individuals within the spectrum fueled by media-inspired fears. Fortunately, those who have sought and seek out my services for themselves, their family, and friends see my Asperger's as the perfect springboard for growth and inspiration.

17

BUYER BEWARE

One of my wishes had been fulfilled, that of beginning my career as a counselor, but a second still niggled at the back of my mind, particularly at times when no help was at hand. Despite a failed first attempt, I was resolved to find myself a suitable husband, and with a greater understanding of myself and this clear vision before me, I pursued my dream with the greatest determination.

Do not think that in my enthusiasm to find myself a mate I threw due caution to the wind. I had lived a lifetime of solitude to varying degrees and had learned to find in my own company a level of contentment sufficient to the day. This hard-won contentment, as poor a substitute to passion as it may seem, became a compass point in that it furnished me with the one criterion that really mattered—that a connection with any man should enhance and in no way diminish the quality of my present single state.

I considered the avenues by which I might achieve my goal. With a young child, random "nights on the town" were neither convenient nor desirable. Having few social connections with people my own age, introductions were also out of the question. By this time, Internet dating had come out of the shadows and into the mainstream. Of all the mediums there were to meet, it seemed to me that this would play to my strengths. What I lacked in social fluidity was more than made up by my Asperger instinct, logic, and powers of observation. It was these qualities I would harness, putting them to the service of my present pursuit.

Cyber-dating slowed down the speed of social interaction, removing the myriad of social expressions that might distract me from taking in the overall picture of a person. Neither did I wish to be hoodwinked by high emotion, the sweet enemy of common sense, for I knew that I had to safeguard my heart. If only I looked and listened, each man I met would, by word and deed, surely reveal the quality of his character.

I lost no time in putting my plan into action. That night I brought out my cosmetic case and applying the makeup with all my skill, created an effect that faithfully reproduced a look in a magazine that pleased me. Holding my mobile phone at arm's length, I smiled and clicked the button, producing a picture ready to upload to the wonderful world of Internet dating.

The stories that I had read or heard about online dating were fairy tales at best and horror stories at worst, and I had no desire to be dashed against the rocks of either extreme, preferring to steer my way into the safe haven of a situation settled and sustainable. I had learned the lessons of the past and I now applied them diligently to my present circumstances. Having sat and written a few words describing my character and interests and having penned a reasonable proposal of qualities that I would seek in a life partner, I uploaded my profile onto a well-established site and waited for the fish to bite.

In no time at all, several suitors presented themselves in my inbox. Sitting there in my dressing gown and slippers, sipping coffee and considering the merits of each, I thought what ridiculous fun it all was, getting to know someone in perfect anonymity until a time of one's choosing. The world of cyber-dating put me in mind of a masquerade ball, where a vast array of men and women went about in the half-light, paying each other compliments and presenting themselves at their best through words alone; but come the stroke of midnight, what face would be revealed?

Some men didn't have the decency to wait that long, ripping off their own masks, declaring their identities, announcing their personal phone numbers and less than chivalrous intentions, and desiring that I do the same. Others were so slow in their romantic deliberations that the "getting to know you" process went from days to weeks and showed every sign of stretching into months. Through all the interactions that presented themselves for my consideration, I kept in mind that no matter how well you think you have come to know a person "on paper," it is seldom any comparison to what you find in the flesh. So settle back and I shall tell you the tale of three men whom I had the misfortune to meet.

THE "LONG ISLAND ICE TEA" LOSER

I came across this fellow's profile late one Sunday evening. The tone of his e-mails suggested a character bright and personable, easygoing and yet with plenty of "get up and go" for he had recently started his own security business. This intrigued me as he was young and good-looking in a "boy band" kind of way. After I'd spoken to him on the phone, the image seemed intact, his conversation mirroring what his profile professed; moreover, after a week's solid e-mailing, he showed a keenness to meet.

That Saturday evening I spritzed my wrist with my favorite perfume and, running a hand over my little black dress, picked up my clutch purse and headed out the door. I had chosen to meet my date in the foyer of a city hotel. I sat beneath a sparkling chandelier on a soft leather sofa. Around me, happy couples sipped their drinks by the light of little low candles. Pulling out my compact, I checked my makeup, blending a spot of eye shadow with trembling fingers as I awaited his arrival.

Turning my head, I saw him stride through the sliding glass doors in all his 3-D splendor. I rose from my seat smiling and lifted a hand in recognition. "Hi, Rachael!" he said, smiling his "boy band" smile, kissing my cheek. He led me back through the foyer door to his waiting vehicle. Opening the passenger door, I got in and fumbled for the seat belt and it was a good thing I did, for the moment he turned the key in the ignition and dropped the handbrake, he sped off like a lunatic, weaving through traffic and taking the turns like a Formula One driver, all the way to a far-off dockside restaurant he had been keen to show me.

Coming to a sudden stop that caused me to do a convincing impression of a crash-test dummy, he turned to me smiling, oblivious of the impact his behavior was having on me. "They do the most fantastic Turkish food here!" he said brightly, climbing out of his car and leaving me to follow in his wake. Pulling my fingernails out of the seat upholstery and releasing the tension on the belt, I got out and crossed the parking lot. I saw that he was talking to the security staff that manned the entrance. When I'd finally caught up with him, he took my hand and led me beneath a ceiling of beautifully embroidered Middle Eastern canopies, leaving one with the impression of passing beneath a stately desert tent.

Looking down, I saw that he had led me straight up to the bar, where I presumed he was about to order pre-dinner drinks, wine perhaps and a beer for himself. Without any consultation, he ordered two "Long Island Ice Teas." I had never heard of this drink, and he spent the waiting moments telling me it was the "best cocktail in the world!" with its potency owing to equal shots of vodka, tequila, white rum, gin, and Cointreau. Presently the barman placed two drinks the size of flower vases before us. I was horrified. My date wasted no time downing half his glass before leading the way to our table. What he did not bank on was the extraordinary capacity I have to hold my liquor; and among those with Asperger's I am not alone in this. Whereas a single glass of wine can leave me feeling seedy and spent, spirits are as water to my constitution, causing neither inebriation in the moment nor any ill effect the following day. With my faculties as clear as a bell, I was given over to the unenviable entertainment of watching my date become increasingly tipsy as the night drew on.

The food we had ordered finally arrived, and ever the optimist, I thought that maybe even at this late stage the date could be salvaged by the satisfaction of a lovely meal. I placed a selection of exotically spiced meats on my plate and asked my date more about his work and his hopes for his new business. "Yes, I've got quite a lot of connections around the city and some good opportunities to grow my business further down the coast," he offered enthusiastically; then all of a sudden a look of preoccupation came over him. With no explanation he rose from the table saying, "I'll just be a couple of minutes." With that he went off, leaving me to sip my "tea" before returning twenty minutes later with yet another round. It was a Long Island Ice Tea evening, and after determining that my date had eaten enough food and had had enough time to sober up, I called it a night.

Leaving the restaurant, he called out to his security colleagues, "We'll talk more about that business next week!" telegraphing that he had doubled up our date with a night of networking. My date managed to get me home in one piece, but to my surprise, seemed genuinely mystified as to why I no longer wanted the pleasure of his company!

THE GREAT PRETENDER

A few weeks later, another potential mate sent me a message. Having made a pact with myself to take each individual on his own merits, I opened his message and perused his profile. This man seemed the polar opposite of my last date. A newly qualified solicitor, he had posted a picture taken the day of his admittance to the Bar. He stood tall in a fine dark suit, his dark, wavy hair swept back in the style of W. B. Yeats. With a sandstone cloister receding behind him, he seemed every inch the quintessential "tall dark stranger," his profile confirming he stood six feet in height.

A week or so had passed when he rang and told me that he would be in Brisbane for business and would I like to meet at the Queensland Art Gallery for Sunday lunch? I eagerly accepted his invitation and spent the following week agonizing over what I would wear to what would surely be my dream date! I watched the weather; it would be warm that day. I settled on a midnight-blue wrap dress, putting my hair back with a tortoiseshell comb.

Crossing the square and within sight of the gallery, I saw in the distance a small solitary figure standing next to the entrance. My gut instinct told me to turn on my heel and walk away, but my head argued that I could not be sure. By the time I could confirm my suspicions it was, alas, too late! There I stood, eye to eye with a man who had shrunk from six feet tall to five-foot three-inches. His dark brown hair, once luxuriant, had receded overnight to a few thin wisps on a balding crown. For the sake of his personality, a charitable woman might forgive a "white lie" or two about appearance. Unfortunately, my date was missing that *certain something* that most women look for in a mate—a pulse. "Woe is me," I muttered to myself. So bitter was my disappointment, so shocked was I by his audacity, that I hardly felt the clammy soft hand that grasped mine in greeting. By the time I recovered my senses, I found myself in a coffee shop, sitting opposite the world's most boring man.

"And might I say how lovely you look," said he, running his eyes over my body in a most unhealthy manner. His compliment, intended to flatter, left me feeling slightly ill. Having finished my coffee, I suggested that we might go and view the art in the main gallery; for who knew what opportunities there might be to slip down a side corridor, thus losing him forever? There was no such chance, however, for he followed hot on my heels, his words a constant stream about his work and the tardy ways of his colleagues, whom he admitted, disliked him intensely. "Why?" I asked, amazed that a man on a first date would paint himself in such a self-deprecating way. "Well, that *would* be telling tales out of school!" he snorted, wringing his hands in the manner of a Charles Dickens character. It turned out he had snitched on his colleagues for the petty crime of relieving the stationery cupboard of a few pens and paper clips. This man's legal turn of mind never slept.

We stood before a painting titled *Monday Morning 1912* that showed two women in voluminous Victorian dresses bent over tubs on washday. "You can almost feel the steam coming off the clothing," I said, lost for a moment in the realism of the scene. "What do you think?" I casually asked, but answer was there none. His mouth opened and closed while his eyes scanned the painting time and time again as if he were considering the legal ramifications of his answer. It seemed his studies had sucked the spontaneity right out of his soul, poor man.

The afternoon dragged on, and after a light lunch, I wished him a safe journey home but made no reference to any further contact. Getting up to leave, he insisted on walking me to the train station. I finally reached the sanctuary of the barrier, and as I turned to say good-bye, he suddenly saw his chance, lunging at me and locking me in an embrace that I managed to struggle out of before giving him a short, sharp shove to remember me by.

A NARCISSIST ONLY SEES HIMSELF

Of all my memories of my "gentleman callers," it is the memory of this man which disturbs me the most. On paper, this man was a picture of success. He ran a busy dental practice and had supplied a photo with a smile fit for a promotional brochure. His life and interests too seemed to have a glow about them, as if everything he had ever done had been done with a Midas touch.

I remember speaking with him on the phone one evening before dinner. He asked me what I was cooking, and I told him I was making a beef curry. "What spices are you using?" he asked. "Curry powder," I replied. That was his in. He began to regale me with the details of a roll of beef that he had encrusted with a dozen exotic spices, reeling off types of which I had no knowledge. For a moment, I wondered whether I was on the receiving end of a petty game of one-upmanship for it was not the first time that he had followed a story of mine with a greater tale. As I was thinking on this, he suddenly suggested that he would make this dish for me and soon, dispelling in an instant my critical line of thought with a pleasing offer.

I had told him a story or two about the places I'd been and the things I'd done, which in his mind branded me "special," but whether this applied to me in my own right or merely as complementary to what I had already perceived as his own particular sense of "uniqueness," I could not tell. So it was that against my better judgment, I agreed to go out on a date, drawn as I was like a moth to a flame's brightness.

I arrived at yet another hotel lobby and took a seat near a busy walkway by the reception desk where I might have a clear view of those who came and went. When I had been left to wait longer than comfort would allow, it was then he made his appearance. He arrived in a suit of expensive cut, making me wonder whether I had dressed sufficiently for the occasion. He looked me up and down in a most perfunctory manner, saying, "Well, you look like your photo." So stark was his delivery that I thought he was making a joke—but the punch line never came.

My date had done no small amount of research into where we would eat, and having hailed a taxi, he spent the journey telling me "how exclusive" the restaurant was and how it was recognized as "the best fine dining in Brisbane." I could make neither head nor tail of the extraordinary amount of energy that he had put into his choice because for all the show, it did not seem to have been done with a view to impressing his date.

It was a Friday night and the restaurant was filled to capacity. A waiter in a long, starched-linen apron ushered us to our reserved table. Once we were seated, my date drew his finger down the wine list until it stopped at the most expensive bottle he could find. He sat back smugly, twiddling his thumbs, and told me of various occasions on which he had partaken of this particular vintage. When the wine arrived, his mood changed again, for as the wine waiter poured this lavish drop, my date watched him as though he were under examination. Raising the glass to the level of his eyes, he made much of its appraisal for the edification of the whole restaurant. I was not entitled to order my own meal, for my date would have me bow to his superior knowledge of the matching of wine and meat.

Furthermore, not content to patiently wait for our food or engage me in conversation, he called the waiter at his busiest hour, instructing him to bring small plates with which we might sample a selection of regional olive oils. So it was that my date spent the next half hour airing his knowledge on "unfiltered virgins" and the aromatic delights of "green bananas" and "grass on the nose." "Do you find this moderately bitter?" he asked, pushing yet another plate before me and nodding at its contents. "I find it very bitter indeed," I replied, dunking a crust of bread into the pale oil.

Turning away, I saw a lovely young couple at the table beside me. By their degree of animation, I figured they had not known each other very long. The young lady wrinkled her nose as she laughed and drew her hand through her long blond hair to the delight of her dining companion. I smiled at the sight. "You should try it sometime," my date said suddenly. "Pardon?" I replied, for I did not know how long he had been watching me. "It's called 'flirting,'" he said, taking a long quaff of his wine. Despite his total lack of interest in anyone other than himself, he thought it fitting that I should "perform" for my supper.

The restaurant emptied until we were the last table left. His vintage drop had done me no good, and at a few minutes to midnight I was beginning to fade. "I'm rather tired," I said, having tried my best to humor the man so as not to spoil his dinner. "Perhaps we could move on?" Raising his gaze from the dregs of his wine, he gave me a look of utter contempt for even suggesting it. When he had finished, he walked me to the nearest taxi rank and on the way confessed that he had never found what he would consider the "perfect woman," a disclosure at which I took no offense; his ideals were a hell of his own making. On arriving home I suddenly felt the urge to jump in the shower and scrub the contamination clean off my skin, for I had come face-to-face with a narcissist of the first water.

The next morning I deleted my profile from the dating site, deciding that I no longer had the stomach for it. In any case, I had no intention of continuing to try to pry open a door that would not yield. I prayed and put the matter in God's hands, vowing I would not lift a finger to change my circumstances now or in the future. I had been "singed" if not "burned" too many times, and if God wanted things to change, it would be His doing, not mine. Of course in saying this, I ran the risk of being left to my own devices and the good Lord would be well within his rights to do so . . . although He may have had other ideas.

Christmas was fast approaching, and I threw myself into the preparations as never before. One afternoon I stood in line outside the post office, waiting to purchase some stamps. I looked down and there, shining at my feet, lay a small silver cupid. I picked it up and took it as a sign that maybe all was not lost.

18

THE PRAWNS OF FATE

All families have their Christmas traditions, and mine is no exception. For many years it had been customary for each member to bring a particular dish to contribute to the feast. I had elected to bring fresh-cooked shrimp (known as prawns in Australia), and so I set off for the shops on the morning of that fateful Christmas Eve.

The shopping center with its noise, crowds, and fluorescent lights in which, at the best of times, I was loath to linger had reached a fever pitch. I grabbed a shopping basket and made a beeline for the deli, determined to purchase my shrimp and beat a retreat. As I stood there waiting, number in hand, I heard a lady with a thick Eastern European accent deliberating with the counter staff over how best to preserve her shrimp. Her accent was catnip to my ears, conjuring up all manner of romantic images from Gypsies to women in jeweled headscarves over-seeing collective farms in Mother Russia.

Fascinated by her accent, I felt motivated enough to engage her in a little small talk. Our exchange revolved around the high quality of Queensland shrimp and the inferiority of imports. In this lady's mind, I had now established a bond and was worthy of being taken into her confidence. Ascertaining my marital status, she began to embark on a spot of matchmaking. "You're a nice girl," she said, cocking her head to one side as if to appraise me the better, and leaning in she got down to business. "My son the scientist, he's just back from New York and *single*, you know!" This she said with a squeeze of my arm and a know-ing smile. Far from being thrown by her audacity, I deduced that here was a woman who grasped at life's opportunities with both hands and so found myself suddenly caught up in my own carpe diem moment.

Just as I was musing on how many "roubles dowry" I would need to cough up for such an arrangement and what form her "son the scientist" would take, she suddenly asked for my phone number and I, throwing caution to the wind, handed her my business card as my deli number came up. A minute later, taking my parcel of shrimp, I turned to find my companion had disappeared, and I wondered for a brief moment if it had all been a dream—but just how real that dream was I was soon to discover.

No sooner had I put my shopping in the trunk of the car and shut the lid than my phone rang and I found myself speaking with the lady's "son the scientist." "Hello Rachael? This is Rudi. I believe you met my mother this morning." His tone was warm and his speech measured, and it was a Sydney accent—that much I could tell. "Yes," I said, "She was pretty persuasive!" At this he laughed; he knew her well. We exchanged a few pleasantries, and if first impressions count for anything, I was interested enough to accept his invitation for coffee the following week. Ending the call, I sat back in the driver's seat, impressed by this man's bold move. "Rudi," I said, repeating it again and, starting the car, headed for home.

The night of my coffee date with Rudi arrived, and as I stood before the dresser, holding up now one pair of earrings, now another, I felt calm, almost relaxed, previous "disaster dates" having inoculated me against investing more emotion than was merited. I chose a pleasing pair of earrings whose amber and clear stones glittered like dewdrops beneath filigree hearts. I laughed back at my reflection, pondering how it was that I had finally succumbed to that most unenviable of all social exchanges—the blind date.

I arrived at a local café a little before the designated hour, and looking around, I saw a few patrons in an otherwise empty place. An old man just finishing his coffee walked by me, but not before complimenting me on my "lovely earrings," which put me in a rather happy frame of mind. "This will be a good night," I thought, "and if not, what will I have lost other than an hour of two of my time?" Consoling myself with sentiments such as these, I found a seat at a table for two and waited for my date to appear.

The time ticked over, and I suddenly saw the silhouette of a young man standing by the door, the young man clad in black, his Eastern European pallor and dark hair highly exotic to my reckoning. Rudi looked so young that I hesitated (had I made a mistake in accepting a date with so little detail?), but the moment he opened his mouth, I discovered a turn of mind so mature that my initial reservations simply melted away. Rudi was a computer scientist, and as true as nature intended, he set out to impress me, explaining the intricacies of his craft. Even though most of what he said was outside of my knowledge, his interest in me was displayed in every word.

Rudi, some years younger than me, had an air of Old World charm and a reserve unusual for his age. We spoke of our families and of things we liked to do and all the while I caught myself leaning in and drawing an absentminded hand through my hair. Having been diagnosed with Asperger's syndrome myself, and well-versed in the recognition of its traits, I had discreetly diagnosed my date before the first coffee cup was drained. Even at this early stage, I recognized in Rudi the makings of a soul mate, and on we went to dinner down the road.

We turned into a curry house and found a cozy alcove, but whether we ate hot, mild, or medium I cannot recall, riveted as I was by the sheer scope of my date's interests. A solitary sportsman, he had spent years perfecting his skills in fencing; on weekends he welded and worked in wood; and in the course of his career, he had read and written millions of lines of code. We spent the rest of the evening sampling curries and exchanging experiences via the alluring language of facts.

At evening's end, he took my hand across the table and told me how beautiful I looked and with his touch imparted a hint of passion. When he brought me home, I presented him with my cheek to kiss, and like a true gentleman, he accepted it and sought no more before he went his way. I was slow to settle that night, and as I walked about I pictured Rudi donning his fencing mask and flexing his foil before his lunge toward and parry with his opponent; I saw Rudi writing code in millions of combinations; I saw him behind his welding mask, forcing metal to meld. Yes, "the man behind the mask"—that is how I pictured him, making him more mysterious now than before.

Rudi began to date me with determination, phoning just ahead of his frequent appearances at my door. By day, he dressed like a university student of the "Che Guevara" variety. At South Bank one Sunday after-noon, I remember him having me choose a selection of small bright badges to adorn his hat. I saw his acceptance of my "Little Miss" badge as the sign of a *real* man; indeed, he had a forthrightness unmatched by any man I had met and would telegraph by word, at least, his intentions at any given time. As we were driving home from a day out, I recall him suddenly suggesting, "Let's go back to my place and have a cuddle on my couch." I found Rudi's lack of preamble most refreshing, precluding my having to second-guess any mixed motives. Rudi's ways were a far cry from those of the kind of suitors who shattered my nerves by their lack of predictability, and his love of routine gave me a sense of reassu-rance.

Homebodies at heart, I loved to cook and Rudi loved to eat. Not wishing to introduce Laurence to Rudi prematurely, I would leave Laurence at my parents' place when I visited Rudi. So it was that I would arrive at his bachelor pad with a bag of ingredients and a recipe at the ready. If love entails making allowances, I learned my lessons in love early. I recall preparing a lasagna layered with béchamel sauce, parmesan, and cheddar cheese, only to discover to my dismay that Rudi was, as I later termed it, "lactose intolerant." I understood that gastric upsets were not uncommon in those on the autism spectrum, however, the "Angel of Digestive Ailments" had passed over me, and from that day forward, what I lacked in cheese I made up for in chilies.

Stomach upsets aside, Rudi was a fine communicator, and in our late-night conversations, I found in him the companionship I craved. It was not so much "the thrill of the chase" as "the thrill of the facts." The desire for detail that Rudi and I indulged in was no dry, soulless dis-semination. For us, there was no dichotomy between facts and feelings. I recall the nights we saw out on my sofa, bathed in the soft glow of candles that burned down to the wick as I lay back on one side and he the other, each of us pouring out as much passion as our subjects would allow.

"You know," I said (taking a sip of the margarita Rudi had mixed), "I was walking past the chemist's the other day, and as I did, the automatic doors slid open, and can you believe I felt guilty because they had expended their energy—alas!—in vain?" I laughed, wiping back a tear. "Don't worry," said Rudi, "fractals will make you feel better." Firing up his laptop, he generated mathematical flowers whose infinite patterns were posies of his affection. Taking my hand, he drew me to him, and as I lay my head on his breast, we talked of atomic clocks and of the elasticity of time, of numbers so large as to render them meaningless, and all the while he held me close as time, like Dalí's melting clocks, pooled in the present moment. Cupid's arrow had finally reached its mark, and so, at the age of forty and for the first time in my life—I fell in love.

I cannot recall the moment I graduated from "date" to "girlfriend," and now that I come to think of it, that moment never arrived, but what I clearly remember was the "marriage talk" that came within a month of our meeting. This was no proposal of impetuous love—love did not come into it. This was an interview, and as I sat slightly taken aback by his line of inquiry, Rudi proceeded to interrogate me on my expectations of Holy Matrimony.

1. What does marriage mean to you?
2. Do you believe it's for life?
3. How do you see your role in a marriage?
4. What are your expectations?

He glared at me as I gathered my thoughts, and through the cross-fire I answered his questions as truthfully and as dispassionately as possible. Poor Rudi, I knew enough of his story to see the raw wounds of his past bleeding into every present word. He seemed reassured by what I'd said, and standing up, he shook off the words like so much dust before departing to do the sorts of things he always did when he was about: upgrading my computer, my cellphone, and indeed, my life!

Rudi was a man of action and showed his care in a thousand practical ways. I remember watching him eyeing my son's small bookcase and muttering about how it might be improved. A short car ride later, he returned with a trunk full of pinewood and proceeded to saw and hammer his way through a whole weekend, not stopping until he had finished making a brand-new bookcase with his own hands. Common was the sight of Rudi soldering toy trains that had had one too many derailments, and the hand that could solder was a hand that could sew. As I placed another pile of repair work at his side, I found myself asking God what I had done to deserve a man of so many talents?

The one area of my life in which I had no desire for Rudi to trespass was that of my beloved filing methods. As he lingered over a pile of my paperwork, I grew faint at the thought of him disturbing a system that was a mystery even to myself. All my weaknesses converged at the point of self-organization, but even here, Rudi stepped in to intervene and act as my personal secretary.

I walked into the garage one afternoon to be confronted by the sight and sound of Rudi feeding my "papers" into a paper shredder. I stood there, frozen a moment, then cried out, "Stop! Stop! What are you doing?" I ripped the pages out of his hand, while Rudi stared at me, flummoxed by the strength of my reaction. "These have no value," he declared, holding up the other half of what I had torn from his grip. "See, look at the dates." As I inspected the age and content of old newsletters and ancient notifications, I saw that he had discarded the debris and filed the forms I wished to keep. "Thank you, darling," I said, breathing a sigh of relief. "You still shouldn't have touched them though!" I frowned, and then kissed him as old paper rained down like celebratory streamers.

Laurence, who on the cusp of his adolescence continued to grow and mature according to his own personality and pace, began to bloom under the influence of a father figure. Rudi's interests, which spanned the generations, were more than able to accommodate those of my young son. Having more electronic pastimes than I thought were possible, he introduced Laurence to "old school" computer games. Together they would enter the pixelated paradise of Monkey Island. Here was a land whose universal laws, by virtue of primitive programming, were bound by a staccato of movement and slowness of exchange that had no match in the real world. The hero, Guybrush Threepwood, a young man with a thirst for adventure and a hunger to make his fortune, made his silent way around the island. Seeking out pirates and others, his only means of communication lay in clicking on one of a handful of possible responses.

Walking by, I saw that a pirate had insulted our hero: "Ha ha ha!!! That's the stupidest name I've ever heard!!" Guybrush had four choices:

1. I don't know . . . I kind of like "Guybrush."
2. Well, what's *your* name?
3. Yeah, it is pretty dumb, isn't it?

4. I'm insulted. Good-bye.

Laurence mulled over his choice and finally clicked on the first and most fitting response. I suddenly remembered Marjorie Bristlehead and thought how much easier my life would have been had I grown up in the mythical world of Monkey Island.

Not content to live out their adventures on-screen, Rudi and Laurence would visit a laser tag venue. Fitted out with computerized vests and "phasers," they would spend happy afternoons running around a darkened maze, a team of two holding their own against a horde of opponents. Rudi could offer Laurence the "rough and tumble" which I could not, and by the end of a day's activity, Laurence, having expended his energies, was content to sit next to Rudi and talk about his interests and soak up his company.

By the time I met Rudi, I was very familiar with the dynamics of how other people on the autism spectrum relate, there being as many expressions as there are individuals; indeed, I had counseled many couples, making of myself a bridge between their Aspergic and neurotypical perspectives. Given that I'm a woman on the autism spectrum, you might conclude that the idea of having a partner who isn't given to much emoting or to showing plenty of physical affection would be appealing to me. But like most women, I sought love, affirmation, companionship and a feeling of togetherness borne of romance.

An unsolicited embrace or a warm, direct smile came to me like manna in the desert over the months, and if a little goes a long way, these fleeting gestures played their part in sustaining my soul. I never doubted that Rudi loved me. His ways were the personification of "actions speaking louder than words," and yet the words were not left unuttered—had he not knelt down before a crackling fire and professed with all his heart undying love and the desire to take my hand in marriage?

After we had exchanged the critical amount of information needed to ascertain compatibility, ours was a relationship with many silences and none of them awkward. In terms of emotional feedback, the only question in my mind was "How badly do I want it and if so, am I prepared to do what it takes to get it?" As unromantic and lacking in spontaneity as it might sound, opening my mouth and asking him to smile at me, or coaching Rudi in "terms of endearment," was the perfect remedy to an otherwise extremely satisfying relationship.

Rudi showed the promise of every quality I would seek in a husband, and time would tell. He was hardworking, loyal, faithful, trustworthy, focused, honorable, and stable. Beyond this roll call of superlatives, all was open to negotiation. My fiancé may not have been the type to wear the sentiments of his heart on his sleeve, but neither did he lean all over me and drain me dry. I had met men with more social savvy than he, but on closer inspection, they often turned it to their own ends. Rudi had been burned by the manipulation of those who took advantage of his good nature, and yet the traits that made him so attractive were never washed away.

Together Rudi and I were more than the sum of our individual parts, and yet who and what he was remained to me a mystery. My fiancé was many things, but boring wasn't one of them, and in accepting his proposal, I said "Yes" to a lifetime of endless discovery.

I pushed a small crystal tiara into my hair, and drawing the tips of my fingers through the fine netting of my veil, I watched its beaded edges fall over my shoulders and follow the smooth brushed satin to my feet. My parents had departed for the chapel. I wandered their house in my wedding finery, waiting for my ride to arrive. Passing my mother's full-length mirror, I turned this way and that and found myself thinking of the departing step that I had taken over the threshold of the monastery twelve years before and of the many that had moved me toward this day. Once again I stood on the cusp of a life change and savored its enormity in the silence. Some minutes had passed when the doorbell suddenly rang, and taking up a bouquet of deep red roses and a small beaded purse, I stepped away from the mirror and into my future.

A little while ago I was interviewed over the phone by a journalist who, knowing me to have Asperger's syndrome, asked me in all seriousness, whether I felt anything on my wedding day, or whether I had gone through the ceremony "like a robot." Her inquiry was ignorant and innocent enough, but she had not been there to witness the beads of perspiration running down my forehead or the trembling hand that reached into my purse, pulling out a small notebook and pencil when I found the time to write my speech on my way to the church (no pressure!). Having waved to every motorist I saw, I chose the red lights at which to pour out the sentiments of my soul.

My darling husband Rudi, from the first time we met over coffee, it didn't seem to be a case of "getting to know you," but a feeling of "being known." There was no "gap," no gulf to cross, but a sense of Homecoming. I never cease to thank God for bringing you into my life and admire your humor, your companionship and support. Rudi, I am happy to become your wife today. Never before have I felt such confidence as I do today, as I place my life and my son's life into your safekeeping, with great surety that together, we will continue to grow in love and grace throughout our years. You are the love of my life and "the best wine till last"—To Rudi!

My driver slid into the parking area where my father was waiting for me; taking my father's arm, I walked with him through the slanting golden light of a fine April afternoon, and looking up past the steeple to the sky, I whispered, "Something blue" before stepping into the dark, stone chapel where Rudi awaited me. On the altar and about glowed bowls of liquid light as stained glass petals shone softly, scattered from a rose window. Then I saw him, black suited and so serious! Putting my bouquet aside, I warmed his cold hand in mine. We were both a little nervous, but each prayer, each blessing brought us back to the present moment ". . . through Christ Our Lord, Amen."

Laurence, with an angelic face like a page of Venus, bore our rings on a silver shell, and as Rudi and I exchanged vows, we kissed and lit a single flame to symbolize that we were no longer two, but one. Following the final blessing, we made a solemn bow, turned, and strode down the aisle to Handel and to the heavy wooden doors which, alas, were locked! "All right everybody, we're here for the night!" Rudi declared. Amid laughter, on we went to celebrate with our family and close friends, toasting, dancing, and smiling until our faces ached. Rudi and I looked knowingly at each other as a shrimp cocktail was placed before each hungry guest.

The following morning, unconstrained by the fetters of corset and zipper, I gave myself over to a buffet breakfast as Rudi and I reminisced over our Big Day and anticipated the honeymoon to come. Then came another dawn, and barely had we put away our wedding attire and swept up the silver cupid confetti which fell from the folds of my clothing (and the candied almond that somehow found its way into my shoe) when it was time to depart. Rudi and I, newlyweds, hopped into the back of a taxi which took us along an almost empty highway toward the airport.

Our destinations included Singapore, Paris, and Rome, but when we arrived in England, all roads led to Quidenham. We made our way, navigating through large industrial cities and small obscure villages, aided by the reassuring voice of Jane, our GPS tour guide. Free to go as we pleased, I pointed randomly to towns on our map, bound by a certain imperative that they, *at least*, be "on the way."

After covering many hundreds of miles, we turned off a main road and drove along country lanes lined by red-bricked walls and open fields. It was a welcome sight and one I knew well. Rounding a bend we came to a crossroads, and there on a signpost, I saw our much-anticipated destination: "Quidenham." We drove up to the monastery and deposited our luggage at the guesthouse before heading to the parlor for a warm and happy reunion. I heard the familiar peal of bells through the air calling me back to this place of prayer.

The Sister who was my companion in the novitiate welcomed us. How excited I was to see her and she, me! "Wow, Rachael, I can't believe you're here, and to think, you've come all this way to spend a few days of your honeymoon with us!" Reaching out to embrace her I replied, "Nicola, we wouldn't have it any other way!" Rudi had heard so much about the community that he was as keen as I to see the place and the Sisters who had meant so much to me. Over the four days of our stay, I was able to reconnect with many of the Sisters, and I was delighted by the opportunity to introduce my husband to them and to thank them for all they had been for me.

It was a particular pleasure to be reunited with Sister Ruth Burrows, who had been my prioress and who continues to be an inspiration in so many ways. As she came through the parlor door, we took up our conversation as if we had never left off, chatting long into the afternoon. Despite the passage of so many years and such different lifestyles, I was surprised at how we had kept pace, both of us, passionate as ever to open ourselves to the fullness of life in our chosen vocations.

Having thanked the Sisters for their hospitality, I took Rudi on a rediscovery of the grounds at the far end of the enclosure, taking the long track that led down to the lake. It was surreal to look out on its familiar blue and gray waters, this time in the company of my husband, but the sight of it was as charming as ever. As the sun began to dip below the horizon, Rudi and I set off back up the track. We were suddenly startled by a colorful pheasant that launched itself from a nearby field. Then as I looked up, whom should I see but the descendants of the sheep who had lined up to greet me on my arrival at the monastery so long ago. This time, they lined the fence to farewell me— I had come full circle.

As we strolled toward the car, our conversation turned to our future together. "How amazing it's been to be able to bring you to this place that has meant so much to me, and even better to know that this time, I have you by my side when I leave." "I'm happy to support you in every way," said Rudi. "You know," I said, I'd like to do more talks and have more time to think and write." "Yes," said Rudi, "it's time you wrote your book."

19

"PHYSICIAN, HEAL THYSELF"

When I was studying to become a counselor at the time of my own diagnosis, it occurred to me, in terms of the treatment of clients with autism spectrum conditions, that here as far as I was aware was an area of therapy that was as yet unpracticed in the counseling and psychotherapy fields. I was further drawn to psychotherapy for two reasons: one, my firmly held belief that autism spectrum conditions could be approached from a position of health rather than pathology; and two, the recognition that knowledge of the autism spectrum cannot be advanced exclusively by examination of its biology and behavior—it must also be advanced by the acknowledgment of its psyche, its "soul." The therapeutic question "What does it mean for the individual client to have autism in a neurotypical world?" opens up a pathway to social, emotional, and spiritual growth.

The pressing question of "meaning making" for those on the autism spectrum can be explored effectively within the context of the therapeutic relationship inherent in psychotherapeutic practice, in conjunction with therapy techniques designed for those on the autism spectrum, as a key to unlocking their potential and so enhancing personal growth.

As with any skill, we learn it as we practice it. So it is for those on the autism spectrum: to learn to relate we must have someone to relate to; and to learn to reflect on our own lives, we must have it modeled to us by another. The importance of the therapeutic relationship in helping those on the autism spectrum cannot be overemphasized.

My desire to work in the field of autism spectrum conditions came like a sense of vocation, as something precious and not to be entered into lightly, but certainly, wholeheartedly. Still, some who are not on the spectrum may say, "Physician, heal thyself."[1] How do you do it? There exists in such a question a "kernel of bias" as to the capabilities that an individual on the autism spectrum may be expected to possess in the objective treatment of others on the spectrum.

Aware as I am that the term "Asperger's syndrome" has dropped out of use in the American diagnostic classification of autism spectrum conditions, nevertheless I cling, rather doggedly I admit, to this term. Human beings are in the business of categorizing everything with which they come into contact, and I am no different in this regard. For those of us diagnosed under this title, it is a familiar term and a distinction that I feel is helpful in pinpointing where we stand on the spectrum.

Within the autism spectrum there is a broad range of capabilities. And because the spectrum *is* so broad, we with Asperger's syndrome must not lose sight of the hardships of those struggling with classic autism—for we are their voice!

Even within the portion of the autism spectrum we call "Asperger's syndrome," there is a vast range of abilities. It is *exactly* by having been in the thick of it, drawing from my experience and the work I have put into knowing myself, my strengths, and limitations, that I bring a certain discipline and objectivity to bear. In this way, I continue to hand on the skills and knowledge that have helped me not only survive but thrive as an "older sister" on the spectrum, tailoring and developing therapies to help my clients overcome challenges while accepting who they are.

Our capacity "to turn away from the everyday world,"[2] as Hans Asperger put it, is not one of shunning the social milieu; it is the expression of a mind caught up in the love of detail. People with Asperger's syndrome, are the Observers par excellence, many making of their powers of observation a lifetime's work. Many of these solitary figures, rather than being isolates, have become, for multitudes, a rallying point, and their discoveries and creativity have shaped the world in which we live—for the better.

Some historical figures for whom the Asperger template fits like a glove include Jane Austen, Emily Dickinson, Marie Curie, and Carl Jung. I'm sure that even if we consider some or all of these examples of humanity as unusual, nobody could deny the richness of their contribution to our society, our health, and our culture to this very day. Their "highly restricted, fixated interests that are abnormal in intensity or focus," as the American Psychiatric Association's fifth edition of its *Diagnostic and Statistical Manual of Mental Disorders* (DSM-V) puts it, are the very traits that enabled them to do the wonderful feats they did.

However, as inspiring as stories of "Aspie Notables" are, it troubles me that in promoting a positive awareness of the Asperger profile, undue focus has been paid almost exclusively to examples of their "brilliance" and "ingenuity." In the midst of war-torn Europe, as Hans Asperger began his observation and study of the development of children on the autism spectrum during the 1930s, his research came to the attention of the Nazis. Appealing to what he noted of his children's precocious intellectual abilities, he managed to convince the Third Reich of his children's usefulness. Thus did Hans Asperger shield his young charges within the University of Vienna. We should not value individuals with Asperger's syndrome because they are clever or useful but because they are human beings, and so require no further justification for their existence.

The perennial argument in psychology continues: Nature or nurture—which has the greater influence? Asperger's syndrome can never be viewed in isolation; indeed, it can only be viewed through the prism of environment, upbringing, temperament, life experience, and personal values. All these aspects are interrelated and revolve around the quality of one's relationships.

All of us, whether on the autism spectrum or not, are called to relate to—that is, to connect with—others, appreciating their uniqueness, letting them be who they are, and rejoicing in the differences. No, we are not all the same and thankfully do not have to be. We are, all of us, so much more than the sum of our mental processes. If that were our only definition, how impoverished our lives would be! Each one of us is called to reach out to the other from the depths of our strengths and limitations, accepting to be who we are, as we are, each step of the way.

I was pondering recently what was the "one thing," the one quality, that I brought to my practice that defined my work and made my work unique, and it came to me: empathy—a characteristic regarded by many as that most elusive of emotions in those on the autism spectrum. Whether vicariously applied through long and compassionate interaction or through personal experience, empathy is the platform on which all effective therapies are constructed, to help clients to grow, to be challenged, to be inspired, as I myself have drawn inspiration from others.

Today an emerging body of research is bringing the female expression of Asperger's syndrome into clear focus. Women and girls on the spectrum share the diagnostic traits of their male counterparts and yet diverge by their capacity to mask their social confusion, observing and mimicking their more socially able peers, drawing on their developed language skills to "get by," and finding solace and pleasure in special interests that tend to be less eccentric than those of males but no less intensely pursued. The coping mechanisms that women and girls on the spectrum employ come at a high price. The mental energy needed for social interaction, organizing oneself, and coping with the constant fear of making a social mistake can leave them emotionally exhausted and can contribute to elevated levels of anxiety as well as a fragmented self-identity, resulting in low self-esteem. Crucial to treating those on the autism spectrum is applying therapies designed to build emotional resilience—imparting a basic sense of stability from a developing sense of self.

In order to counsel and treat clients on the autism spectrum rightly, it is imperative that we understand them rightly. I remember a mother of a teenage girl asking me, quite sincerely, "How long will it take to fix her?" I questioned what she meant by that, and indeed she just wanted her daughter to be like "the other girls" at her school. No doubt this mother was motivated by a desire to spare her daughter the social confusion and anxiety that comes with the territory of autism spectrum conditions, but how do you tell a mother her daughter will "not be like the other girls—not now, not thirty years from now"?

In the general perception, people with Asperger's syndrome are categorized in terms of their inferiority to the neurotypical type, a type that is perceived routinely as more socially able and aware than its Asperger counterpart. I think it needs to be mentioned that in focusing on the social deficits inherent in autism spectrum conditions, one can get a false impression that neurotypicals have a perfect ability to relate, while people on the autism spectrum will always lag behind. This is not always so. From my own observation, many neurotypical people have very poor social skills and little empathy for others. At the same time, because of their knowledge of their weak points in social interaction, people on the spectrum can consciously work at developing their ability to relate and can reach a level of quality social interaction equal to, if not surpassing, that of their neurotypical peers.

The neurology of an individual with Asperger's syndrome is *different*, and if we *really* understand this, we will respect that difference and will no longer endeavor to use the neurotypical perspective as a yardstick for treatment and outcomes but instead will treat within the framework of a healthy "Asperger archetype." I coined this term as a way of describing more accurately and faithfully the Asperger profile as Hans Asperger understood it and as it is coming to be expressed today: as part of a natural continuum of abilities that merges with those experienced by the majority—a frame of reference that honors individuals on the spectrum.

This proper frame of reference builds on and acknowledges the strengths of the Asperger profile and plants seeds of change in the vulnerabilities inherent in that profile. If Asperger's syndrome is its own kind of normal, as I believe it is, then it begs the question "How do we identify what healthy, functioning Asperger's looks like?"

A part of the difficulty is that many, maybe most, people who are on the higher end of the spectrum never receive a formal diagnosis; indeed, they never darken the doorway of a psychology clinic simply because they have muddled their way through their childhood and teens, coming out the other side as adults with hard-won skills and have worked with their strengths until finding their place of belonging in society, as was my own experience.

These are the individuals on the spectrum who may now be considered outside the clinical range. For many clients referred for therapy, it is not their Asperger's per se that finds them in the clinical setting but comorbidities, additional disorders which may exacerbate and accentuate their expression of Asperger's, and it is these mental health issues that pull at the equilibrium that would otherwise exist and require urgent attention. Either way, once the individual has reached a certain level of social and emotional competence, they are no longer perceived as having research value.

The questions "How is it that you are as well as you are?" and "How do you maintain your equilibrium on a daily basis?" are equally as fascinating as the definition of any pathology.

A part of the difficulty in identifying the nature and attributes of a healthy Asperger archetype is that it has been only twenty years since Asperger's syndrome came to prominence in 1994 with its introduction in DSM-IV. Thanks to the research, I believe that we have practically exhausted the deficits; and when we dig down to the bedrock of the condition we call "Asperger's syndrome," we come to discover not only health, but advantage! And so I am developing a new school of psychotherapy dedicated to treating clients with autism spectrum conditions from a position of health rather than pathology, and I believe that this is the direction that future research—and certainly my own theories, therapies, and writing—will take.

Some of the qualities that I have identified as present in a healthy Asperger archetype are a developed sense of self, an ability to reflect, and a capacity to regulate emotions as seen in the ability to respond rather than react to life while still being subject to Asperger traits.

The Asperger and neurotypical perceptions of reality are not mutually exclusive. These experiences are, in fact, inextricably linked: both expressions need to be witnessed. Like day and night, or action and contemplation, the differences inherent in the Asperger and neurotypical perspectives are a binary that gives balance to the human condition.

EPILOGUE

FULL CIRCLE

Julian of Norwich, the fourteenth-century English mystic, wrote in her *Revelations of Divine Love*, "He did not say, 'You will never have a rough passage, you will never be over-strained, you will never feel uncomfortable,' but he did say, 'You will never be overcome.'"[1]

The story of my life has been, for me, a journey from isolation to communion, from fragmentation to ever-increasing wholeness. I have learned to forgive others for their misunderstandings of me and to forgive myself for the ways I did not read social situations aright, which invariably brought about errors in judgment and opportunities missed. No doubt I shall always struggle with certain aspects of my autistic nature. My expression of the condition has not disappeared but has been integrated within the totality of my personality.

I have learned to shoulder a certain degree of anxiety and have renounced the tendency to analyze myself to death. Life, as has often been said, is not a problem to be solved, but a mystery to be lived! The fragments of my experience are the raw material of the beauty, which emerges at each turn in my kaleidoscopic life, clicking and coming into place. Even the fragments that seemed to make no sense, held up to God's light, find a purpose in a pattern which He alone sees.

I have been restored to myself many times over through the twists and turns of my life and have long since dispensed with the need to pretend to be anything other than who I am, comfortable and at home in my own skin. Some years ago, I walked my son down to his school in his Spiderman outfit for Dress Differently Day—raising autism awareness. As I walked back through the school toward the parking lot, I had an overwhelming sense of gratitude to see the children dressed in their wild and wonderful outfits, and I thanked God that the knowledge and acceptance of the autism spectrum was here to stay.

Many years have passed since the day I chose to leave the monastery, catching the train that hurled me into that unknown future. It may be over a decade and a half now since I sat on my bed back home in Queensland, unpacking my suitcase, but I have never ceased to unpack and incorporate the lessons that I learned as a member of that community. The paradoxical nature of the monastery taught me this:

In losing myself in its hidden life, I found myself; in embracing silence, I found my voice; in seeking solitude, I became connected to all; in enduring anxiety, I was restored to peace and in every moment was met by God's grace.

I do not believe, as some might conclude, that I have simply "done my spade-work." I am far too weak to merit the title of one who has "pulled herself up by her own bootstraps." No, only grace could resolve what would have taken a thousand years of my own efforts to achieve. Grace has come quickly, sometimes slowly and painfully, but has always, in all circumstances, come to meet me.

The most valuable lesson that I have learned in the school of my lived experience is this: how important it is for people on the autism spectrum, and indeed all people, to have a basic awareness of their own value and goodness and self-worth, *independently* of how others perceive them, or even of how they perceive themselves. For me, this is realized through my faith in God and His faith in me.

No one would deny the challenges faced by those on the autism spectrum, but I believe that the quality of my life is richer and deeper for the unique perspective that Asperger's syndrome has graced me with, and I wouldn't swap my genetic inheritance for anything—how could I? I was wired for wonder, and autism was not the lock, but the key!

BIBLIOGRAPHY

Apollinaire, Guillaume. "1909." In *Alcools*, 182. Berkeley: University of California Press, 1974.

Asperger, Hans. "Problems of Infantile Autism." *Communication, Journal of the National Autistic Society* (1979): 49.

Asperger, Hans. "The Mentally Abnormal Child." *Viennese Clinical Weekly* 49 (1938): 1–7.

Austen, Jane. *Pride and Prejudice*, 9. London: Vintage Books, 2007.

Carroll, Lewis. "The Pool of Tears." In *Alice in Wonderland*, 23. Bath, UK: Parragon, 2003.

Daly, William Joseph. "The First Born." 1894.

Forster, E. M. *A Room with a View*, 9. London: Edward Arnold, 1924.

Hopkins, Gerard Manley. "That Nature Is a Heraclitean Fire and of the Comfort of the Resurrection." In *Poems and Prose of Gerard Manley Hopkins*, 66. London: Penguin Books, 1985.

Julian of Norwich. *Revelations of Divine Love*, translated by Clifton Wolters, 185. London: Penguin Books, 1966.

Nesbit, E. *The Railway Children*, 23. London: Puffin Books, 2010.

Peers, E. Allison. "La Noche Oscura del Alma." In *St. John of the Cross and Other Lectures and Addresses, 1920 – 1945*, 20. London: Faber & Faber, 1946.

The Penguin English Dictionary, 4th edition. s.v. "career." London: Penguin Books, 2002.

Rossetti, Christina. "Up-Hill." In *The Penguin Book of Religious Verse*, edited by R. S. Thomas, 171. Harmondsworth, UK: Penguin Books, 1963.

Royal Brunei Airlines. "Doa Safar" [Travel Prayer]. www.flyroyalbrunei.com/wp-content/uploads/downloads/2012/06/BI_IFEG_JUL12_WEB.pdf.

The Sayings of the Desert Fathers, translated by Benedicta Ward, 139. Kalamazoo, MI: Cistercian Publications, 1984.

Wordsworth, William. "Intimations of Immortality from Recollections of Early Childhood." In *The Penguin Book of Religious Verse*, edited by R. S. Thomas, 78. Harmondsworth, UK: Penguin Books, 1963.

WEBSITES

www.rlharrispsy.com

Visit my official website. Here you can learn about my clinical work as well as upcoming speaking engagements and retreats.

www.tonyattwood.com.au

Professor Tony Attwood's website is an excellent hub of information, as well as resources and related topics, for parents, professionals and people with Asperger's syndrome.

www.aspiengirl.com

I am delighted to share Tania A. Marshall's beautiful and informative pictorial books displaying Asperger's syndrome from the female perspective. Watch out for more!

www.wccm.org

The simple practice of Christian meditation has been both an anchor and compass on my journey. On this site there are many interesting resources to be found.

NOTES

INTRODUCTION

1. Hans Asperger, "The Mentally Abnormal Child," *Viennese Clinical Weekly* 49 (1938): 4.

I. THE WANDERER

1. William Wordsworth, "Intimations of Immortality from Recollections of Early Childhood," in *The Penguin Book of Religious Verse*, ed. R. S. Thomas (Harmondsworth, UK: Penguin Books, 1963), 78.

3. CURIOUSER AND CURIOUSER

1. Lewis Carroll, "The Pool of Tears," in *Alice in Wonderland* (Bath, UK: Parragon, 2003), 23.

6. A TURN FOR THE WORST

1. Jane Austen, *Pride and Prejudice* (London: Vintage Books, 2007), 9.

7. "IT'S A LIVING"

1. *The Penguin English Dictionary*, 4th ed., s.v. "career" (London: Penguin Books, 2002).

8. THE OLD COUNTRY

1. E. Nesbit, *The Railway Children* (London: Puffin Books, 2010), 23.

9. A FORK IN THE ROAD

1. Matthew 13:46 (Authorized Version).

10. PARIS

1. Guillaume Apollinaire, "1909," in *Alcools* (Berkeley: University of California Press, 1974), 182. Author's translation.

11. THE MONASTERY

1. Christina Rossetti, "Up-Hill," in *The Penguin Book of Religious Verse*, ed. R. S. Thomas (Harmondsworth, UK: Penguin Books, 1963), 171.
2. Gerard Manley Hopkins, "That Nature Is a Heraclitean Fire and of the Comfort of the Resurrection," in *Poems and Prose of Gerard Manley Hopkins* (London: Penguin Books, 1985), 66.
3. *The Sayings of the Desert Fathers*, trans. Benedicta Ward (Kalamazoo, MI: Cistercian Publications, 1984), 139.
4. E. Allison Peers, "La Noche Oscura del Alma," in *St. John of the Cross and Other Lectures and Addresses 1920–1945* (London: Faber & Faber, 1946), 20. Author's translation.
5. E. M. Forster, *A Room with a View* (London: Edward Arnold, 1924), 9.
6. Jeremiah 31:15 (Jerusalem Bible).

12. MIRAGES AND MINARETS

1. "Doa Safar" [Travel Prayer], Royal Brunei Airlines, www.flyroyalbrunei.com/wp-content/uploads/downloads/2012/06/ BI_IFEG_JUL12_WEB.pdf.

15. LIKE MOTHER, LIKE SON

1. William Joseph Daly, "The First Born," (1894). Written for his daughter Elizabeth.

19. "PHYSICIAN, HEAL THYSELF"

1. Luke 4:23 (Authorized Version).
2. Hans Asperger, "Problems of Infantile Autism," *Communication, Journal of the National Autistic Society* (1979): 49.

EPILOGUE

1. Julian of Norwich, *Revelations of Divine Love*, trans. Clifton Wolters (London: Penguin Books, 1966), 185.

INDEX

ABOUT THE AUTHOR

Rachael Lee Harris is a registered psychotherapist specializing in Asperger's syndrome and high functioning autism providing a unique contribution to the field of autism spectrum conditions (ASC) therapy and research from her perspective as a woman who has been diagnosed with Asperger's syndrome. She is the only psychotherapist in Australia diagnosed as being on the autism spectrum and specializing in this field. She continues to improve the quality of life of children and adults on the autism spectrum as well as their carers and partners through her private practice, speaking engagements and retreats. She has also given several academic presentations.